ISBN: 1492769207
ISBN 13: 9781492769200

Library of Congress Control Number: 2014909799
CreateSpace Independent Publishing Platform
North Charleston, South Carolina

18 19 20 21 10 9 8 7 6 5 4 3 2

FOR MY PARENTS:

the son of Oklahoma Creek Freedmen
and the daughter of North Carolina sharecroppers

Vanguard

[T]he childhood pledges that you tossed about
And then forgot in vain frivolity,
Must now be kept in strict sincerity;
For you are children of the brave, devout!
They cry to you—pleading, lest you forget
The charge you received before your birth:
"Avenge for us the crimes that made us weep,
Collect for us this long, outstanding debt;
Not with the sword, but with your strength—your worth
Fail not, this is a sacred charge to keep!"

— J. Tolbertte Lacy

African American youth leader, high school principal,
and college dean of students at Paine College, 1971–1976

CONTENTS

PREFACE

Maybe I should learn how to meditate.
This is the thought that arose in my mind several years ago as I was going through a divorce, burdened with all the usual challenges that come with it, involving family, custody, support, property, money, and emotional and spiritual pain. Overwhelmed and afraid that I might fall deeper into despair, feeling I had no resources but myself, I decided to give meditation a try.

What I learned helped me to free my attention from a cascade of tormenting thoughts and to rest it on my breath. That journey from my thoughts to my breath helped me to see through the chaos that clouded my mind and life. It helped me to become more aware of what really needed my attention. Gradually, I was able to uplift my mind and my personal situation, and resume fulfilling my life purpose.

As I continued to meditate, and in my work at the Baltimore jail, I became acutely aware that something else needed closer attention: my African American brothers and sisters who were overrepresented in the jail population. They were living with challenges much greater than my own that they had to overcome in order to obtain release from confinement and to avoid finding themselves in the same situation again. But even in the visitation lines that snaked from the jail towards the streets, and among the people in low-income African American neighborhoods through-out the city, it was clear that our people were struggling to meet many other challenges related to education, employment, housing, health, policing, and so forth. Even people I knew who outwardly appeared to be doing quite well were discontent and frustrated with their lives.

Over the years, as I journeyed from my thoughts to my breath, from my meditation seat to the jail, and throughout Baltimore, I cannot count all the times that I thought about the troubles that could be alleviated, and the inherent goodness, genius and potential that could be brought forth, if more African Americans meditated. This is not to say that I believe meditation to be "the solution" to the individual or collective problems of African Americans. To the contrary, since the challenges we face are multifaceted, so are the remedies that are needed.

But simply because our problems are complex does not mean they can't be addressed with simple approaches. Meditation does not cost anything, yet it has great value. And it does not take long to learn, even if you are doing it for the first time.

My personal experience leads me to the conclusion that regular meditation practice can help us bring forth the excellent qualities with which we are naturally endowed. It can help us to live complete, rich, and fulfilled lives. Yet, as I have visited meditation and yoga centers in Baltimore and around the country, searched meditation and yoga websites, and perused meditation and yoga books and magazines, I have found only a few African Americans.

Free Your Mind is an attempt to contribute to the efforts of others to address this situation. It is an attempt to convey to African Americans this message: Meditation is for *us*!

Actually, meditation is for everyone regardless of race, age, gender, physical size, nationality, ethnicity, religion, income, educational level, or sexual orientation. And I encourage everyone to learn how to meditate. However, I have written this guidebook with African Americans in mind.

In particular, I have written this for African Americans who have an affinity for African American history and culture, who want to bring their heritage more fully into their lives while learning how to meditate. I have also written it to suggest an approach that can be used and adapted by anyone who wants to introduce meditation in our community. Indeed, "black lives matter," and meditation can help us to uplift black lives.

I chose the journey that slaves took to freedom during the Antebellum Period in the United States as the theme for introducing meditation. I did this for several reasons.

First, learning about our history can help us begin to free our minds. Many of the challenges we face are rooted in our past. Understanding how we got here, what our forebears went through, and what we need to do can help us to go forward both in our lives and, as this book demonstrates, in our meditation practice.

Second, aspects of the flight that runaways took—beginning in bondage, stepping on a path of liberation and journeying forward, and then, after facing and overcoming many challenges, attaining freedom—are comparable to the journey that meditators make. Certainly there is much we can learn from the runaways' journey that we can apply to what we do both as meditators and as human beings living in the world today.

Third, although faced with extreme oppression, the enslaved men and women of the Antebellum Period never gave up. It is nothing less than a heroic achievement that our people have survived the extraordinary efforts to dehumanize us. This is particularly true of the men, women and children who escaped to freedom. As the former slave William Wells Brown noted, "No country has produced so much heroism in so short a time, connected with escapes from peril and oppression, as has occurred in the United States among fugitive slaves, many of whom showed great shrewdness in their endeavors to escape from this land of bondage."[1] These heroes and heroines can inspire us to be brave and to keep going in our meditation practice and everyday lives.

Fourth, we have a lot in common with the people who were enslaved: we are all trying to find a way out of some form of bondage—to thoughts, habits, things, situations, people, organizations, and so forth. We are all trying to become free, each in our own way. Moreover, many of the reasons we are trying to become free are comparable to the reasons our ancestors ran from slavery.

In our efforts to become free, heroes and heroines of the Antebellum Period such as Frederick Douglass and Harriet Tubman serve as beacons, eternal reminders that no matter how great the disadvantages, misfortunes, or opposition we face, no matter what or who is keeping us shackled and bound, we can still uplift our minds, uplift our personal lives, uplift our families, uplift our communities, and uplift human dignity.

The meditation principles and techniques in this guidebook can help us to grow and improve our situation. I learned them over the course of many years of study, contemplation, and practice. They are varied, from traditions that originate in Africa, Asia, Europe and North America. But they are not exactly the same ones that I learned. That's because I have placed the ones I learned in the crucible of the African American experience in order to produce an approach to freeing the mind that African Americans might find informative, inspiring, and beneficial.

This does not mean that the meditation principles and techniques in this guidebook are without universal applicability. After all, they have been used in one form or another by people of all backgrounds. Moreover, it is *because* they are universal—have been used by people of all backgrounds—that they are also true to the African American experience. Our ancestors sat, gazed, walked, stretched, contemplated, cared, helped, chanted, prayed, sang, danced, served, and were devoted to their elders and ancestors. Through these activities they brought forth their inherent goodness, genius, and potential, which enabled them to deal with challenges in their lives, and to lift our people out of slavery. By relating to them as an integral part of meditation practice, we can journey on an authentic path of liberation.

Meditation can help us as individuals to relate to everyday life challenges with caring and wisdom. It can also help us to guard against threats to the freedom of our people. The external threats—such as racism—are well known. However, another threat lies right in our own minds. It is our human tendency to fix and hold our attention on our thoughts rather than to rest it on what is actually happening right *here,* right *now.* Not only does this tendency cloud our minds and cause suffering, it makes it difficult for us to see and respond appropriately to what is actually happening in our community and the world.

This tendency is clearly evident today in the Digital Age. Distraction is becoming an epidemic. We are overwhelmed by sensory input, information, sound, and activity. (Have you received a phone call or a text or checked your cell phone while reading this?) The many sources of distraction are making it difficult for us as a people to give our full attention to what is *really* going on and what we need to do.

Many of us are, at most, giving only partial attention to what's happening around us and to what we and others are thinking, saying, and doing, and the probable effects and implications for our lives. We, as individuals, are not only losing sight of the sunrises and the sunsets, the state of our health, the development of our children, and so forth—we, as a people, are losing sight of the larger forces shaping our future.

As a result, what we and our leaders think, say, and do is often more a testament to distraction and social conditioning than to a clear vision. If we have allowed our minds to simply conform, rather than be transformed, how can we bring forth the authentic and collective wisdom within us? How can we as a people, in this generation and the next one, discern and respond *effectively* to external threats to our freedom?

We need to understand the state of black America and the inner cities, and we need to develop remedies to alleviate disparities in income, health, justice, education, and so forth. But we must have as one of our remedies the freeing of forty million black minds. After all, much of what we see in the state of black America today is not merely the result of historical and external factors. The state of black America is also the result of what we are dwelling on, fixating on, and holding onto in our minds. And a lot of what we are holding onto are beliefs, attitudes, and behaviors from slavery and Jim Crow times that have been transmitted to us intergenerationally and that do not support our efforts to uplift our lives.

"As long as the mind is enslaved, the body will never be free."[2] In our efforts to address the challenges we face, we will be well served to remember those words of Martin Luther King, Jr. Our minds have been embedded in a diseased culture for a long time. One way we can free our minds and bodies is with meditation. In meditation, we remove our attention from thoughts that hold us down and rest it on our breath, allowing our minds to connect with what is actually happening right *here,* right *now.* By regularly practicing in this way, you can develop the clarity and vision to bring forth the goodness, genius, and potential that can help you move forward in life. In other words, you can *free your mind.*

I welcome your comments and questions at freeyourmindguide@outlook.com.

HOW TO USE THIS GUIDEBOOK

You cannot keep the human mind forever locked up in darkness. A ray of light, a spark from freedom's altar, the idea of inherent right, each, all, will become fixed in the soul; and that moment his "limbs swell beyond the measure of his chains," that moment he is free; then it is that the slave dies to become a freeman.

—William Wells Brown, *Narrative of William W. Brown*
Former fugitive slave

This guidebook is organized into eleven sections. Each section is named after a city (terminal) through which Harriet Tubman, the great Underground Railroad conductor, traveled as she led people to freedom during the Antebellum Period in the United States (1789 to 1861). As you probably know, the "Underground Railroad" was not a real railroad. The term simply referred to a network of people (agents), safe houses (stations), and routes (tracks) that were used by guides (conductors) prior to the US Civil War to help enslaved black people (passengers) escape to freedom (the Promised Land) where aid workers (brakemen/women) helped them to settle down in new lives.

As you read this guidebook, it is recommended that you take your time. Start at the beginning and read one chapter each day or each week. Take one step at a time. That's how Tubman made her journey to freedom. If you use this approach, you will make greater progress than if you try to go through the entire book quickly.

Reflect on the historical sketches. They are intended to inform and point to sources that can be used for further study. Also reflect on the principles and quotes, do the exercises, and practice the techniques as they are presented. At the conclusion of each chapter, contemplate the material you have read. Reflect on whether there is an area of your life where the information or techniques are relevant and useful. If they are helpful, look for ways to apply them in your everyday life.

Of course, you may decide to just look at the photos, go through the terminals out of order, reflect on certain quotations, or practice a technique that you are particularly interested in. Perhaps a poem or story will attract your interest. Honor that and go from there.

As you work with the meditation principles, techniques, and exercises in this guidebook, you will need to be practical. Although you may be well served to follow the instructions in the guidebook, nothing in it should be considered a hard-and-fast rule. This is a *guidebook,* not a rulebook. Avoid placing too much emphasis on doing anything "right." Such an attitude will only impede your efforts to free your mind. Use the information in this guidebook "as best you can," with heart and gentle discipline, in a way that is helpful to *you.*

Although we may have a common African heritage, each of us is a unique person. We have unique personal histories, dispositions, needs, preferences, and issues. In many ways we come from and live in different realities. How a person who meditates thinks, speaks, and behaves will depend on what they are dealing with in their life and where they are on their journey. None of us experiences and responds to meditation in the same way. Therefore, avoid comparing your meditation practice with that of others, or thinking that a meditator is supposed to think, speak, or behave in a certain way. Each person's meditation practice is uniquely their own, just as yours is your own. So be genuine.

Although meditation can help you to free your mind and uplift your life, the information in this guidebook should not be used as a substitute for professional treatment or therapy. If you need either of these, please obtain them from people who can help.

Frederick Douglass
Source: Library of Congress

INTRODUCTION

SLAVERY! How much misery is comprehended in that single word. What mind is there that does not shrink from its direful effects?

—David Walker, *Walker's Appeal*
African American antislavery activist

The struggle of African Americans for freedom in the United States is not over. Although (at this time) President Barack Obama is in the White House, and First Lady Michelle Obama is one of the most admired women of our time, the legacy of slavery continues.

There are still many racial disparities in social mobility, material conditions, and everyday life. For example, recently, the Pew Research Center reported that in the United States, in 2013, the median net worth of white households was $141,900, while for African American households it was $11,000, and this gap is widening.[1] Over the past 25 years, the wealth gap has tripled. The black unemployment rate remains at least twice that of whites and the poverty rate among blacks nears 30 percent compared to 10 percent for whites.[2] Although African Americans represent about 13 percent of the US population, according to the Bureau of Justice Statistics, they represented nearly 36 percent of the total population in US jails in 2013.[3]

The racial disparities in the United States indicate that the structure of white supremacy/black subordination is still in place in America. This is further indicated by the efforts to dismantle programs designed to offset the impact of slavery and Jim Crow segregation and discrimination on present-day African Americans. It is indicated by racial profiling, voter suppression, "stop and search" tactics, race-segregated private spheres (such as social intimates, neighbors, churches, and friends), and race-segregated social networks that all too often exclude blacks from access to opportunities and resources. It is indicated by the fact that, "although things are changing," "racial segregation within religious congregations remains high."[4]

The American dilemma has not been resolved. Many African Americans feel that, even if they get a good education, find a job and work hard, support their family and raise their children, and remain law-abiding, they still will not be able to rise above the legacy of slavery. Many of us do not see a Promised Land in our future. Moreover, many of us are losing confidence in the promise of America as well as in the inherent goodness, genius, and potential that lies in ourselves and our people.

Aware of this, in addressing the National Association for the Advancement of Colored People at its hundredth anniversary celebration in 2009, President Obama reported that the federal government is working "to overcome the inequities, the injustices, the barriers that still exist in our country." "But," he added:

> [I]nnovative government programs and expanded opportunities will not, in and of themselves, make a difference if each of us, as parents and as community leaders, fail to do our part by encouraging excellence in our children.

Government programs alone won't get our children to the Promised Land. *We need a new mindset*, a new set of attitudes—because one of the most durable and destructive legacies of discrimination is the way we've internalized a sense of limitation; how so many in our community have come to expect so little from the world and from themselves.

We've got to say to our children, yes, if you're African American, the odds of growing up amid crime and gangs are higher. Yes, if you live in a poor neighborhood, you will face challenges that somebody in a wealthy suburb does not have to face. But that's not a reason to get bad grades—that's not a reason to cut class—that's not a reason to give up on your education and drop out of school. No one has written your destiny for you. *Your destiny is in your hands*—you cannot forget that. That's what we have to teach all of our children.[5] [Italics mine]

What We Must Do Now

In order to develop a new mindset, and restore our confidence in our inherent goodness, genius, and potential, we—children and adults—have to free our minds from limiting thoughts that hold us down. What this means is that, in the words of African American political activist Angela Davis, "We need to talk about liberating minds as well as society."[6] Even Martin Luther King, Jr. recognized that in order to overcome the legacy of slavery and Jim Crow segregation and discrimination, we need to free our minds:

Psychological freedom, a firm sense of self-esteem, is the most powerful weapon against the long night of physical slavery. No Lincolnian Emancipation Proclamation or Johnsonian Civil Rights Bill can totally bring this kind of freedom. The Negro will only be free when he reaches down to the inner depths of his own being and signs with the pen and ink of assertive manhood his own Emancipation Proclamation. And, with a spirit straining toward true self-esteem, the Negro must boldly throw off the manacles of self-abnegation and say to himself and to the world, "I am somebody. I am a person. I am a man with dignity and honor. I have a rich and noble history. How painful and exploited that history has been. Yes, I was a slave through my foreparents and I am not ashamed of that. I'm ashamed of the people who were so sinful to make me a slave." Yes, we must stand up and say, "I'm black and I'm beautiful," and this self-affirmation is the black man's need, made compelling by the white man's crimes against him.[7]

Because the inner depths of our being lie in the mind, it is to the mind that each of us must go to sign our own freedom papers. It is to the mind we must go to unlock the shackles and cell doors that continue to arrest us. Once there, we must turn the key to freedom. The key is turned by letting go of thoughts that cloud our minds and hold us down. The key to freeing our mind, and body, is meditation.

Using Meditation

Meditation is simply *a technique;* it is a way to accomplish something. In this guidebook, you are invited to use meditation to free your mind.

Basically, when we meditate this is what we do:

1. take our attention off our thoughts;

2. rest our attention on a neutral object such as our breath, and

3. repeat steps 1 and 2 whenever we become aware our attention is dwelling on our thoughts.

We take our attention off our thoughts and rest it on our breath because doing this helps us to keep our mind on what's happening in the present, *here* and *now*. With our attention on the breath, rather than on our thoughts, we are more aware of what's going on within and around us, and we gain insight. Thus, we are better able to relate to what's happening in our lives and satisfy our wants and needs.

When we regularly practice meditation and reflect on our insights, a change begins to occur. We naturally begin to view ourselves, our situation, and the world differently. With greater awareness, we begin to see more possibilities, have a more positive attitude, make wiser choices, and behave in ways that help us to live more satisfying lives. We let go of our limiting thoughts about ourselves and our world. When we do that, a new life, and a new world, begins to come into existence.

This transformation is one of the reasons meditation is often associated with religion. However, in truth, meditation is no more religious than bread or water. Just as bread is used for Communion as well as for sandwiches, and just as water is used for baptism as well as for washing clothes, meditation is used in religious practices as well as to nurture personal well-being and improve performance. In fact, meditation is used for many purposes. For example, meditation is often used by people to help them to de-stress, relax, and chill out.

You, however, may not have the luxury of using meditation to simply de-stress, relax, and chill out. You may need a larger view of meditation, one that is appropriate to your needs and situation. This larger view is what is being presented in this guidebook.

You are invited to use meditation to help you to free your mind regardless of the beliefs you may hold. When you practice meditation, you will be better able to use your *mind* and *body,* together, to do the things you want and need to do in order to uplift your life. Since you will have freed your mind from your limiting thoughts, you'll be able to direct your mind and body to think, say, and do what is needed. This is what the black nationalist and Pan-African Movement leader Marcus Garvey was talking about when he said, "Liberate the minds of men and ultimately you will liberate the bodies of men."[8]

However, in order to liberate your mind and body you'll have to do more than follow the meditation techniques in this guidebook. You'll also have to follow them with a genuine and heartfelt desire to free your mind so that you can uplift yourself, your family, and your community. This means you'll need to exert yourself by applying the information in the guidebook and regularly practicing one or more of the techniques over an extended period of time. To keep going, you'll need to draw on the inspiration of your ancestors, in particular, the sacred charge you received before your birth. When you relate to the historical sketches, quotes, poems, principles, exercises, and meditation techniques in this guidebook in this way, with heart, you will surely make progress on the path of meditation. You'll free your mind, and body, too.

African Roots of Meditation

Meditation is an ideal technique for African Americans to use. After all, meditation originated in Africa.

As far back as two hundred thousand years ago, in Africa, early *Homo sapiens* engaged in various campfire rituals—meditative focused-attention activities such as flame gazing, chanting, clapping, and dancing. These activities sharpened mental focus. Over time, such meditative activities helped *Homo sapiens* develop the brain and mind that all human beings are born with. It produced a mind that was superior to the one possessed by earlier species. It produced a mind that was better able to adapt to the environment and overcome challenges. This is how we became fully human.[9]

Today, focused-attention activities are used in all societies for health, spiritual, and religious reasons, as well as for self-improvement. There is a simple reason that meditation is used all over the world: it works! It helps people to live their lives more fully, and it can certainly help people of African ancestry as it did our early ancestors. It can help us free our own minds of an internalized sense of limitation. It can help us to uplift our personal existence, family and community. It can help us fulfill the hopes and dreams of our ancestors with our lives.

Although our capacity for growth, well-being, achievement, fulfillment, and happiness is infinite, we can only experience the benefits of meditation by regularly practicing it. This is because we have deeply ingrained thoughts that continually arise in our minds. These habitual thoughts don't really go away, and we don't easily stop dwelling, fixating, and holding on to them. So we have to keep practicing letting go, resting our attention on the breath, and remaining present in each moment, until the habit of holding on is displaced by the new habit of letting go and simply *being* with whatever arises.

This is how you can develop a new mindset, a new set of attitudes. This is how you can overcome a sense of limitation. This is how you can bring forth your inherent goodness, genius, and potential. This is how you, and your children, can escape enslavement and reach the Promised Land.

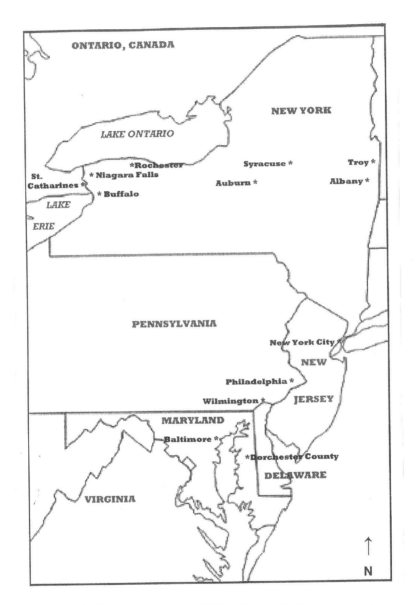

Map of Underground Railroad Terminals Through Which Harriet Tubman Journeyed

PART I:
FREE YOUR MIND

BURY ME IN A FREE LAND

Make me a grave where'er you will,
In a lowly plain or a lofty hill;
Make it among earth's humblest graves,
But not in a land where men are slaves.

I could not rest, if around my grave
I heard the steps of a trembling slave;
His shadow above my silent tomb
Would make it a place of fearful gloom.

I could not sleep, if I heard the tread
Of a coffle-gang to the shambles led,
And the mother's shriek of wild despair
Rise, like a curse, on the trembling air.

I could not rest, if I saw the lash
Drinking her blood at each fearful gash;
And I saw her babes torn from her breast,
Like trembling doves from their parent nest.

I'd shudder and start, if I heard the bay
Of a bloodhound seizing his human prey;
And I heard the captive plead in vain,
As they bound, afresh, his galling chain.

If I saw young girls from their mother's arms
Bartered and sold for their youthful charms,

My eye would flash with a mournful flame,
My death-pale cheek grow red with shame.

I would sleep, dear friends, where bloated might
Can rob no man of his dearest right;
My rest shall be calm in any grave
Where none can call his brother a slave.

I ask no monument, proud and high,
To arrest the gaze of the passers by;
All that my yearning spirit craves
Is—*Bury me not in a land of slaves!*

By Frances Ellen Watkins Harper (1825-1911)

["Bury Me in a Free Land" in Frances Smith Foster, *A Brighter Coming Day: A Frances Ellen Watkins Harper Reader,* New York: The Feminist Press at The City University of New York, 1990.]

TERMINAL: Dorchester County, Maryland

Araminta Ross was born into slavery in Dorchester County, Maryland, on the Thompson plantation, around 1822. She was one of the nine children born to Benjamin Ross and Harriet "Rit" Green.

Harriet "Rit" Green's mother, Modesty, was probably Ashanti. Modesty may have arrived in Maryland in the late 1700s, after surviving the Middle Passage of the Atlantic slave trade. She may have taught aspects of Ashanti culture to her children and grandchildren.

At the time of Araminta's birth, her father was enslaved by Anthony Thompson, and her mother was enslaved by Edward Brodess. Araminta lived for a couple of years with both parents and her brothers and sisters on the Thompson plantation. They all lived in a shack that one of her biographers, Earl Conrad, described as being "rain-soaked, discolored, without windows, almost airless."[1]

When Araminta was about two years old, Brodess separated her family by moving her mother and children to his farm near the town of Bucktown, leaving her father behind. At that time tobacco farming in Maryland was on the decline, and the demand for slaves was waning. So Brodess hired his slaves out to the owners of neighboring farms.

When Araminta was around six years old, Brodess began hiring her out to work for nearby white families. As a child laborer, she apprenticed as a weaver, worked as a maid, provided child care, and waded into marsh waters to check muskrat traps. She was often scolded and whipped, and frequently ill. As is true of any child, she longed to be in a home with her family. Occasionally, when she was ill, she was allowed into her mother's care, but only long enough to recover. Then she was forced to return to work.

One day, when she was in her early teens, Araminta stood between a friend and an iron weight being thrown at him by an angry employer, and she was struck in the head. The head injury was serious, and for the rest of her life it would cause her to have episodes of narcolepsy, falling asleep unexpectedly throughout the day.

Later in her teens, Brodess hired Araminta out to work for John Stewart, a merchant. At first she was employed as a domestic worker in the Stewart home and a laborer in his store. Later she was assigned to more strenuous work, such as plowing fields, cutting timber, and hauling logs, work that enabled her to develop great physical strength and endurance.

The five or so years she spent working for Stewart allowed her to mingle with free and enslaved black laborers. It also allowed her to reunite with her father. By 1840, Benjamin Ross had been freed by Thompson. This meant that he was free to hire himself out to Stewart, and that is what he did. He worked as a supervisor of timber cutting and hauling and spent time with his daughter.

From her father and other men employed by Stewart, Araminta learned that there was a secret network of safe houses and routes that runaway slaves could use to escape to freedom in the North. She learned about the dangers that were involved in the runaways' journey; the codes, disguises, and ruses they sometimes used; and the fortitude and courage they needed to reach their destination—the Promised Land.

Seeing that Araminta was self-reliant, industrious, and trustworthy, Brodess decided to allow her to hire herself out in return for sixty dollars annually. She undoubtedly saw this arrangement as an opportunity to earn enough money to purchase her freedom and the freedom of family members. So, with approval from Brodess, she obtained two head of steer, made a small business out of plowing fields and hauling produce, and began saving money. As she became more self-confident and self-assured, she began referring to herself by a new name, "Harriet."

In 1844, Harriet—herself still a slave—married John Tubman. He was a free black laborer who worked in the area. Although married, she continued to work for Stewart and hire her labor out. Eventually she began hiring herself out to Dr. Anthony C. Thompson, the son of her father's former owner.

When Brodess died in 1849, Harriet began to worry that his widow was going to sell her to pay his estate-related debts. When she shared her concerns with John, he saw no reason for alarm. When she kept suggesting that they should flee north, to the Promised Land, he ridiculed her.

Harriet began to have sleepless nights. She had dreams and visions of horsemen coming and terrified women and children screaming, and she would awaken in the night, screaming, "Oh, they're coming, they're coming, I must go!" She also dreamed of green fields and lovely flowers on "the other side" where beautiful white ladies were waiting for her with outstretched arms.[2]

When Harriet went to work in the mornings, she heard rumors that she and her brothers were going to be sold, separated from their family, and taken south where conditions for slaves were known to be more severe than in Maryland. She listened deeply, gave her full attention to what she was hearing and experiencing, and began taking the rumors seriously. After all, her sisters—Mariah Ritty, Soph, and Linah—had already been sold and taken away to the Deep South. Harriet surely knew that if she was sold, she'd be taken there too. And, since she was young, relatively healthy, and childless, there was a good likelihood that she would be used for sexual and childbearing purposes.

Although Harriet had only known life as a slave, she began to awaken to the fact that, in actuality, she had always been free, and didn't have to remain enslaved if she didn't want to. She saw that her destiny was in her hands. But in order for her to become free she had to do more than have this enlightened understanding.

Harriet began letting go of the mindsets and habits typical of many of those who were enslaved. As she did, she gained greater confidence in her inherent goodness, genius, and potential, and began bringing it forth. She decided to flee.

Harriet Tubman
Source: Library of Congress

1. Being

On the one hand, there stood slavery, a stern reality, glaring frightfully upon us—its robes already crimsoned with the blood of millions, and even now feasting itself greedily upon our own flesh. On the other hand, away back in the dim distance, under the flickering light of the North Star, behind some craggy hill or snow covered mountain, stood a doubtful freedom—half frozen—beckoning us to come share its hospitality.

—Frederick Douglass,
Narrative of the Life of Frederick Douglass
Former fugitive slave

The "Promised Land" was any place that people of African ancestry could be free from slavery and enjoy the blessings of liberty.

In the early years of the United States, many slaves viewed Spanish Florida, Haiti, and lands occupied by the indigenous people of North America as the Promised Land; these lands were safe havens for runaways. Others looked upon the Everglades and the Okefenokee Swamp, Great Dismal Swamp, and Congaree Swamp, where communities of fugitive slaves lived, as the Promised Land. Canada was viewed as the Promised Land too, especially after slavery was outlawed there in 1834. Even Mexico and faraway Sierra Leone and Liberia were considered to be the Promised Land.

Mostly, though, slaves considered the non-slaveholding states and territories in the north and northwest regions of the United States as the Promised Land. By 1860, these regions, referred to as "the North," consisted of nineteen states and seven territories, including the District of Columbia. "The South" consisted of fifteen states and two territories, all of which held slaves.

Since slave owners would go to any lengths to keep people of African ancestry from reaching the Promised Land in the north, traveling on the Underground Railroad—the secret network of people, safe houses, and escape routes—was the only way many of them could become free.

We can be inspired by the Underground Railroad agents who provided our ancestors safe passage. We can also be inspired by our brave ancestors who used the Underground Railroad, as well as their own resources and ingenuity, to make the perilous journey to freedom. These men, women, and children helped to compel this nation to live up to its most sacred creed.

Just as the Underground Railroad provided many of our ancestors with a way out of physical slavery, meditation is like an Underground Railroad. It can provide us, with a way out of another kind of slavery—an enslaved mind.

Our mind is enslaved when our attention dwells, fixates, and holds on to thoughts. When our attention dwells, fixates, and holds on to our thoughts, our attention becomes attached or bound to them. Our thoughts then are able to control our mind, what we think, say and do. If you have ever allowed your attention to dwell on hateful or lustful thoughts, then you know that the thoughts on which your attention dwells can oppress you, and become like a master over you.

Meditation provides us a way out of an enslaved mind to a free mind. Instead of dwelling, fixating, and holding on to thoughts, we remove our attention from them, rest it on the breath, and allow our thoughts to naturally rise and fade without making any judgments about them. When we free our minds in this way, we go beyond our thoughts and enter the Promised Land. We are then able to think, speak, and act like free men and women.

Although we may enter the Promised Land, that does not mean we will no longer experience troubles. "The promised land guarantees nothing. It is only an opportunity, not a deliverance," writes African American writer, educator and journalist Shelby Steele.[1] The same is true of the Promised Land to which we journey through practicing meditation. It merely provides us with an opportunity to further uplift ourselves in freedom.

In order for us to journey to freedom and uplift ourselves, we'll need resources. We'll need the same ones our ancestors used, and the only ones they had: the body, the breath, and the mind. Let's look at the mind.

The Mind

One of the things the mind does is *perceive*. It perceives visible forms, sounds, scents, tangible objects, tastes, and thoughts. You don't have to take my word for this. You can examine this for yourself. Just stop reading for a few moments and quietly observe what is happening within and around you.

***

What you observed were your perceptions. Perhaps you observed the color of the walls, the sound of a horn outside, the texture of this book in your hand, the flavor of a beverage you just drank, or your thoughts about the instructions you were just given.

You may have noticed something else: thoughts arose about what you perceived. We perceive, recognize, name, and judge by thinking. It all happens very fast. In case you didn't observe this, let's do the exercise again. But this time, observe your sensory perceptions *and* the thoughts that accompany the perceptions.

***

Upon close observation you'll find that the thoughts that arise are mostly your opinion, description, judgment, or interpretation of your perceptions—the *rhythmic* sound, the *beautiful* sight, the *sweet* smell, the *delicious* taste, the *pleasant* thought, and so on.

Giving our attention to our thoughts is what we do when we think. It's how we make sense of our world. It's how we are able to reason, remember, and make rational decisions in many everyday situations. For example, imagine you heard a loud noise in the next room. Accompanying your perception of the sound, thoughts will arise in your mind about what caused it. If your attention comes to rest on the thought that a lighted candle has been knocked to the floor, the thought that your home could go up in flames may arise, and you probably will stop what you are doing, enter the room to investigate, and take whatever action is appropriate.

Although giving our attention to thoughts can be helpful, it can also be harmful. It can make it difficult to see what's going on, because our attention is on our thoughts rather than on what's actually happening. For example, if your attention is dwelling on your thoughts about an argument you had recently, you might not even hear the noise in the next room until the smell of smoke from the fire draws your attention away from your thoughts to what is actually happening.

Indeed, when you hold your attention on thoughts, you are less attentive to what's happening around you. The longer you hold your attention on thoughts, the more thoughts *about* your thoughts your mind will generate.

The more thoughts your mind generates, the more clouded your mind will become. The more clouded your mind is, the more likely it is to lose touch with reality. The more you lose touch with reality, the more likely you are to mistake your *thoughts* for *reality*. The more you mistake your thoughts for reality, the more likely you are to think, speak, and act inappropriately. The more you think, speak, and act inappropriately, the less likely you are to satisfy your wants and needs. If you are unable to satisfy your wants and needs, you cannot uplift yourself and contribute toward uplifting your community. If you cannot do what you want and need to do to uplift yourself and your community, you are probably enslaved, to some person, some thing, or some thought.

In meditation, we train our attention to refrain from dwelling and fixating on thoughts. We train our attention to let go so our mind can remain in touch with reality. We train by taking our attention off thoughts and placing it on an object, such as the breath. When we do this, our minds become less clouded with thoughts. They become calm and clear. This allows us to see with clarity our internal and external experiences as they arise through our senses. Since our mind is not clouded by clouds of thoughts, it is more in touch with reality. We are more conscious. But, in order to synchronize our mind and body so that we can skillfully engage reality, we need another resource. We need the breath.

The Breath

In meditation, we train our attention to refrain from dwelling, fixating and holding on to thoughts by giving it a different object to rest on—the sensation of the breath. Whenever we become aware that our attention is dwelling, holding, or fixating on thoughts, we take it off our thoughts and gently rest it on the breath. This helps us to move forward on our journey to freedom.

Take a break from reading and spend a few moments becoming familiar with your breath. Just sit and observe your body breathing. In particular, notice that your breathing has two parts: the inhalation, or in-breath, and the exhalation, or out-breath. There is also a gap at the end. Just be aware of your body inhaling and exhaling your breath.

***

In meditation, we use the sensation of our breath as the object on which we rest our attention for several reasons:

- The breath is always available.

- The breath is always happening right now.

- The breath is relatively easy to find.

- The breath is an object toward which we have a neutral attitude.

- The breath is soothing.

- The breath is rhythmic, like a *djembe* drum, calling the attention away from thoughts.

When we remove our attention from our thoughts without judging or analyzing them and place it on the breath, our mind generates fewer thoughts *about* our thoughts: fewer opinions, judgments, interpretations, and analyses. As a result our mind becomes less active, less agitated, less clouded with thoughts, and we experience calm, stability, clarity, and peace.

Although this might sound like a philosophy or theory, it's an observation that you can make on your own. Follow these instructions:

1. For a minute, think about something that is pleasant and all the reasons it is pleasant to you. This can be an event, a person, a kind of food, a piece of music, a movie, a work of art, an opinion, or a place.

2. Next, let go of those thoughts and for a minute simply rest your attention on your breath as you exhale and follow it. Allow your awareness to join with your environment, and your environment to join with your awareness.

3. For a minute, think about something that is unpleasant and all the reasons it is unpleasant to you. This can be an event, a person, a kind of food, a piece of music, a movie, a work of art, an opinion, or a situation.

4. Next, let go of those thoughts and for a minute simply rest your attention on your breath as you exhale. Follow each exhalation out into the space around you. Allow your awareness to join with your environment, and your environment to join with your awareness.

Did you notice a shift in your awareness when you moved your attention from your thoughts to your breath? When the shift occurred, what did you become more aware of?

When we move our attention from our thoughts to our breath, we are:

- letting go of notions and concepts about ourselves, others, and the world that can limit us;

- strengthening our mind's connection to our body;

- shifting our perspective and outlook;

- resetting our mind;

- *being*—right *here* and right *now*;

- seeing things with deeper understanding as they really are;

- *being* authentically who and what we are; and

- experiencing moments of freedom.

The Body

When we rest our attention on the breath, we are bringing our mind and body together. Actually, a connection always exists. We experience this mind/body connection every day. For example, sometimes, when our mind is agitated, we sweat, or our heart beats faster and stronger. Likewise, when we accidentally bump our knee or hand on a table, it upsets and disturbs our mind. And when we are not worrying about anything, it is easier to physically relax.

Not only are our mind and body connected, our mind can only perceive what's going on *through the body*: through our eyes, ears, nose, tongue, skin, and brain—all of which are a part of the body. Investigate this for yourself. Look around: see, hear, touch, smell, taste, and think. Your mind cannot perceive anything without your body.

When we let go of our thoughts and rest our attention on the sensation of our breath, we are deepening our mind and body connection. We are allowing our mind to permeate our body, to come all the way to our *senses*. We are allowing our mind to perceive with increasing clarity various sounds, sights, odors, tastes, sensations, and thoughts, without having our perception obscured, filtered, labeled, interpreted, analyzed, or judged by our thoughts. We are allowing ourselves to experience our lives and world directly, freshly. As a result, we become more awake. We become more conscious. We enter the Promised Land.

In the Promised Land we are healthier and happier, and we think, speak, and act with greater wisdom, caring, and skill. As a result, we are able to uplift our lives in freedom.

The Promised Land we enter as meditation practitioners is not a mythical place, a utopian existence, or a haven in a remote celestial sphere. It's not years or miles away. It's right *here*. It's right *now*. It's *reality,* unobstructed by our thoughts. It's always been and always will be right *here*, right *now*. That is a promise.

The best way to really understand all of this is by practicing meditation. Merely reading about it and talking about it just won't do. The only way you can truly understand how meditation works and determine whether it is something beneficial for you is to follow the examples of Beyonce, Halle Berry, Kobe Bryant, Lebron James, Russell Simmons, Tina Turner, Alice Walker, Oprah Winfrey, Tiger Woods, and many other African Americans, and *practice meditation.*

Indeed, we have truly phenomenal people living in our time from who we can at least learn that meditation is an "OK" thing to do. As professional athlete Kobe Bryant observed, "It's crazy to me that meditation is viewed as hokey. Just look at the people who've done phenomenal things. Do they meditate? Absolutely."[2]

2. Calming

Every night of the year saw runaways, singly or in groups, making their way slyly to the country north. Traps and snares were set for them, into which they fell by the hundreds and were returned to their homes. But once infected with the spirit of freedom, they would try again and again, until they succeeded or were sold south. This whole borderland was continuously stirred with strife and hatred over the runaways who were endeavoring to break through…. But in spite of the odds against them, there were a surprising number who did make good their escape. Once they started, no obstacle was too great for them to overcome.

—John P. Parker, *His Promised Land: The Autobiography of John P. Parker*
Former fugitive slave

People of African ancestry enslaved in North America always wanted to be free. It is not surprising, then, that many of them seized any opportunity to flee. Some fled without help, without any idea of where they were located geographically, without knowing what lay ahead. They just trusted in their inherent goodness, genius, and potential, and fled. Others decided to flee using the Underground Railroad.

Often, runaways who decided to flee using the Underground Railroad began their journey by meeting their conductor at a secret place, often on Saturday at nightfall. With Sunday being the only day they didn't have to work, fleeing late on Saturday allowed their conductor to get them off to a good start before their escape could be discovered the next workday. When the sun came up on Monday morning, there would be a great deal of commotion as slave owners, overseers, drivers, and slave patrollers went searching for their missing "property" and ranted about the audacity of any slave to escape. But there was a satisfying silence among the slaves who had helped the runaways to flee.

Though most of our ancestors remained on the plantation, it doesn't mean that they had resigned themselves to slavery. They were very intelligent human beings. They simply recognized the reality of the constraints under which they existed. They used every opportunity to stay alive and live a dignified existence while confronting, resisting, and undermining the institution of slavery.

They worked slowly, did not complete tasks, refused to follow orders, threatened overseers, stole livestock and produce, set buildings afire, damaged wagons, broke equipment and implements, pretended to be ill, refused to work, and hid for several days. Undoubtedly, if they had been physically able, thought escape was actually feasible, or felt they were not needed by other slaves, they would have run away too. But instead, they remained. They remained to care for parents, siblings, and children as well as the elderly, disabled, and ill who could not make the difficult journey, while helping those who could to get away.

Unlike many runaways, you don't have to wait until next Saturday after dusk to begin your journey to freedom. You can get started today, right *here*, right *now*. All you'll need is to:

- have a mind, breath, and body;

- acknowledge that you possess inherent goodness, genius, and potential;

- rely on your guide, the instructions;

- be willing to exert yourself; and

- be willing to face your hopes and fears.

Let us begin our journey.

Taking Your Seat

There is an African proverb that says, *"A na etugwuru ala ma bia dabiri"* ["You must find a seat before relaxing in a chair"]. Likewise, in meditation, you must find a sitting posture that helps you to relax in your chair.

Find a quiet place that has a chair or similar surface and sit down.[1] Sit in a dignified and relaxed manner. This posture is easy for anyone to assume. Moreover, it is closely associated with the sitting postures of the black pharaohs of Ancient Egypt and the kings and queens of sub-Saharan Africa who sat in chairs and on benches and stools. Sitting in a chair can also align you with

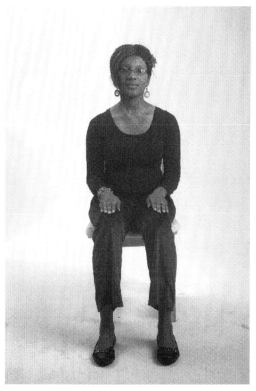

great African Americans such as civil rights activist Rosa Parks, who sat with great dignity on Bus No. 2857 in Montgomery, Alabama, on December 1, 1955, refusing to give up her seat, and through her dignified presence provided the impetus for the modern civil rights movement which made possible many of the liberties you enjoy today.

To align yourself with the greatness of your ancestors, sit in a chair with your feet flat on the floor, about shoulder's width apart, and face forward with your eyes open. Sit upright by

aligning your upper body with gravity. In other words, sit vertically rather than leaning sideways, backward, or forward—or slouching. To help you sit vertically aligned with a natural curve in your back, sit away from the back of the chair and ensure that your pelvis is slightly higher than your knees. For this, you may need to place a firm cushion or small pillow on the seat of the chair.

Once your upper body is properly aligned, relax your shoulders by allowing your arms to naturally hang down by your sides. Now, bend your arms at the elbows, bringing your forearms up and placing your hands in your lap or palms down, on your thighs. Tuck your chin in slightly to further align your head with your upper body. When you do this, your head should be positioned like an African woman balancing a basket on her head. Slightly open your mouth, and relax your jaws. Next, without lowering your head, look downward about six feet in front of you to the floor. Just look downward with a soft gaze without staring at anything in particular. Take a few deep breaths and relax your entire body in this posture.

You're now in the sitting meditation posture.

When you are sitting properly, your muscles don't have to work too hard to keep your upper body upright. As a result, you can begin to relax. Relaxation happens when you allow the natural motion in your body and mind to occur without resisting it.

As your body relaxes, muscles release tension, and thoughts arise and fade, you may feel the urge to scratch an itch or reposition your body in some way. Since you are not trying to be still like a bronze, clay, or wooden African sculpture, a minimal amount of movement is natural—and in some instances appropriate, such as if you are experiencing pain. But remember that your head, neck, shoulders, arms, hands, back, chest, abdomen, legs, and feet are all interconnected. You really can't move one part of the body without moving the others, thereby affecting your meditation posture, your upper body alignment, and your ability to calm your mind and physically relax.

Therefore, when faced with discomfort, first try to allow it. Notice the discomfort and allow it to happen. In other words, try to simply *be* with what you are experiencing—without generating a lot of thoughts about it. Usually whatever you are experiencing will do what everything else in the universe does: it will arise, it will stay for a while, and it will eventually go away. It will fade as long as you don't prevent that from occurring by dwelling, fixating or holding on to it. But if it seems like your discomfort won't fade, go ahead and adjust and realign your body and then start or resume your meditation practice.

Calming Meditation

Although a good sitting posture will help you to sit comfortably in a chair, in order to prevent distracting thoughts from compelling you to get up, you'll need to do what Rosa Parks did: calm your mind and allow it to remain that way. In meditation, one way to calm your mind is by following the three steps below:

The Body

1. Sit in a chair with your body in this relaxed, uplifted, and dignified posture:

   a. *Head* facing forward.

   b. *Feet* flat on the floor.

   c. *Knees* slightly lower than your hips.

   d. *Upper arms* naturally hanging downward.

   e. *Hands* palms down on your thighs, or resting in your lap.

   f. *Back* vertically aligned, not touching the back of the chair.

   g. *Chin* slightly tucked in (slightly back) so that the entire length of your spine is naturally aligned.

   h. *Mouth* slightly opened, and *jaws* relaxed.

   i. *Eyes* open and gazing downward at the ground about six feet in front of you.

The Breath

2. As you sit, notice that your body is breathing. Feel the sensation of your breath. Just experience the breathing process for a few moments. Next, place your attention on the sensation of your breath inside the opening of your nostrils. Do this in a gentle way. As you exhale, allow your awareness to follow your breath all the way out as it dissipates in the space around you. (If you've ever been outside on a very cold winter day, you've probably actually seen your breath dissipate in this way.)

   Note: If you find it difficult to follow your breath out into space, you can instead practice resting your attention on the flow of your breath as you breathe in and breathe out. Both ways of relating to your breath will help you to calm your mind.

The Mind

3. As you sit, whenever you become aware that your attention is not on the sensation of your breath—that you have lost awareness of what is going on around you because your attention has been on your thoughts—relate to the thoughts in this way:

    a. recognize the thoughts (a "thought" in this technique, and in other forms of meditation, is anything that distracts your attention from your breath, including fantasies, memories, ruminations, or even your thoughts and judgements about sounds, sensations, and other perceptions that arise while you are meditating);

    b. label the thoughts silently as what they are, "thoughts," without judging or analyzing them;

    c. gently take your attention off your thoughts, return it to the sensation of your breath, and follow your exhalation out into the space. Note: If you are instead practicing by resting your attention on the flow of your breath as you breathe in and breathe out, simply take your attention off the thoughts and return it to the flow of your breath as you breathe in and breathe out.

As you practice this calming meditation technique, you'll probably encounter a lot of thoughts. You might think, "This isn't getting me anywhere!" or "I am wasting my time doing this!" or "Why am I doing this while everyone else is running around having a good time?" All sorts of thoughts will arise. They will make it difficult for you to continue the journey. When this happens, you simply need to take it easy, relax, and see such thoughts for what they are. They are merely a part of the landscape of meditation. They are an inescapable part of the terrain through which you must journey to free your mind.

Continue observing your mind. Continue labeling your thoughts as "thoughts" and letting them go. Continue returning your attention to your breath. Continue following your breath out as it dissolves in the space around you.

The habit of giving attention to thoughts, especially unhelpful ones, and thereby granting them authority over our lives, is very difficult to overcome. But just as our ancestors overcame enslavement, you can overcome the habit of dwelling, fixating, and holding on to thoughts.

In time, with regular practice, the volume of thoughts generated by your mind will begin to decrease. Your mind will become less agitated, more stable and calm. As it does, you will be able to start relating to distracting thoughts, emotions, perceptions that arise while you are meditating with greater skill and ease.

As you continue to regularly practice calming your mind, your mind will not only become easier to calm, it will start remaining calm for longer periods of time, beyond the time you spend practicing. When this happens, you'll then be able to take the calm mind you've developed by practicing this technique with you into other areas of your life.

Having a calm mind as we go through the day is a momentous development, because when we have a calm mind that remains that way, generally we are better able to relate with skill and ease to what's happening in our lives. With such an uplifted mind, we can uplift our personal situation. With an uplifted personal situation, we can uplift our family. With an uplifted family, we can uplift our community. With an uplifted community, we can uplift societal conditions of every kind.

But don't expect immediate results from practicing this calming technique. The path of meditation can be a long and difficult journey. Yes, you will have difficulty and doubts. But don't allow them to keep you from reaching your destination. Be steady, gentle and tough. Keep going forward. No turning back. OK? If our ancestors can survive the brutal conditions of slavery and then make the perilous journey from slavery to freedom, surely you can sit in a chair for a few minutes each day and work with a simple technique that can help you to calm and, ultimately, free your mind.

One of the things you can do to reduce the likelihood that you will give up on meditating is to slow down. Reduce your daily activities. Remove your mind from chaotic and challenging environments. Seek solitude. Sit down. Give your mind and body a rest.

We spend so much time running around, hanging out, talking, caught up in emotional disturbances, and engaging in pursuits and diversions that keep our minds agitated rather than calm, and which do absolutely nothing to uplift our existence or foster for us happy lives. We have to pay attention to how we are moving through our days. We have to ask ourselves: "How is all this running about and talking working out?" "As a result of all my comings, goings, and conversations, am I any closer to fulfilling the purpose of my life?" and "What is the purpose of my life?" While you have your life, stand back and take a look at it. Ask yourself, "What am I doing?" If you are not satisfied with the answers to these questions, seek quiet spaces.

Pull back a little from busyness, activity, and engagement. Instead of giving all your attention to everyone and everything, give it to the real sustainer of your life—your breath. Instead of spending all your time doing things, give yourself time in which to simply *be* in silence.

The growth and change you want to experience in your life can come through regular, gentle, and patient practice and confidence in your inherent goodness, genius, and potential. So don't give up. Commit yourself to becoming free, no matter how long it takes, one breath at a time. Over and over again, let each breath be a step toward freedom.

3. Developing

Men and women whom I helped on their way came from Tennessee, requiring weeks to make the journey, sleeping under the trees in the daytime and slowly picking their dangerous way at night. How they crossed the numerous creeks that lay waiting for them like a trap was unbelievable to me. As a matter of fact, they became backwoodsmen, following the North Star, or even mountains, to reach their destination, the Ohio River. Once there they felt they were in view of their promised land, even if they had no way to cross into it. Few had shoes, and these were so worn out by the time they reached me, the soles were held together by twine—making loose-fitting sandals.

These long distance travelers were usually people strong physically, as well as people of character, and were resourceful when confronted with trouble, otherwise they could have never escaped.

—John P. Parker, *His Promised Land:*
The Autobiography of John P. Parker
Former fugitive slave

Fleeing on the Underground Railroad was a life-altering experience. Each step runaways took carried them deeper into unfamiliar territory. As they trekked, they discovered things they had not known. They encountered new people and places as well as new challenges. The challenges they encountered compelled them to bring forth many qualities of their character that had lain dormant during their years in slavery—qualities that they needed in order to keep moving forward. Gradually, the qualities that arose became distinctive and enduring aspects of their personality. The person that left slavery and reached freedom was not the same.

Meditation and Character

Because you possess inherent dignity, you also possess good character. It is already in you. But in order to bring it forth into all aspects of your life, you have to develop it. After all, the potential for greed, hatred, and indifference also exists in us. Therefore, we need to develop our good character so we can displace our negative tendencies. If we don't, they can grow and take over our minds and lives.

You probably know of brothers and sisters in whose minds greed, hatred, and indifference are growing. Such individuals do not exhibit their good character. If you take note of their thoughts, speech, and behavior, this might be clear. From them we learn an important lesson: What makes black "beautiful" is not merely skin color. What makes black really "beautiful" is good character, what the late African American entertainer and civil rights activist Ruby Dee called the "hard-to-get kind that comes from within—strength, courage, dignity."[1]

The first step toward developing good character is to refrain from following in the footsteps of people who do not exhibit it. Rather than leading you to the Promised Land, they are likely to lead you into some form of bondage. Consider this advice of African American professional basketball great and businessman Magic Johnson:

> If people around you aren't going anywhere, if their dreams are no bigger than hanging out on the corner, or if they're dragging you down, get rid of them. Negative people can sap your energy so fast, and they can take your dreams from you, too.[2]

Some of our people have lost confidence in their inherent dignity. They do not see their inherent goodness, genius, and potential—and they do not see these attributes in you or others, either. They are confused. They don't know what to do with their lives, and they certainly don't know what to do with yours. But, unless you are willing to have your mind enslaved by people with confused minds, *you* must know.

Don't allow people to blind you to your inherent goodness, genius, and potential. Don't allow your associations to cause your mind to become so clouded that your good character ceases to shine through what you think, say, and do. You can reduce the likelihood that this will occur by following the example of people who exhibit good character.

One person who exhibited good character and whose example is worthy of being followed is the South African anti-apartheid revolutionary and president Nelson Mandela. During his twenty-seven years in prison, he used meditation to further develop his character. He wrote about this from his prison cell:

> In judging our progress as individuals we tend to concentrate on external factors such as one's social position, influence and popularity, wealth and standard of education. These are, of course, important in measuring one's success in material matters and it is perfectly understandable if many people exert themselves mainly to achieve all these. But internal factors may be even more crucial in assessing one's development as a human being. Honesty, sincerity, simplicity, humility, pure generosity, absence of vanity, readiness to serve others—qualities which are within easy reach of every soul—are the foundation of one's spiritual life. Development in

matters of this nature is inconceivable without serious introspection, without knowing yourself, your weaknesses and mistakes. At least, if for nothing else, the cell gives you the opportunity to look daily into your entire conduct, to overcome the bad and develop whatever is good in you. *Regular meditation, say about fifteen minutes a day before you turn in, can be very fruitful in this regard.*[3] [Italics mine]

Developing Positive Qualities

As a meditator, you will encounter challenges, and you will get to know "your weaknesses and mistakes." You will also get to "overcome the bad and develop whatever is good in you." In the process, you might become a somewhat different person. Your friends might have difficulty recognizing the new you.

- By relating to your thoughts without judging them, you will be developing *impartiality* and *acceptance.*

- By observing, recognizing, and acknowledging the content of your thoughts, you will be developing *knowledge* and *understanding.*

- By softly resting your attention on the breath, you will be developing *gentleness* and *kindness.*

- By repeatedly returning your attention to the breath, you will be developing *persistence* and *strength.*

- By letting go of thoughts that hold you down, you will be developing *lightheartedness* and *generosity.*

- By being sincere in your motivation to free your mind, you will be developing *honesty* and *genuineness.*

- By meditating so that you can uplift yourself and help your people, you will be developing *loyalty* and a *readiness to serve others.*

- By practicing meditation regularly, you will be developing *steadiness* and *reliability.*

- By relating to all aspects of yourself with an attitude of friendliness and caring, you will be developing *caring* and *love.*

- By following your breath out as it dissolves into the space around you and observing your moment-to-moment experience, you will be developing *peace* and *wisdom.*

- By persevering in the practice of meditation when faced with fear and obstacles, you will be developing *courage* and *self-reliance.*

- By practicing without becoming proud about what you have attained, you will be developing *humility* and *selflessness.*

- By taking delight in the fact that you have found a way to free your mind, you will be developing *joy* and *happiness.*

Through regular meditation practice, these and other attributes of good character can develop in you and yield many benefits. However, they cannot be developed in one day. Just as it takes a while for exercise to strengthen the body, it takes a while to "develop the good in you." But, with regular meditation practice, good character will develop in you. This will happen naturally, whether or not you make developing it your aim or goal. Gradually you'll overcome greed, hatred, and indifference and more of the positive aspects of your character will shine through everything you think, say, and do.

TERMINAL: Wilmington, Delaware

Harriet Tubman and two of her brothers fled to freedom in the summer of 1849. After being on the run for several days, her brothers became weary and were overtaken by fear and doubt. They argued with their sister about the wisdom of their decision to flee. Ultimately, they persuaded her to help them get back to the Eastern Shore of Maryland.

A few days later, after accompanying her brothers back, Tubman decided to flee alone. On the evening of her departure, she pretended to be doing a chore that gave her reason to go to the slaveholder's house, where her mother worked. Her intention was to tell her mother that she was about to leave, but she was unable to tell her because the slaveholder unexpectedly showed up. With no time to spare, she began singing a song with a coded message that the slaveholder would not understand but which conveyed to her mother that she was about to flee. She sang:

> I'll meet you in the morning,
> Safe in the promised land,
> On the other side of Jordan,
> Bound for the promised land.[1]

Tubman began her journey that evening at dusk by following the North Star. She stayed off the main roads to avoid being seen by slave catchers. Using her knowledge of the wilderness, she made her way through the forests and thickets and along the waterways of Maryland and Delaware, both of which were slaveholding states. As she moved northward, she used notes, owl hoots, hand signals, and other gestures to get the attention of Underground Railroad agents, who provided her with shelter, food, clothing, and guidance to help her continue on her way.

She had to be careful, though. There were always spies and informants in the region, who would pretend to be Underground Railroad agents and then, after gaining runaways' trust, would turn them in for rewards.

Although many of the details of Tubman's journey to freedom are not known, it is likely that her northward escape route took her in the vicinity of towns with free blacks—perhaps Denton in Maryland, as well as Sandtown, Camden, and New Castle in Delaware—and that she received help from African American Underground Railroad agents all along the way. No one knows for sure, because many African American agents in the South remained anonymous; they were known only to runaways and other Underground Railroad agents.

They remained anonymous for good reasons. Many runaways had been traumatized by white Southerners, and they were not predisposed to run into the outstretched arms of unknown white people without assurances from a trustworthy black person—often an African American agent—that the white agents could be trusted. Even Tubman recalled that before making her escape, "Every time I saw a white man I was afraid of being carried away."[2]

Thus, African American agents remained anonymous. If it became publicly known in the South that they were working for the Underground Railroad, they'd have to flee in order to avoid imprisonment or death, and their station would, in effect, cease operating. They would no longer be available to runaways looking for help as they trekked through the area. Therefore, they lay low, and in Tubman's case, it is very likely that African American agents forwarded her northward to a true, tried, and tested white man in Wilmington, the legendary stationmaster Thomas Garrett, and his wife, Rachel.

Thomas Garrett was a businessman and untiring antislavery activist who helped fugitives escape from slavery. In 1848, a federal court handed down several costly judgments against Garrett for helping Samuel and Emeline Hawkins escape to freedom with their children. When given the opportunity to speak at the end of the trial, he rose and defiantly said, "Judge, thou has not left me a dollar, but I wish to say to thee, and all in this court-room, that if anyone knows a fugitive who wants a shelter and a friend, send him to Thomas Garrett, and he will befriend him."[3]

In addition to financial loss, Garrett endured public ridicule and death threats. But he never wavered. Garrett and his wife sheltered runaways, arranged for them to be transported, and paid their transportation costs. They helped forward thousands of black men, women, and children across the Mason-Dixon Line to freedom. There is a very good likelihood that Tubman was one of them.

Garrett, who helped Tubman during her career as an Underground Railroad conductor, recalled one of their encounters:

> [O]n one occasion when I had not seen her for three months, she came into my store. I said, "Harriet, I am glad to see thee! I suppose thee wants a pair of new shoes." Her reply was, "I want more than that." I, in jest, said, "I have always been liberal with thee,

and wish to be; but I am not rich, and cannot afford to give much." Her reply was: "God tells me you have money for me." I asked her, "if God never deceived her?" She said, "No!" "Well! How much does thee want?" After studying a moment, she said: "About twenty-three dollars." I then gave her twenty-four dollars and some odd cents, the net proceeds of five pounds sterling, received through Eliza Wigham, of Scotland, for her.[4]

When Garrett died, in the winter of 1871, the one thing that distinguished his funeral service from many others was the presence of many blacks faces—many of them were the men and women and children of those he had helped escape from slavery. A group of them actually met to discuss how they could fittingly honor him. As an expression of their admiration, eight strong black men, working in two groups of four, carried the bier, on which his casket was placed, on their shoulders as they slowly made their way through the crowded streets of Wilmington to his final resting place, with the family and a long procession of friends following.

Thomas Garrett
Source: Historical Society of Delaware

4. Breathing

I had long since made up my mind that I would not trust myself in the hands of any man, white or colored...there were traitors, even among colored people. After dark, I emerged from the woods into a narrow path, which led me into the main travelled road. But I knew not which way to go. I did not know north from south, east from west. I looked in vain for the North Star; a heavy cloud hid it from my view. I walked up and down the road until near midnight, when the clouds disappeared, and I welcomed the sight of my friend—truly the slave's friend—the North Star!

—William Wells Brown, *Narrative of William W. Brown*
Former fugitive slave

To navigate their way from "the land of whips and chains" to "the land overflowing with milk and honey"—the North and Canada—runaways used the North Star. In order to find it, they had to first locate the Big Dipper in a clear night sky. The two stars on the very edge of the "cup" of the Big Dipper align with and point to the North Star. The North Star is the *end* of the handle of the Little Dipper. Upon locating the North Star, runaways simply needed to faithfully follow it until they reached the Promised Land.

The North Star is actually 10,000 times brighter and 100 times larger than our Sun, although it appears to be small and dim from Earth. This view from Earth, however, does not diminish the star's importance, as African American abolitionist Frederick Douglass notes in explaining his reason for naming his antislavery newspaper the *North Star*:

Of all the stars in this "brave, ever hanging sky," the NORTH STAR is our choice. To thousands now free... it has been the STAR of FREEDOM. To millions now in our boasted land of liberty, it is the STAR OF HOPE. Dark clouds may conceal, but cannot destroy it. Tempests may toss the sea, earthquakes convulse the globe and storm-bolts shake the sky; it stands as firm as Heaven. In its meek and twinkling rays are Faith, Hope and Freedom.[1]

Your Breath as Your North Star

In meditation, when we return our attention to our breath, we are using our breath as our "North Star." We are using it to guide us to freedom, and even though we may lose awareness of it, it is always there. However, sometimes our attention dwells so intently on thoughts that it's difficult to take it off our thoughts and rest it on our breath. As a result, it may become difficult for us to practice, to continue the journey. To help us let go, to rest our attention on the breath, we can use the breathing and counting exercises below.

The first breathing exercise is relatively simple. It's intended to help you familiarize yourself with your breath so that when your mind is overcast with clouds of thoughts, your breath—your North Star—will be easier to find. This exercise can be done anytime, especially as you begin your meditation session.

Breathing Exercise #1: Becoming Familiar With Your Breath

1. Sit or stand in a comfortable, upright posture.

2. Breathe naturally.

3. Place the palm of one hand on your belly.

4. As you inhale, allow your belly to expand.

5. As you exhale, allow your belly to contract.

6. Practice inhaling into your abdomen and exhaling from your abdomen.

7. Place both hands by your thighs, and practice inhaling and exhaling from your abdomen for a minute. Keep your attention on your belly, though. Feel your belly expand while inhaling and contract while exhaling.

8. Move your attention from your belly to your nostrils and rest your attention on the sensation of your breath as you inhale and exhale through your nostrils.

9. When your mind stabilizes, begin or resume meditation.

During your meditation session, counting your breaths can also help you to find and rest your attention on them. This is where the following exercise can help.

Breathing Exercise #2: Counting and Noting Your Breaths

To count your breaths, sit, relax, and begin calming meditation. Begin mentally counting each exhalation, up to four. Then start over again. For example: Exhaling, count "one." Inhale.

Exhaling again, count "two." Inhale. Exhaling again, count "three." Inhale. Exhaling once more, count "four." Then start this cycle over again, repeatedly counting your exhalations from one to four while observing your breath.

When you are comfortable counting breaths as described above, there are similar techniques you can use. For example:

> Mentally count each inhalation *and* exhalation consecutively from one to ten while observing your breath, for example, in (one), out (two), in (three), out (four) and so forth.

or

> Stop counting altogether, and begin noting your breath by mentally saying a word or phrase during each exhalation. For example, instead of counting one, two, three and four, you might say, "Be," "here," "right," "now." Mentally pronounce the syllable or word as you exhale. See if you can tie the words to your breath.

As you do these exercises, breathe as you usually do, without altering your natural breathing pattern. If your attention wanders, start over again at the beginning of the counting or noting cycle.

Remember that mentally counting or saying a word or phrase in this way is intended only to help you find and rest your attention on your breath. Counting and noting the breath are not a part of the meditation technique. Therefore, when your attention is able to rest on your breath with ease, stop counting or noting. Resume the meditation technique. Follow the instructions. Continue to follow your breath, your North Star.

***

The following breathing exercise can be done before you begin your meditation session or at any point during the day when your mind is oppressed by thoughts. Oppressed? Yes. Sometimes, thoughts merely cloud the mind; at other times, they toss the mind like the sea, convulse it like an earthquake, and rattle it like thunderbolts. If you have ever been upset and were tempted to say or do something that you knew you would regret, then you know that being able to move stormy clouds out of the way can be a useful skill to develop.

Breathing Exercise #3: Using Your Breath to Calm the Storm

1. Sit or stand in a comfortable posture, with your feet flat on the floor, your spine straight, and your shoulders relaxed.

2. Lower your head forward until your chin rests on your chest and empty your lungs of air by exhaling though your mouth.

3. Without straining, gradually inhale through your nostrils while lifting your chin/head off your chest and moving it backward until your lungs are full.

4. After your head is back (and you are looking upward), pause. Then exhale forcefully through your mouth, emptying your lungs, as you bring your head forward, returning it to the starting position with your chin resting on your chest.

5. Do four more repetitions of steps three and four. Then take two normal breaths.

6. Do five repetitions of steps three and four. Then take two normal breaths.

7. Do three repetitions of steps three and four. Then take two normal breaths.

The breathing exercises above can help you to remove your attention from thoughts that cloud your mind. They can help you to find your breath and rest your attention on it. Rest your attention on your breath lightly, enough to stay in contact. From then on, all you have to do is to follow the example of the heroic men and women of the Antebellum Period who made the journey from slavery to freedom: continue following your North Star. Keeping it in your awareness as you go through each day will enable you to go far.

A Final Note About the Breath

If you smoke tobacco products, you can also use the breath to help you take your attention off thoughts about lighting up. Stopping smoking is not easy. But look at Sojourner Truth, the former fugitive slave, abolitionist, and women's rights activist. If she could stop smoking, so can you. Look at Barack Obama, the president of the United States of America. If he can stop smoking with all he has on his shoulders, you can, too.

Consider, too, the history. The tobacco industry in the Antebellum Period brought many of our ancestors to an early death on tobacco plantations. The industry used its profits to buy more black people to replace those who perished. Today the same industry is reaping $3 billion in profits annually from the black community while contributing to forty-five thousand African American smoking-related deaths each year.[2] Its profits are used to market tobacco products that lure black people into bondage to nicotine addiction.

Don't be a slave to the tobacco industry (or to anything that is detrimental to your health and welfare). If you smoke, reclaim your existence. Use your breath to help you escape from slavery to freedom. Find a smoking cessation program or talk with your physician about starting nicotine replacement therapy. Think of your efforts to stop smoking as honoring the suffering and sacrifices of your ancestors.

Make better use of your breath and your life by meditating.

5. Thinking

He asked me what I wanted him to do. I said, "To get me away to Canada".... When I mentioned Canada to the gentleman, he sat for a full twenty minutes thoughtfully, and at last said, "Now, if I promise to take you away out of all of this, you must not mention a word to anyone. Don't breathe a syllable to your mother or sisters, or it will be betrayed." Oh, how my heart jumped for joy at this promise. I felt new life come into me.... I went home and passed an anxious day. I walked out to my poor old mother's hut, and saw her and my sisters. How I longed to tell them, and bid them farewell. I hesitated several times when I thought I should never see them more. I turned back again and again to look at my mother. I knew she would be flogged, old as she was, for my escaping. I could foresee how my master would stand over her with the lash to extort from her my hiding-place. I was her only son left. How she would suffer torture on my account.... At length I walked rapidly away, as if to leave my thoughts behind me....

—Francis Fedric, *Slave Life in Virginia and Kentucky*
Former fugitive slave

The slaves who gathered at the "secret place" to begin their journey to freedom sometimes carried a bundle, knapsack, or satchel containing food and personal belongings. Otherwise, all they carried with them was their body, breath and mind.

But *in* their minds, they carried plenty of thoughts about the past and future. They carried thoughts about the life they were leaving behind; thoughts about loved ones they'd never see again; thoughts about the bloodhounds and the slave catchers on their trail; thoughts about the dangerous insects, poisonous snakes, alligators, wolves, and bears that they were likely to encounter; thoughts about how they were going to obtain food, shelter, and clothing; and thoughts about the cruel punishment they would receive if they were captured.

To keep from being apprehended by slave catchers, runaways had to stop dwelling on their thoughts. They had to let go of thoughts about the past and future, so they could be attentive to what was happening around them. Then they'd be able to respond with skill and wisdom to threats to their freedom.

When you sit down to meditate, you'll have a lot of thoughts, too, although the concerns in your mind will be very different from those of the runaway slave. But as your session gets underway, you'll have to keep following the meditation technique. You'll have to let go of thoughts about the past and future, and rest your attention on your breath. This will calm your mind. As a result, you will become aware of some things about your thoughts you might not have noticed.

What might you become aware of? Let's find out.

Stop reading this, calm your mind, and just observe your mind for five to ten minutes.

***

One of the things you probably became aware of is that, not only do you have a lot of thoughts, you have many kinds of thoughts. You have thoughts that:

- vary in length—some are short, and others are long;
- are of various types—beliefs, memories, daydreams, fantasies, worries;
- vary in intensity, emotional and unemotional;
- concern the past or future, for the most part;
- are about our hopes and fears, what we want and don't want;

- originate from external influences such as advertising, popular music, movies, news, novels, school, church, work, friends, home;

- originate from our own experiences;

- explain or interpret our reality; and

- arise, stay a while, and fade; are not solid or lasting.

The Problem with Holding Thoughts

In the above exercise, you might also have noticed that some of your thoughts are about your "problems." However, sometimes those problems are not as difficult as our thoughts make them out to be. Indeed, if there is a problem, it often is our tendency to dwell, fixate, and hold our attention on our thoughts—thoughts that are unpleasant or pleasant, thoughts about the future or the past.

Dwelling, fixating, and holding on to thoughts about the past or future only generate more thoughts that agitate and cloud the mind. They keep our attention away from where we want it to be—on what is happening right *here*, right *now*, and on what we need to do, right *here*, right *now*, to resolve the actual problem.

Now actually is all we have. It is the only moment in which anything can happen, the only moment in which we can do anything, the only moment in which we can address our problems, the only moment in which we can uplift our lives. This is the reason you want to reside in *now*.

If your mind is not in the present moment, right *here*, right *now*, where is it? Is it in the past, shackled to fond memories, regrets and resentments, or is it in the future, manacled to worries, hopes, or cravings? When you take your attention off thoughts about the past or future and place it on your breath, you are able to see more clearly (and do more skillfully) the things you need to do, and are more available to do what is needed to uplift your life.

For example, when you come back to *now*, you might see that you need to wash the windows in your home, pay your bills, return a call, or even lose some weight, and actually do what is needed. Coming back to *now* can also allow you to notice a beautiful spring day, how glad you are that your mother is still here for you, and how wonderful it is to be in relatively good health. Awareness can influence the way we relate to our situation.

When our attention becomes distracted by thoughts about the past or future—when we dwell, fixate, and hold on to our thoughts—we often become confused, and mistake our thoughts for reality. If you have ever had a strongly held opinion about something that you thought had happened or would happen, only to find out that what you thought was incorrect, then you know how easy it is to mistake thoughts for reality. A quotation commonly attributed to African American professional basketball player Charles Barkley speaks to this limitation that we all have: "I don't care what people think. People are stupid."[1]

Of course, we are not really stupid. But often our minds are not in touch with things as they actually are because we are holding on to thoughts such as beliefs and opinions that are not in accord with reality, that actually cloud our minds and prevent us from seeing things clearly. This is another reason to free your mind: so you don't fall prey to your own or other people's "stupidity."

Also, holding tightly to our thoughts, as we tend to do with our precious beliefs and strong convictions, doesn't make them true. It's more likely to make it difficult to hear others' truth, to learn things, to grow, to behave in ways that are appropriate or helpful. Painful and tragic things happen every day because people hold too tightly to thoughts—their ideas, beliefs, opinions, and judgments about themselves, situations, and others—especially others of a different race, sex, age, sexual orientation, religion, political affiliation, nationality, ethnicity, social group or status, or even gang. Having the approval of respected and influential people and tradition doesn't make our thoughts true either.

We don't want to become delusional. This is one of the reasons we want to *calm* our mind and then *observe* it. What thoughts are causing you to think, speak, and behave in harmful or unhelpful ways? They are probably thoughts on which your attention habitually dwells. They are probably the ones that you want to let go because they are probably the ones that are controlling your mind and likely to imperil your journey, your efforts to become free.

When we let our thoughts go, return our attention to our breath, and follow our breath out as it dissolves in space, we are, metaphorically speaking, leaving the land of bondage. In the moment to moment experience of letting go, we are leaving behind thoughts, including hateful, greedy, sad, resentful, fearful, lustful, doubtful, and jealous ones, that have kept us shackled and bound. We enter a free state. In this free state our minds are in touch with the reality of what is actually happening, right *here*, right *now*—in each moment of *now*. We experience sanity. With such a free mind, we can then use it—with our breath and body—to create the sane life we want. We can uplift lives as free men and women.

Please note, though, that we are talking about letting go of thoughts. We are not trying to stop thoughts or stop thinking or get rid of thoughts. Thoughts and thinking really cannot be stopped. There are a couple of reasons for this.

First, thoughts and thinking are part of our nature. They make us human. Thoughts enable us to solve our problems, even ones that are caused by dwelling, fixating, and holding on to thoughts.

Second, even if having thoughts were not our nature, we wouldn't be able to stop them because they arise too quickly:

- We perceive (notice) sights, sounds, tastes, smells, touch, and thoughts.

- We recognize our perceptions—we notice that we notice!

- Then, we name our perceptions.

- After that, often based on past experiences, we judge our perceptions as pleasant or unpleasant.

- Finally, we act in some way, choosing either to let go of our thoughts about the experience or to hold on to them and begin weaving a story about them.

These phases occur so fast—in nanoseconds—that for the most part, the best we can do once we become aware that a thought has arisen is to refrain from generating additional thoughts by taking our attention off of it.

Rather than trying to stop thoughts and thinking, our practice is simply to observe our mind, acknowledge our thoughts without judgment, take our attention off the thoughts on which it is affixed, and gently rest it on the breath. When we let go of thoughts without judging or analyzing them, return our attention to the breath, and follow the breath out as it dissolves in the space around us, fewer thoughts arise. Then our mind is more present, open, and receptive to what is really going on and important in our lives.

Of course, this is subversive work that undermines the habit we have of attaching our attention to habitual thoughts and rigid notions about ourselves and the world. But when we loosen our attachment to them, clouds of thought dissipate, more light comes in, and it becomes easier for us to see and know what to do and to then skillfully do it. We are able to keep moving in the direction of freedom. As we move forward, we are better able to uplift all areas of our lives: relationships, health, education, work, and so forth. Rather than having a mind that is enslaved, we can come away to freedom and gain mastery over our lives.

TERMINAL: Philadelphia, Pennsylvania

Harriet Tubman became free upon crossing the Mason-Dixon Line into Pennsylvania. The Mason-Dixon Line was a boundary that separated the non-slaveholding states in the North from the slaveholding states in the South. When she crossed that line, her mind was no longer clouded with the fixed notions she had held about herself as a slave:

> When I found I had crossed that line, I looked at my hands to see if I was the same person. There was such a glory over everything; the sun came like gold through the trees, and over the fields, and I felt like I was in Heaven.[1]

From the Mason-Dixon Line, Tubman, now also physically free, continued traveling northward. No one knows for certain where or how she traveled. After all, the organization and efficiency of the Underground Railroad varied. In many areas there was no Underground Railroad at all, not even abolitionists, only supporters of slavery. As a result, fugitives often had to rely on their own ingenuity and resources.

Whatever way she traveled, Tubman reached Philadelphia. When she arrived, the "City of Brotherly Love" was the fourth largest city in the United States with a population of about 120,000 people, of whom nearly 20,000 were free blacks building a thriving community. Nevertheless, her heart ached. She was lonely for her people still in slavery:

> [M]y home, after all, was down in Maryland; because my father, mother, my brothers, and sisters, and friends were there. But I was free and *they* should be free. I would make a home in the North and bring them there, God helping me.[2]

Tubman decided to take action to free her people. But, first, and foremost, she uplifted her mind and personal situation. For example, with the help of the black community, she found work as a scrubwoman and maid in Philadelphia and Cape May, New Jersey, found a place to reside, and saved her earnings. She met key abolitionist figures and learned everything she could about the agents, stations, routes, stationmasters, stockholders, terminals, and brakemen/brakewomen of the Underground Railroad. And she began thinking about how she could use the underground network to bring her people to freedom.

In December 1850, Tubman received word that her niece, Kessiah Jolley Bowley, and her two children were going to be sold and taken further south. That was the very thing that had happened to Kessiah's mother, Linah.

Tubman had a plan. She traveled to Baltimore, Maryland, without being detected by the slave patrols that guarded the roads. The patrols checked black travelers for "free papers" to ensure there was no unauthorized travel by fugitives from slavery. Tubman hid in the city among free blacks, and waited for Kessiah's husband, a free black named John Bowley, to bring his family up the Chesapeake Bay. When they arrived, Tubman conducted them to freedom.

In the spring of 1851, Tubman returned to Maryland and brought her youngest brother to freedom. Then in the fall, she decided to embark on a more dangerous mission. She traveled all the way back to Dorchester County to get her husband, John Tubman. In making this trip, she was putting herself at risk of being seen by unsympathetic former neighbors who probably would have been delighted to run and tell the authorities that they had seen her.

Arriving after nightfall, Tubman found that her husband was now living with another woman and was unwilling to return with her to the North. She was very angry and disappointed, and upset enough to cause a scene, but she had to let go of her disappointment, and of the dream she had of life in freedom with her husband. Although she had gone there intending to conduct him to the North, she let go of the plan. Instead, she left with five other men who wanted her to show them the way out of slavery. So, through cold and wet autumn nights she conducted them to freedom.

When her friends found out what she had done, they were shocked and let her know they were concerned about her safety. They had good reason to be concerned. It was well known that such incursions into the South had resulted in the capture, imprisonment, and even death of the conductors involved.

Her friends' fears may have caused Tubman to hesitate. Tubman recalled that at one point,

> I said, "Oh Lord, I can't—don't ask me—take somebody else." Then I could hear the Lord answer, "It's you I want, Harriet Tubman"—just as clear I heard

him speak—and then I'd go again down South and bring up my brothers and sisters.[3]

In the twelve months after delivering her five passengers in Philadelphia, Tubman made several more trips into the South, bringing away about twenty people.

According to folklore, Tubman made as many as nineteen trips to the South (or "down into Egypt," as she often called the region), and enabled as many as three hundred slaves to become free. This does not include the seven hundred and fifty slaves she would help to free later as a scout with the Union army.

William Still, an African American stationmaster in Philadelphia, in describing Tubman's work as a conductor wrote:

> Harriet was a woman of no pretention, indeed, a more ordinary specimen of humanity could hardly be found among the most unfortunate-looking farm hands of the South. Yet, in point of courage, shrewdness and disinterested exertions to rescue her fellow-man, by making personal visits to Maryland among the slaves, she was without equal.[4]

Tubman may have been without equal; however, that did not keep her friends from worrying about her safety. In fact, as it became more apparent that she was extraordinary and precious, they became even more concerned. Thus, Thomas Garrett wrote, in a letter to Still:

> I have been very anxious for some time past, to hear what has become of Harriet Tubman. The last I heard of her, she was in the State of New York,

on her way to Canada with some friends [passengers], last fall. Has thee seen or heard anything of her lately? It would be a sorrowful fact, if such a hero as she, should be lost from the Underground Rail Road.[5]

Garrett was justifiably concerned about whether Tubman was safe, as this account, told to Sarah H. Bradford by Tubman, makes clear:

Sometimes, when she [Tubman] and her party were concealed in the woods, they saw their pursuers pass, on their horses, down the high road, tacking up the advertisements for them on the fences and trees.[6]

Still also conveyed to Tubman his concerns about her safety. But it was to no avail. Still wrote,

Great fears were entertained for her safety, but she seemed wholly devoid of fear. The idea of being captured by slave-hunters or slave holders, seemed never to enter her mind. She was apparently proof against all adversaries. While she thus manifested such utter personal indifference, she was much more watchful with regard to those she was piloting.[7]

Father of the Underground Railroad

Like Tubman, William Still was also fearless. He and his wife, Letitia George, were stationmasters in Philadelphia.

Additionally, Still was a leading member of the Pennsylvania Anti-Slavery Society and chairman of the Philadelphia Vigilant Committee. Working with abolitionists such as African American Robert Purvis, he helped oversee the best organized and most efficient Underground Railroad system in the country. Thousands of runaways were directed from Philadelphia to New York City, New Bedford, Boston, and points beyond. Others were forwarded to points northwest, including Syracuse, Rochester, Buffalo, and St. Catharines.

To keep the system operating smoothly, Still coordinated with a vast network of influential railroad agents in the South, the North, and Canada. When necessary, he also directly intervened to help slaves flee. For example, once, he was informed by a black hotel worker that there was an enslaved woman in town who was telling other black workers that she wanted to become free. The woman was Jane Johnson, who had her two children with her. They had arrived in the city with their slaveholder, the US Minister to Nicaragua.

Still and a white abolitionist, Passmore Williamson, caught up with Johnson and her slaveholder after they boarded a steamboat that was about to leave for New York City, from which they were to set sail for Nicaragua. Basically, they told Jane that any slave entering Pennsylvania was free, and that if she wanted to become free all she had to do was to let go of the thought that she was a slave and walk away a free woman. When the US minister protested, they told Johnson:

> You are entitled to your freedom.... If you prefer freedom to slavery, as we suppose everyone does, you have the chance to accept it now. Act calmly—don't be frightened by your master—you are as much entitled to your freedom as we are, or he is—be determined and you need have no fears but that

you will be protected by the law.... Of course, if you want to remain a slave with your master, we cannot force you to leave; we only want to make you sensible of your rights. *Remember, if you lose this chance you may never get such another....* [8]

Still, who would later face trial along with Williamson and five black porters who got into a tussle with the minister, walked away with Jane and her children. He got them away to New York City. Later, Johnson and her children settled in Boston.

The *New York Times* would later call Still "the Father of the Underground Railroad."[9] The extensive records he kept of Philadelphia's Underground Railroad activities proved invaluable to fugitive slaves seeking their loved ones and as a rich historical record for the future. In 1872, he published his records, which consist of correspondence with leading Underground Railroad agents and interviews with hundreds of runaways who passed through Philadelphia on their way to freedom. His book, *Underground Railroad*, is a national treasure.

William Still
Source: Wikipedia

6. Reading

"Now," he said, "if you teach that nigger [speaking of myself]
how to read, there would be no keeping him. It would forever
unfit him to be a slave...." I now understood what had been
to me a most perplexing difficulty—to wit, the white man's
power to enslave the black man. It was a grand achievement,
and I prized it highly. From that moment, I understood the
pathway from slavery to freedom.

—Frederick Douglass,
Narrative of the Life of Frederick Douglass
Former fugitive slave

By 1840, most of the US slave population had been born in America. However, many of them did not know much about their African past. Their means for learning—African tribal, communal, and familial bonds—had been severely weakened, almost destroyed. Without strong communal and family bonds it was difficult for them to learn about African history and culture and to transmit it to their descendants.

Although some aspects of African culture survived in the United States, such as music, dance, and religion, much of what the enslaved population learned about Africa and anything else came from the slaveholding society. And the society taught blacks that they were inferior.

Frederick Douglass recalled some of the lessons he was taught:

[W]e had been taught...the duty of obedience to our masters; to recognize God as the author of our enslavement; to regard running away an offense, alike against God and man; to deem our enslavement a merciful and beneficial arrangement; to esteem our condition, in this country, a paradise to that from which we had been snatched in Africa; to consider our hard hand and dark color as God's mark of displeasure, and as pointing us out as the proper subjects of slavery; that the relation of master and slave was one of reciprocal benefits; that our work was not more serviceable to our masters, than our master's thinking was serviceable to us.[1]

The purpose of the "education" that Douglass received was to keep him ignorant and content with being a slave. Its objective was to prevent him from seeing that he possessed inherent goodness, genius, and potential. However, Douglass decided to undo the miseducation he had received by doing the very thing that would make him *forever* unfit to be a slave. He decided to gain knowledge about the world—and correct knowledge about himself—by learning how to read.

Like Douglass, we can learn about our world, ourselves, and our possibilities by reading. Obviously, there are millions of subjects and types of writing you might explore, either online or in books, magazines, newspapers, and so on. You might want to go to the library or a bookstore and just see what captures your interest. That can be a good way to begin, if you are not already in the habit of reading.

In addition to whatever you may already be interested in, it can be of great benefit to explore African, and African American, history. Reading about our history can help us restore the ancestral bonds that were severed during slavery, and can enable us to receive wisdom from our ancestors. The more we read, study, and reflect on our history, the more we find out about who we are today. This can enable us to shed a European-centered consciousness—still stained with notions of white superiority and black inferiority—and develop more of an African-centered consciousness, one that heals, inspires and empowers us to break free from many harmful thoughts to which our minds have been bound.

Here are a few things you can do to gain knowledge about who you are:

- Explore the many books, periodicals, magazines, newspapers, films, and documentaries that discuss and show African and African American history and culture. If you're not sure where to start, you could get some ideas for this by exploring the Bibliography section at the end of this book, or check online. You may also find that there is an African American bookstore in your area.

- Research genealogical records concerning members of your family, write the history of your family using a pedigree chart, and distribute this information to several family members for safekeeping.

- Conduct recorded interviews with your elders about their memories and perceptions of important historical events, notable people, and their everyday lives. Listen deeply. Share copies of your recordings.

- Develop genuine relationships with native Africans and descendants of Africans who were enslaved and shipped to the Americas, Middle East, Europe and Asia who are living in the United States. Learn about their native cultures and their experience in America.

- Look for opportunities to use art, music, dance, songs, poems, proverbs, and reenactment to learn and tell inspiring stories about African American history and culture.

To gain knowledge about ourselves, we not only need to read about our history and culture, we also need to "read" our minds. In other words, we need to look into our minds and closely observe our thoughts and patterns of thinking. What thoughts are going through our minds?

When you look into your mind and observe your thoughts, you are observing what African American entertainer Sammy Davis, Jr. called, "The ultimate mystery... one's own self."[2] Have you ever done something and then thought, "Why did I do that?" You might, indeed, be a mystery to yourself if you do not regularly take time to closely observe your mind. If you do regularly observe, you will become increasingly aware of what makes you uniquely who you are, what drives your behavior—your habitual thoughts about the past and future, your hopes and fears. You'll become aware of the habitual thoughts—both helpful and unhelpful—that influence what you think, say, and do.

In the following reading meditation we are going to allow ourselves to *be* so that we can *read*. We are going to sit relaxed in a quiet place. We are going to calm our mind and look into it. We are simply going to observe the content of whatever arises in the mind without dwelling, fixating, or holding on to it. Instead of labeling thoughts as "thoughts," we are going to call them what they are about (for example, if we are thinking about the rent being due, we might inaudibly say "about rent"). We are then going to let go of our thoughts and return our attention to the full cycle of our breath, our North Star. We are going to repeat this process whenever we become aware of our thoughts.

This technique is similar to the calming meditation technique, except that we are bringing a little bit more awareness to what we are thinking *about* rather than simply recognizing our thoughts and letting them go.

Reading Meditation

1. Take a seat in a quiet place and practice the calming meditation technique for several minutes.

2. When your mind is calm, transition to reading meditation:
   a Without lowering your head, lower your gaze to an area on the floor that is about three feet in front of you.
   b Rest your attention on the sensation of your breath. But rather than following your exhalation out as it dissipates, simply allow your attention to rest on each full cycle of breathing (inhalation and exhalation).
   c When you become aware of thoughts, recognize what the thoughts are *about*—say to yourself what your thoughts are about without dwelling, fixating, or holding on to them—and then gently return your attention to the full cycle of breathing.
   d Continue practicing in this way.

When you look at yourself in the mirror of your mind, you become more familiar with many habitual thoughts. Some of the thoughts influence your notions of who you are and the world you're in. Some of them influence your behavior. You are not going to like everything you see. You may find it difficult to simply *be*. Emotions may arise. You might even have difficulty keeping your seat. Whatever arises, continue reading with an attitude of acceptance and kindness towards your experience and yourself. Continue reading. If you become overwhelmed or lost in thoughts, you can always return to the calming meditation technique for a while, and then resume this technique.

"Check out your mind," as the rhythm-and-blues group the Impressions sang. Checking out your mind is the way you get to "know thyself." It can help you discover who you truly are and what you can do to create a new life in freedom.

Check out your mind. You may become aware of the habitual thoughts, beliefs, and behaviors that make you who you are and that made your present situation what it is. *Check out your mind.* You may become aware of choices you've made—some wise, some unwise—as well as the effects of those choices, and that perhaps there are different choices available to you. *Check out your mind.* You may become aware that much of what you think is going on in your world is actually only going on in your mind, and that you can change your relationship with your world for the better simply by shifting your perspective, developing a more positive attitude, or being a little more caring and skillful. *Check out your mind.* Although you may feel that someone is oppressing you, you might discover, to quote African American writer and educator Toni Morrison, that in actuality, "You are confined by your own system of oppression."[3] *Check out your mind.*

You are not powerless. You always have power. This is because you always have freedom of choice, even in the worst situations. As President Obama said, "[Y]es, if you're African American, the odds of growing up amid crime and gangs are higher. Yes, if you live in a poor neighborhood, you will face challenges that somebody in a wealthy suburb does not have to face. But.... No one has written your destiny for you. Your destiny is in your hands—you cannot forget that."[4]

The question is, how are you going to use the power you have? What choice are you going to make? Are you going to dwell, fixate, and hold on, and thereby defeat the very power you possess to uplift yourself? Or are you going to let go and return your attention to the breath, to the present moment, to right *here*, right *now*, so you can become free?

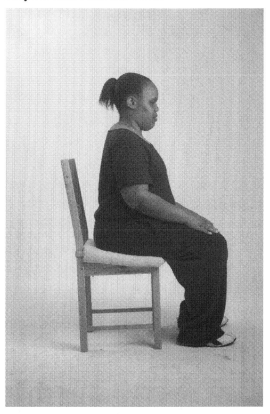

"Read! read! read! and never stop until you discover the knowledge of the Universe," said the black nationalist Marcus Garvey.[5] An important part of this "knowledge of the Universe" is you yourself. Keep reading, keep looking. The more often you do this, the more you will see and understand, and the freer you will become.

7. Awakening

The silver trump of freedom had aroused my soul to eternal wakefulness. Freedom now appeared, to disappear no more forever. It was heard in every sound, and seen in everything. It was ever present to torment me with a sense of my wretched condition. I saw nothing without seeing it. I heard nothing without hearing it. I felt nothing without feeling it. It looked from every star. It smiled in every calm. It breathed in every wind, and moved in every storm.

—Frederick Douglass,
Narrative of the Life of Frederick Douglass
Former fugitive slave

Arguments over slavery that were made during the founding of our nation continued for decades after the US Constitution was ratified. As the debate changed attitudes and laws, the enslaved population shifted accordingly.

In 1790, about 40,000 of the approximately 694,000 slaves in the United States were located in the North, but over the next seventy years this number decreased. By 1860, the only African Americans in the North were about 226,000 free blacks (of which about 70,000 were mulattos). Most of the nearly 3,954,000 people living in slavery in the United States that year (of which about 411,000 were mulattos) were located in the South (which was also home to about 261,000 free blacks, of which about 107,000 were mulattos). Also in the South, there were about 8,300 African Americans enslaved in the Indian Territory.[1]

Two factors contributed to the dramatic increase in the slave population throughout the South: the invention of the cotton gin by Eli Whitney in 1793, and the global demand for cotton. The cotton gin could quickly remove seeds from cotton, without the time-consuming process of having slaves do it by hand. For example, whereas it would take one slave an entire day to manually remove the seeds from one pound of cotton, with a cotton gin, the seeds from fifty pounds of cotton could be removed in one day.

What this technological breakthrough signaled to Southern cotton planters, especially in the Deep South, was that they could now make huge profits. All they had to do was to grow and export more cotton with the labor of more slaves. Although fewer slaves were now needed to remove the seeds, more slaves were needed to cultivate and grow the cotton on the large tracts of land acquired by the planters. Slaveholders obtained more slaves through births, buying slaves from slave traders in the north, and illegally importing slaves from Africa. Thus, the slave population in the South steadily grew. By 1860, 13 percent of the US population was enslaved.

Although slavery was illegal in the North, the Northern economy remained intimately tied to the domestic and international slave trade and the institution of slavery. The North was heavily involved in the construction, financing, and outfitting of ships involved in the slave trade, the refinement of Southern slave-grown goods, and the transport of goods produced by slave labor to world markets. Slavery was not merely the source of many Northerners' livelihood. It was the driving force behind the US economy, and generated immense wealth for all areas of the country.

Slavery was so important to the US economy that, by 1860, slaves had become the second largest form of capital investment, after real estate. Cotton grown by slaves accounted for 60 percent of the country's exports and 75 percent of the cotton produced in the world. The blood, sweat, and tears of people of African ancestry enabled whites to prosper and the United States to emerge on the world stage as an economic power.

As the nation's slave-based economy grew, a religious awakening swept through the country. What it awakened mostly were the country's divergent views on slavery. Supporters of slavery used Bible scripture such as Genesis 9:25-27, Ephesians 6:4-9, Titus 2:9, Leviticus 25:44-46, Colossians 3:22, and 1 Peter 2:18 to argue that there was nothing wrong with slavery. Opponents of slavery, on the other hand, used the Bible to argue that more important than scripture were basic Christian principles, such as "Love thy neighbor as thyself," and that the institution of slavery was a violation of all of them.

Our ancestors, most of whom were illiterate, did not need religious scripture or principles to know that slavery was evil. Thus, their escapes, acts of resistance and rebellion continued. With them, religion-inspired antislavery activity increased, too.

For a time, the American Anti-Slavery Society was a leading force in the fight to abolish slavery. The Society was founded in 1833 by sixty-three delegates from eleven states. Many of the local affiliates of the Society were racially segregated because many white antislavery activists, although against slavery, were also against interracial mixing. Such racial prejudice did not deter the antislavery work of African Americans. In particular, African American women continued to divide their time between their jobs and running households in which fugitives were sheltered. They organized financial support for abolitionist newspapers such as the *Liberator,* led petition drives, distributed meeting notices, and with increasing regularity spoke against slavery at public gatherings.

One of the early publications that contributed to Northern abolitionist sentiment was *Letters on American Slavery,* a book written by the white Presbyterian minister John Rankin. Published in 1826, at a time when most white abolitionists believed that colonization was the solution to the "race problem" in the United States, the book was one of the earliest calls by a white person for immediate emancipation. Within a few years, it had become essential reading for anyone involved in the abolitionist movement.

Another early publication was *Walker's Appeal, in Four Articles; Together with a Preamble, to the Coloured Citizens of the World, but in Particular, and Very Expressly, to Those of the United States of America*. This pamphlet was published in 1829 by African American abolitionist David Walker, a year before his "mysterious" death. *Walker's Appeal* refuted the notion that white people are superior, called for the enslaved population to revolt against their masters, and urged free blacks to reject white racist schemes to get them to emigrate to Africa. Walker wrote,

> America is more our country, than it is the whites'— we have enriched it with our blood and tears. The greatest riches in all America have arisen from our blood and tears:—will they drive us from our property and homes, which we have earned with our blood? They must look sharp or this very thing will bring swift destruction upon them. The Americans have got so fat on our blood and groans, that they have almost forgotten....[2]

Walker's Appeal reaffirmed for blacks and for white abolitionists that no matter how slavery and colonization might be justified, they were completely unacceptable. *Walker's Appeal* angered Southerners so much that his pamphlet was banned. In Georgia, substantial rewards for Walker's capture, dead or alive, were offered. Nevertheless, his pamphlet continued to be distributed up and down the Atlantic Coast, thanks to free black sailors. The circulation of the pamphlet caused quite an alarm, but not as much as Nat Turner's insurrection in 1831.

Another publication was the *Liberator*, a newspaper founded in 1831 by the white abolitionist and social reformer William Lloyd Garrison. The paper, which was largely financed by free blacks, took a radical, inflammatory, and uncompromising stance on the issue of slavery. It argued that the US Constitution was nothing but a slavery document, condemned schemes to colonize free blacks in the strongest possible terms, called for the immediate emancipation of all slaves, opposed compensating slaveholders for emancipating slaves, and urged the use of moral persuasion rather than political action such as voting to bring about the abolition of slavery.

Frederick Douglass's autobiography, *Narrative of the Life of Frederick Douglass, an American Slave*, was published in 1845. It gave an elegantly written firsthand account of slavery. Douglass's book was so thoughtful and well written that critics—under the delusion that white people are superior—could not believe that a person of African ancestry who had never attended a single day of school could have written it. Thus, they tried to discredit the book and its author.

Another influential book was *Uncle Tom's Cabin*, an anti-slavery novel written by Harriet Beecher Stowe. Published in 1852, the novel was fiction based, in part, on the real stories told by fugitive slaves. Several hundred thousand copies of the book were sold within twelve months of its release. Even a play was produced, based on the book. However, Harriet Tubman was not particularly impressed. She remarked, "I've heard *Uncle Tom's Cabin* read, and I tell you Mrs. Stowe's pen hasn't begun to paint what slavery is as I have seen it [in the] South. I've seen the real thing, and I don't want to see it on stage or in the theater."[3]

One year later, in 1853, *Twelve Years a Slave* was published. The book was written by Solomon Northup, a freeborn black living in the North. He gave an account of being kidnapped, enslaved in the South for twelve years, and freed. Thousands of copies of his book were quickly sold. One of the most powerful depictions of slave life can be found in the film *Twelve Years a Slave*, which won the Academy Award for Best Picture in 2014.

Seeing Things Freshly

Before any supporter of slavery could buy, read, or appreciate the various antislavery publications, they had to let go of their biases. They had to relate to their own preconceived notions about slavery in an objective way—without dwelling, fixating, or holding on to them. Many proslavery Northerners did, and in the process they became more aware of how degrading slavery was and how poorly informed they had been about it, and about black people. With this greater awareness, many of them abandoned their misinformed views and joined the abolitionist movement.

A similar process occurs in meditation. When you relate to your thoughts—what you think, believe, and have been told—in an objective, impartial, unbiased way, without dwelling, fixating or holding on to them, your mind becomes clear. You become more conscious. You become more aware of things as they actually *are* in reality, rather than simply as you think, were told, and were led to believe. You begin to awaken.

You can move in the direction of awakening by practicing the meditation technique below.

Awakening Meditation

1. Take a seat and practice the calming meditation technique for several minutes.

2. Transition to awakening meditation: Continue to give some of your attention to your breath and follow it out as it dissipates in the space around you. But mostly be aware of the space around you. To do this, lift your gaze so that you are still looking forward but with a wider awareness of the space in the room you are seated in.

3. When thoughts arise, instead of viewing them as distractions or labeling them as "thoughts," view them as signals or cues for you to remain aware of the space around you—and do that. Stay awake. Do not allow your attention to dwell, fixate, or hold on to thoughts or to become drawn to distraction. Relate to thoughts and distraction without bias.

4. Continue practicing in this way. Stay awake. If this technique becomes too challenging after awhile, resume calming technique, and later transition back to awakening meditation.

When you stay awake with a mind that is open to your world, you begin to see more clearly, and can see a lot. Who knows? You might begin to see that the difficult person in your life is actually a human being, just like you. You might begin to see that the people around you need love and kindness, just as you do. You might begin to see previously unnoticed opportunities to accomplish the things you're trying to do. You might see thoughts and beliefs that have held you back, and you may notice ones that are helpful, and wise. You might see that someone wanted to tell you something that you were not open to hearing which you need to listen to now.

When you awaken, repeatedly, to the wisdom of letting go and being fully present in each moment, it is just a matter of time before the intelligence you were born with summons into existence a "new you." Little by little you become aware of ideas and beliefs about reality—thoughts—that have kept you asleep, have impeded the unfolding of your inherent goodness, genius, and potential.

Every time you notice and let go, the true *you*, the authentic *you*, more aware of your inherent dignity, comes further into being. It is the *you*, yourself, without labels: tall, short, slim, overweight, black, male, female, father, mother, son, daughter, attractive, unattractive, student, married, unmarried, employed, unemployed, ex-offender, citizen, good, bad, nice, mean, and so forth. This is *you* without what African American poet Paul Laurence Dunbar called "the mask that grins and lies." This is the *you* who, instead of cultivating a mind that conforms, is allowing your mind to be transformed, awakened, freed from habits of thought so *you* can become aware of what is true. This *you* is the unfabricated *you*, without concepts, labels, and masks; with fresh ways of seeing the world and new ways of thinking, speaking, and behaving. You may well see that both you and your world are much more vibrant and interesting than you realized.

Meditation is about allowing our thoughts, concepts, beliefs, opinions, judgments, and labels—all the notions we have about reality that are keeping us bound—to rise, abide, and fade. It's about being without bias, waking up to a new day, and seeing yourself, others, and the world as they actually are, and using that realization to uplift yourself and your people.

TERMINAL: New York City, New York

Harriet Tubman initially thought she could safely resettle her family and friends in the abolitionist cities of the North. After all, the Fugitive Slave Act of 1793, which contained provisions for the return of runaway slaves, was rarely enforced. However, the situation changed when the Fugitive Slave Act of 1850 became law.

The 1850 law made it easier for slave owners to retake runaway slaves and it was more rigorously enforced. This development convinced Tubman that her loved ones were not safe anywhere in the United States. "I wouldn't trust Uncle Sam with my people," she declared. So she decided to take her family and friends "clear off to Canada."[1]

Tubman took different routes. Sometimes she went through New York City—in 1850, the largest US city, with a population of about 700,000 people. There, to raise funds to help with transportation, food, clothing, and resettlement expenses for her passengers, she performed odd jobs and asked friendly abolitionists for donations. One white abolitionist in the city, Oliver Johnson, remembered her visits:

> During the period of my official connection with the Anti-Slavery office in New York, I saw her [Tubman] frequently, when she came with the

companies of slaves, whom she had successfully piloted away from the South; and often listened with wonder to the story of her adventures and hair-breadth escapes.

She always told her tale with a modesty which showed how unconscious she was of having done anything more than her simple duty. No one who listened to her could doubt her perfect truthfulness and integrity.

Her shrewdness in planning the escapes of slaves, her skill in avoiding arrest, her courage in every emergency, and her willingness to endure hardship and face any danger for the sake of her poor followers was phenomenal.[2]

Tubman was phenomenal because she was very familiar with the geography through which she traveled; knew a great deal about the operation of the Underground Railroad; was courageous, intelligent and self-disciplined; was a master of subterfuge, possessed good character, and had the ability to lead others. These attributes enabled her to move between Canada, the North, and the South, and from station to station, year after year, unnoticed and untouched by her enemies.

Among the runaways Tubman would eventually bring with her to New York City, on the way to Canada, were her brothers, Ben, Henry, and Robert. However, it took the powers of premonition, ruse, and shrewd conducting to get them there.

One day Tubman received a premonition, a message from her higher power, that misfortune was about to come to her brothers. So she decided to let them know that she was coming for them.

She got a friend to write a letter for her to a free, literate black man, Jacob Jackson, who lived near her brothers. She knew that Jackson's son had recently escaped to the North and that, for this reason, everything Jackson did was closely observed by local authorities. She also knew that the authorities opened and read Jackson's mail before delivering it to him. Therefore, she dictated a carefully worded letter, and placed it in the mail.

The letter that the local authorities read discussed various mundane matters. But it ended with words that Tubman knew only Jackson would understand: "Read my letter to the old folks, and give my love to them, and tell my brothers to be always watching unto prayer, and when the good old ship of Zion comes along, to be ready to step on board."[3] The letter was signed deceptively with Jacob's son's name. The local censors could not make sense of the letter and turned it over to Jackson.

True to her word, Tubman arrived in Dorchester County a few days before Christmas. The first thing she discovered was that her brothers were going to be sold at auction the day after Christmas. She promptly sent word with a trusted friend to her brothers to meet her at their father's cabin that evening. When it was time for her to depart, Ben and Henry were present but not Robert.

Robert wasn't there because his wife was in labor and about to deliver a baby. Although Tubman loved Robert, his wife, and the soon-to-be-born baby, she *never* waited for anyone who did not arrive on time after being presented with an opportunity to become free. Therefore, she departed without him. Fortunately for Robert, he was able to leave his family and catch up with his siblings.

On December 29, 1854, Tubman's brothers were interviewed in Philadelphia in the Anti-Slavery office by William Still. They proceeded on to New York City, where African American station master Jacob R. Gibbs was active in harboring runaways forwarded to him by Still. From there, Tubman led her brothers west across the state, through Albany, and on to Canada.

According to journalist Franklin B. Sanborn, the brothers faced a severe winter in Canada, but their sister helped them get through:

> They earned their bread by chopping wood in the snows of a Canadian forest; they were frostbitten, hungry, and naked. Harriet was their good angel. She kept house for her brothers, and the poor creature[s] boarded with her. She worked for them, begged for them, prayed for them...and carried them by the help of God through the hard winter.[4]

Tubman was not the only noteworthy African American woman who traveled through New York City. In the 1830s, Maria W. Stewart, who had begun speaking publicly in the North on behalf of the rights of women and African Americans, also spoke in the city. At the time, a woman speaking in public—no matter what she was saying—would be met with resistance and aggression, and because of it Stewart finally stopped giving public speeches. But later others, such as Sarah Forten, Sarah Parker Remond, Mary Ann Shadd Cary, and Sojourner Truth, followed in her footsteps by speaking publicly on behalf of their people.

Another outspoken African American antislavery lecturer was Frances Ellen Watkins Harper. She was born in Baltimore, in 1825, where after her mother's death she was raised by an uncle, William Watkins, and his wife, Harriet. Watkins was a free black minister and highly regarded educator, as well as an influential figure in the abolitionist movement. Through the Watkins' influence, Harper received a thorough academic education and vocational training in the domestic sciences (sewing, cooking, and other household skills), obtained a job in a bookstore, where she immersed herself in reading, and began writing poetry. She published her first book of poems, *Forest Leaves,* at age 20.

Harper took a job teaching at a school for blacks, called Union Seminary, forerunner to Wilberforce University. After a couple of years there, she accepted a similar position at a school in Little York, Pennsylvania, all the while continuing to write her poetry. However, continual exposure to the comings and goings of runaways and the operation of the Underground Railroad, and the passage of a Maryland law authorizing the enslavement of any free black person entering the state, influenced her to undertake a new vocation.

Harper moved to Philadelphia, where she became an associate of William Still, and began reading her poetry and speaking out against slavery at abolitionist gatherings. These activities took her to Boston, where she gave several praiseworthy lectures. She was eventually hired by the Maine Anti-Slavery Society to join its abolitionist speaking circuit. While she was becoming a popular and sought-after speaker throughout New England, she published, in 1854, *Poems on Miscellaneous Subjects.* Her book sold thousands of copies.

Eventually, Harper broke away from the Maine Anti-Slavery Society and began to lecture independently throughout the North, and write poetry and prose on the subject of slavery and equal rights. As her appeal grew, proslavery Northerners started sabotaging public events where she was to speak. They didn't want anyone to hear what she had to say. But instead of quieting down, she continued to eloquently speak up for her people. Thus, in May 1857, she rose to speak at a gathering organized by the New York Anti-Slavery Society, telling it,

A hundred thousand newborn babies are annually added to the victims of slavery; twenty thousand lives are annually sacrificed on the plantations of the South. Such a sight should send a thrill of horror through the nerves of civilization and impel the heart of humanity to lofty deeds. So it might, if men had not found out a fearful alchemy by which this blood can be transformed into gold. Instead of listening to the cry of agony, they listen to the ring of dollars and stoop down to pick up the coin. (applause) [5]

Foremost an abolitionist, Harper would go on to become one of the most prolific African American writers of poetry and prose in the nineteenth century. She authored "The Two Offers," the first short story published by an African American woman, and *Iola Leroy, Or, Shadows Uplifted*, the first novel published by an African American woman. And she became a leading lecturer in the United States on the subjects of racial equality and women's rights.

Frances Ellen Watkins Harper
Source: Maryland State Archives

8. Walking

We started without money and without clothes, except what we wore, (not daring to carry a bundle) but with our hearts full of hope. We travelled by night, and slept in the woods during the day. After travelling two or three nights, we got alarmed and turned out to the road, and before we turned on to it again, it had separated again and we took the wrong road. It was cloudy for two or three days, and, after travelling three nights, we found ourselves just where we were three days before and almost home again. We were sadly disappointed, but not discouraged; and so, turning our faces northward, we went on.

—James Curry, Former fugitive slave
quoted in *Slave Testimony*,
edited by John W. Blassingame

Slaves fleeing from Southern plantations on foot had to be self-reliant, determined, brave and intelligent. They usually traveled without maps, adequate clothes, footwear, or protection from wild animals. They ate roots, herbs, nuts, and berries, if they were available; treated their own injuries and illnesses; dealt with whatever challenges arose during their trek; and retreated to woods, swamps, caves, or unoccupied buildings to avoid being captured.

The flight of runaway slaves was not easy, as Wilmington College professor emeritus of history Larry Gara makes clear:

In 1844, a slave who had walked all the way from Louisiana arrived in New England. The fugitive was "very shy and would not trust himself in any kind of vehicle." For several months another fugitive, this one a woman, made her way alone from Mississippi to Canada. She was not aided on her way until she reached Illinois. One fugitive took a year to go from Alabama to Ohio, and another young fugitive from that state covered twelve hundred miles "traveling only in the night, feeding on roots and wild [berries]," before reaching Pennsylvania.[1]

The journey of runaways was always challenging, as this account from William Wells Brown portrays:

Travelling along the road, I would sometimes speak to myself, sounding my name over, by way of getting used to it, before I should arrive among civilized beings. On the fifth or six day, it rained very fast, and froze about as fast as it fell, so that my clothes were one glare of ice. I travelled on at night until I became so chilled and benumbed—the wind blowing into my face—that I found it impossible to go any further, and accordingly took shelter in a barn, where I was obliged to walk to keep from freezing.

I have ever looked upon that night as the most eventful part of my escape from slavery. Nothing but the providence of God, and that old barn, saved me from freezing to death. I received a very severe cold, which settled upon my lungs, and from time to time my feet had been frostbitten, so that it was with difficulty I could walk. In this situation I travelled two days, when I found that I must seek shelter somewhere, or die.[2]

The difficulty that Brown and many other fugitives experienced points to an often overlooked fact: Generally, runaways did not receive any help from the Northern abolitionists, if they received any help at all, until they had completed the most difficult phase of their journey through the South and crossed over into the North. The adversity they experienced, however, did not make them weak. It made them stronger. Every step they took developed their character; it strengthened their resolve and confidence in their inherent goodness, genius and potential.

Similar to our ancestors, you can strengthen your resolve and confidence by walking to freedom. Let's try it.

Walking-to-Freedom Meditation

1. Find an area where you can walk back and forth on a straight path without tripping over anything. Although a twenty-to-thirty-foot path is ideal, any amount of space you have will do.

2. Stand at the beginning of the path. Face straight forward with your eyes open. Your head should be positioned like an African woman balancing a basket on her head. Without lowering your head, look at an area of the floor that is about ten feet in front of you. If your space does not allow this distance, maintain your gaze as if it did. Gently hold this soft gaze.

3. Bring your attention to your breath. Observe your body breathing. Then, bring your awareness to each part of your body, observing, moment to moment, without judgment, the sensations you find. Begin with the soles of your feet and your heels and toes, then your ankles, calves, knees,

thighs, pelvis, abdomen, chest, shoulders, back, arms, hands, neck, head, and face; then reverse the order and move your awareness downward, moment to moment, in a non-judgmental way.

4. Next, rest your attention on the sensations in the soles of your feet.

5. Start walking slowly in a relaxed, unhurried, and fluid way, holding your closed left hand with your right hand on top of it at the abdomen as shown in the photo below.

6. As you take each step, continue to rest your attention on sensations in the soles of your feet, while maintaining an awareness of what's happening within and around you, moment to moment, without judgment.

7. Whatever you become distracted by—a compelling thought, aroma, sound, sight, sensation, and so forth— just notice it, without judgment, and gently return your attention to the sensations in your feet as you continue to walk forward with awareness of your environment.

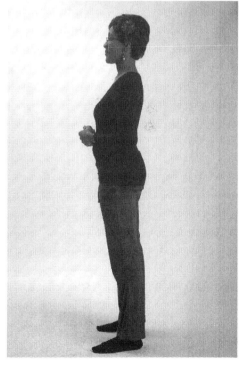

8. When you reach the end of the

path—however long or short it is—turn around and in the same way walk back to the other end. Continue walking back and forth like this—dignified and awake—for several minutes, mindful of the sensations in your feet, and aware of your environment.

You will find walking-to-freedom meditation especially helpful on those occasions when you forget or don't have time to practice sitting meditation. You can use this technique when you walk to or from the area where you meditate, between rooms, or down a hallway in your home or at work, outdoors on a sidewalk, at the bus stop, in a park, or in an open field. You can practice this technique almost anywhere! Just be aware of the sensations in your feet as you walk.

But don't put yourself or others in danger. When you practice

this technique away from the safety of your meditation space, you must remain alert to obstacles in your path, bicycles, cars, other people, etc. Raise your gaze so that you are more aware of what's going on around you. Be discreet. Let your arms hang naturally by your sides and just walk forward. Allow perceptions such as sounds, sights, and scents to enter your awareness without labeling them. Relate to them as reminders to stay awake as you walk forward.

You can also walk to freedom by walking in a circular path similar to what is done in a ring shout. The ring shout is a traditional African practice brought to the United States during the slave trade. It was practiced by the Gullah people in Florida, Georgia, North Carolina, and South Carolina. Men and women moved in a counterclockwise direction as they shuffled their feet, sang, shouted, clapped hands, and prayed. Because the counterclockwise direction is associated with the rising and setting of the sun, the seasons of the year, and the cycle of life, it is said to be a practice that helps us to move in harmony with the rhythm of nature, bringing renewal and restoration within ourselves.

To practice walking-to-freedom meditation as a *ring walk*, place two intersecting sticks or strips of paper of equal length on the floor, in an unobstructed area, with each end of the strips pointed in one of the cardinal directions: east, north, west, and south. These can also be thought of as the crossroads or points of transition we make in our lives. Now stand next to the strip pointing to east (at which point you'll be facing north). State your intention for doing this practice. For example, you might be doing it to clear your mind, or to become grounded, or to strengthen your confidence in your dignity. While you are standing there, bring your ancestors to mind, momentarily. Then let go and walk.

Follow steps 2 through 7 of the preceding walking-to-freedom meditation. Walk in a counterclockwise, circular direction to the top of the north point (at which time you'll be facing west), west point (at which time you'll be facing south), and south point (at which time you'll be facing east). You don't need to stop at these cardinal points; instead, keep walking in a fluid counterclockwise direction.

As you walk, simply keep your attention on the sensations in your feet while remaining aware of the space around you. Of course, as this is a ring walk rather than a ring shout, refrain from singing, shouting, or clapping hands. Just follow the instructions in steps 2 through 7 of the walking-to-freedom meditation for several minutes. As you walk, if you get caught up in the wilderness of distractions, remember you are not really lost. Arouse your resolve to leave what enslaves you behind. Recall the charge you received before your birth. Find your North Star. Resume the technique. Keep moving forward in space and time.

Every step you take is a continuation of your ancestors' journey. See their faces, hear their voices: black men, women, and children walking. See them walking out of hut-filled African villages for the last time, through thick, humid forests to the slave pens on the African coast, on slave ship decks, and down into the crowded inner hull. See them walking on the piers in unfamiliar lands, around the interior yards of slave pens. See them walking upon the auction stand in chains before the rowdy crowds, in the dreadful coffles parading through city streets. See them walking down the byways of the South, and in hot cotton, rice, and tobacco fields. See them walking through the night with the North Star in their eyes. Can you see them as they arrive in the Promised Land? African American educator, author, and diplomat James Weldon Johnson did, when he wrote the second stanza of his poem, "Lift Every Voice And Sing":

> Stony the road we trod,
> Bitter the chastening rod,
> Felt in the days when hope unborn had died;
> Yet with a steady beat,
> Have not our weary feet
> Come to the place for which our fathers sighed?
> We have come over a way that with tears has been watered,
> We have come, treading our path through the blood of the slaughtered,
> Out from the gloomy past,
> Till now we stand at last
> Where the white gleam of our bright star is cast.[3]

Always walk in the spirit of freedom. This is what our ancestors did. This is what Minnijean Brown did when she entered Central High School in Little Rock, Arkansas. This is what James Meredith did when he entered the University of Mississippi. This is what John Lewis did at the Edmund Pettus Bridge in Salem, Alabama. Follow the examples of our ancestors and elders, walk with dignity to freedom.

9. Exercising

I heard a man say "let us rap upon the box and see if he is alive"; and immediately a rap ensued and a voice said, tremblingly, "is all right within?" to which I replied—"all right." The joy of the friends was very great; when they heard that I was alive they soon managed to break open the box, and then came my resurrection from the grave of slavery...I had arisen as it were from the dead.

—Henry "Box" Brown,
Narrative of the Life of Henry Box Brown
Former fugitive slave

Runaways used many ingenious methods to reach the North that revealed their intelligence and courage. For example, Frederick Douglass disguised himself as a sailor and boarded a train. Charlotte Giles and Harriet Eglin boarded a train disguised as grieving women, wearing dark heavy veils over their faces. Ann Maria Weems disguised herself as a male carriage driver using the alias "Joe Wilson," and drove herself to Pennsylvania from Washington, DC, the slave capital of the nation.

Among the most ingenious methods of escape were those used by Harriet Jacobs, William and Ellen Craft, and Henry Brown:

- Harriet Ann Jacobs escaped from North Carolina in 1842. She secretly boarded a northbound ship after slipping out of her grandmother's attic, where she had been hiding for seven years.

- Ellen and William Craft escaped from Georgia in 1848. They used William's dark complexion and Ellen's near-white complexion to disguise themselves as a slave attendant and slave owner and boarded a northbound train.

- Henry "Box" Brown escaped from Virginia in 1849. He arranged for a friend to seal him inside a small wooden box and to ship him to the North. The dimensions of the box were three feet one inch long, two feet wide, and two feet six inches high.

Although these escapes were sensational, most runaways used methods that were not viewed as astounding. They traveled on foot at night and hid during the day. They not only walked; they ran, crawled, climbed, and swam. When necessary, they were completely still. They knew that in order to become free they had to be flexible and adaptable.

Harriet Tubman recalled that, during one of her rescue missions, while traveling north along a river bank, she got a premonition that trouble lay ahead. She knew it was a message from her higher power to be flexible, adapt, and detour. "Brothers," she said to the men she was escorting, "we must stop here to cross this river." The men, seeing no bridge or boats, and being unable to swim, were terrified. However, having complete trust in their conductor, they followed her as she descended into the river. "For me the water never came above my chin," Tubman recalled. "When we thought surely we were all going under, it became shallower and shallower, and we came out safe on the other side."[1]

Solomon Northup, a Northern black freeman who had been kidnapped and enslaved in the Deep South, recalled a similar incident when he attempted to flee. His experience illustrates that runaways had to be really flexible and adaptable if they wanted to become free.

My clothes were in tatters, my hands, face, and body covered with scratches, received from the sharp knot of fallen trees, and in climbing over piles of brush and floodwood. My bare foot was full of thorns, I was besmeared with muck and mud, and the green slime that had collected on the surface of the dead water, in which I had been immersed to the neck many times during the day and night. Hour after hour, and tiresome indeed had they become, I continued to plod along on my north-west course.... [2]

Runaways not only had to be flexible and adaptable while traveling through the wilderness. They had to be flexible and adaptable while fleeing in Southern cities, as this account from Henry Bibb describes:

[J]ust as he turned his eyes from me; I nerved myself with all the moral courage I could command and bolted for the door, perhaps with the fleetness of a much frightened deer, who never looks behind in time of peril....

In running so swiftly through the public streets, I thought it would be a safer course to leave the public way, and as quick as thought I spied a high board fence by the way and attempted to leap over it. The top board broke and down I came into a hen-coop which stood by the fence. The dogs barked, and the hens flew and cackled so, that I feared it would lead to my detection before I could get out of the yard....

After running across lots, turning corners, and shunning my fellow men, as if they were wild ferocious beasts, I found a hiding place in a pile of boards or scantling, where I kept concealed during the day....

I retained my position there until 9 or 10 o'clock at night, without being discovered; after which I attempted to find my way out, which was exceedingly difficult. The night being very dark, in a strange city, among slaveholders and slave hunters, to me it was like a person entering a wilderness among wolves and vipers, blindfolded.[3]

Flexibility and adaptability were also needed by runaway Isaac D. Williams, who with the assistance of a white steward succeeded in boarding a ship heading north.

I crowded in between the [cotton] bales, through a little narrow place, where I could hardly get my head in, and I went away back till I got to a place where there was a little more room,—but there was not room to lie down or sit upright and I could move round only a very little. In the morning the steward came down and stopped up all the chinks by jamming wood into them, so that nobody could see me. Every day he used to bring me water in a bottle and a cracker, and sometimes bread with raisins in it....

We were four weeks in getting to Boston. I laid in that hole three weeks without going out or even seeing the light, only when they lifted up the scuttle to get wood....

At last he told me we were there..., and I might come out. I was so weak I could hardly walk. He then went with me up into the street and then stopped me and said, "now, my friend, I have brought you so far, safely, and that is all I can do for you: go down this street and inquire for a boarding house for colored people, and some of your colored friends will tell you what to do." He shook my hand and said "God bless you," and went back to the vessel....

After he left me, I went along holding on by the houses, and when I had got down the street a good ways, I met a colored man and asked him where the boarding house was. He asked me if I was a sailor, I told him not much of one, but that I had just come from a ship. He said "I understand it all." He knew from my dress and the cotton on my head and clothes, that I was a runaway.... He sent me into the country to stay with some colored people.[4]

Although we may not be traveling on foot through rivers and marshes and city streets or hiding behind bales of cotton on ships, we too need a flexible mind and body. A healthy, flexible mind promotes a healthy, flexible body, and a healthy, flexible body supports our efforts to develop a healthy, flexible mind. We need both so that we can respond to challenges that arise in our meditation practice and in our lives. We need both in order to become and remain free.

Physical Exercise

One thing we can do to develop good health—mental and physical—is to do some kind of physical exercise. Playing basketball, walking briskly, dancing, lifting weights—even carrying groceries and climbing stairs—all these can help get rid of stress, and build strength and endurance. Allow yourself to find enjoyment in using your body. Like your breath, it is always there for you.

Another form of exercise, which is also a form of meditation that has been practiced for centuries, is yoga. Yoga incorporates stretching, breathing, and meditation as well as ethical principles.

It improves the way our body uses oxygen; increases our physical strength, flexibility, and balance; calms our mind; and helps us to relate to ourselves and others with caring and wisdom.

Although yoga is practiced all around the world, according to international yoga master Babacar Khane, it was practiced thousands of years ago in Africa.[5] Many yoga postures are found in Ancient Egyptian scriptures; in papyri; on temple walls; and on stelae (stone or wooden slabs), statues, and obelisks.[6] What this means for us as African Americans is that we can connect to our African heritage by practicing yoga. In the process, we can cultivate our own healthy, flexible body and mind so that we can respond with skill and wisdom to whatever arises during our meditation session or in our everyday lives.

Yoga Meditation Preliminaries

Before you begin yoga meditation, here are a few things to know and do:

1. If you are in poor health or are unsure whether you should do the exercises, obtain a doctor's advice before beginning. This will help to reduce the likelihood of injury.

2. Approach these exercises with a calm, open mind.

3. Wear clothes that allow you to move comfortably while doing these exercises. For example, you might wear shorts, sweat pants, or tights. Or as is shown in the photos below, you might wear stretch jeans. As these exercises are relatively simple, whatever you feel comfortable wearing in public will probably do—provided it does not bind you or restrict your ability to move. You may choose to do these exercises wearing socks, as our model did, or barefoot. Just make sure you're standing on a stable level surface in good repair.

4. As you go through the postures, position yourself in each one without forcing or pushing yourself and without locking your knees or elbows.

5. Breathe *out* as you do movements that *contract* the belly and the front side of your body. Breathe *in* as you do movements that *expand* the front side of your body and contract the back.

6. Be aware of your breath as well as your posture, movement, and the sensations in your body as you move from posture to posture—mind, breath, and body in unison.

7. Stay in each posture the specified number of breaths or for the time it takes you to relax into the posture.

8. After you have relaxed in a posture, slowly and carefully position yourself in the next posture, without pushing or forcing.

9. You can begin and/or conclude this yoga exercise with an exercise called Restoration (step 12 in the sequence below).

10. Be sure to drink water as needed.

Now, let's embody the heroic spirit of our ancestors and make the transcendent journey.

Yoga Meditation
Step #1: Taking a Stand

1. Stand with feet hip-width apart, arms/hands at sides, and eyes looking forward. Ever so slightly: raise the arches in your feet, tighten your thighs muscles, move your navel towards the spine, lift your chest, move your shoulders back, and tuck your chin in. Reach the top of your head towards the sky while rooting your feet in the ground.

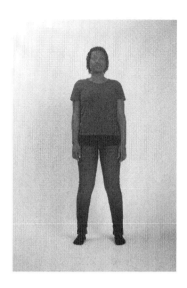

2. Hold this posture while taking several full breaths. As you breathe, bring to mind an aspiration; what you ardently want to happen as you do this exercise or in another area of your life. Allow your aspiration to settle in your heart and mind.

3. Now, begin moving your awareness to each part of your body, one at a time, beginning with your feet—the sensations in your toes, then your soles, your heels, and the top of your feet. Be aware of the rest of your feet, then move your awareness to your ankles, calves, knees, thighs, genital area, pelvis, abdomen, back, chest, shoulders, arms, elbows, wrists, hands, fingers, neck, head, and finally your face, including your ears, cheeks, eyelids, nose, lips and chin. Move your awareness to and through each of these areas very slowly, experiencing and observing the sensations inside and outside. Then reverse the order, moving your awareness methodically through each part of your body from your scalp to the soles of your feet.

Step #2: Finding the North Star

1. Inhale while lifting and extending your arms shoulder-width apart in front of you, all the way above your head.

2. Turn your palms to face each other, with fingers together and pointing upward.

3. Look in the space between your palms as though you see the North Star there.

4. Hold the posture for three full breaths.

Step #3: Praying to the Ancestors for Guidance and Protection

1. Inhale while bringing your palms together over your head.

2. Exhale while lowering your hands straight down to your chest.

3. Hold the posture for three full breaths.

Step #4: Renouncing All Forms of Slavery

1. Inhale while lifting and extending your arms and hands over your head, shoulder-width apart.

2. Exhale while bending forward at the hips as far as you can comfortably go. Your arms should hang downward from your shoulders, with your fingers pointed in the direction of the floor. Bend your knees if necessary.

3. Hold the posture for three full breaths.

Step #5: Preparing to Take Flight

1. Come out of the above posture by slowly curling upward.

2. Leave your head hanging down until your back is straightened up.

3. Stand facing forward with your arms by your sides.

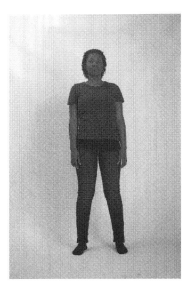

4. Hold the posture for three full breaths.

Step #6: Following the North Star at Dusk

1. Move your left foot a few inches to the left, placing it on the floor at a forty-five-degree angle.

2. Turn your hips to the left so that your torso is facing in the same direction as your left foot.

3. Inhale while raising your arms straight overhead as though you are holding a ball, with your palms facing each other but several inches apart.

4. Focus your attention on the space between your palms; imagine you can see the North Star there.

5. Take three full breaths.

6. Turn your hips and left foot to the right, back to their initial position. Exhale while lowering both arms and hands to your sides.

Step #7: Following the North Star until Dawn

1. Move your right foot a few inches to the right, placing it on the floor at a forty-five-degree angle.

2. Turn your hips to the right so that your torso is facing in the same direction as your right foot.

3. Inhale while raising your arms straight overhead as though you are holding a ball, with your palms facing each other but several inches apart.

4. Focus your attention on the space between your palms; imagine you can see the North Star there.

5. Take three full breaths.

6. Turn your hips and right foot to the left, back to their initial position. Exhale while lowering both arms and hands to your sides.

Step #8: Facing Anxieties, Doubts, and Fears

1. Stand with your feet hip-width apart and your arms and hands at your sides.

2. Look forward. Stand tall.

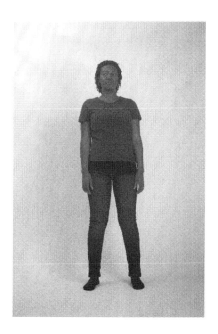

3. Hold the posture for three full breaths.

4. Now, move your awareness to each part of your body, one at a time, beginning with your feet—the sensations in your toes, then your soles, your heels, and the top of your feet. Be aware of the rest of your feet, then move your awareness to your ankles, calves, knees, thighs, genital area, pelvis, abdomen, back, chest, shoulders, arms, elbows, wrists, hands, fingers, neck, head, and finally your face, including your ears, cheeks, eyelids, nose, lips and chin. Move your awareness to and through each of these areas very slowly, experiencing and observing the sensations inside

and outside. Then reverse the order, moving your awareness methodically through each part of your body from your scalp to the soles of your feet.

5. Pause for a few moments and be mindful of your thoughts and state of mind.

Step #9: Eluding Hunters Approaching from All Directions

1. While inhaling, raise and extend your arms in front of you, all the way over your head, in one sweeping movement.

2. In the same motion, gently arch your back as far as feels comfortable and safe.

3. Exhale while bending forward at the hips as far as you can comfortably go.

4. Your arms should hang downward from your shoulders, with your fingers pointed toward the floor. Bend your knees if necessary.

5. Come out of the pose by slowly curling your torso upward.

6. Leave your head hanging down until your back is straight; then, raise your head.

7. Stand facing forward with your arms by your sides.

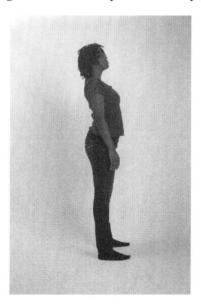

8. Inhale and sweep your arms out to the side and then overhead.

9. Turn your hands so that the palms face each other.

10. Interlace your fingers and straighten your arms, without locking your elbows.

11. While exhaling, move your left hip to the side and bend your upper torso to the right while gently lifting up and out through your whole spine and arms. Keep your feet grounded.

12. Hold the posture for three full breaths.

13. While exhaling, move your hip to the right side and bend your upper torso to the left while gently lifting up and out through your whole spine and arms. Keep yourself grounded.

14. Hold the posture for three full breaths.

15. Inhale while returning to the center with your arms overhead and fingers interlaced. Ground and lengthen upwards.

16. Hold the posture for three full breaths.

17. Exhale while sweeping your arms back down to the sides of your body.

Step #10: Being Cleansed in the Niagara Falls

1. Stand with your feet hip-width apart and your arms and hands at your sides.

2. Look forward. Reach the top of your head towards the sky while rooting your feet in the ground.

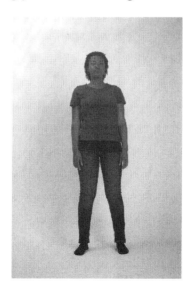

3. Hold the posture for three full breaths.

4. Now, imagine that your whole body is being showered under the Niagara Falls, that the continuous downpour of powerful current is washing away all of the impurities of your body, speech and mind. While you are doing this, be aware of sensations in your body, beginning with your scalp, face, neck, shoulders, and continuing downward though each part of your body, all the way to the soles of your feet. Continually sweep your awareness downward—from your scalp to your toes—as you are being cleansed. Do this for about a minute.

Step #11: Entering the Promised Land

1. Inhale while lifting and extending your arms and hands in front of you, upward over your head.

2. Lift your chin, smile, and bring the palms of your hands together, while connecting with a sense of splendid

achievement, accomplishment, fulfillment, triumph, and victory that is bestowed through providence.

3. Exhale while lowering your hands straight down to your chest in a prayer gesture.

4. Continue to lower your hands, allowing them to hang by your sides with your palms facing forward.

Step #12: Restoration

1. Having arrived in the Promised Land, with the attitude that you are now going to restore yourself to optimal physical and mental health, lie down on your back. Let your feet rest 12 to 15 inches apart, your toes turned out, your arms at your sides a few inches from your body, and your palms turned upward. Notice that your body is breathing.

2. Breathe naturally. Be aware of your breath as your abdomen or chest rises and falls or as your rib cage expands and contracts. Be aware of the quality of your breath, whether it is short or long, even or uneven, deep or shallow, rough or smooth. Notice any changes that occur.

3. Next, move your awareness through each part of your body, one at a time, beginning with your feet—the sensations in your toes, then your soles, your heels, and the top of your feet. Be aware of the rest of your feet, then move your awareness to your ankles, calves, knees, thighs, genital area, pelvis, abdomen, back, chest, shoulders, arms, elbows, wrists, hands, fingers, neck, head, and finally your face. Move your awareness to and through each of these areas of your body very slowly, experiencing and observing the sensations inside and outside your body.

4. Now, reverse the order. Move your awareness from your face to your toes, moving slowly through each part of your body while observing your sensations. Notice what parts of the body are touching the floor or mat and where there is no contact.

5. Finally, just be aware that your body is breathing. You are alive. Relax and be still, but stay alert, with your eyes open. Avoid going to sleep while doing this exercise.

When you feel that you have been restored, conclude this exercise. Then, like Henry Brown leaving his box, rise slowly. Bring to mind your aspiration. Resume your activities, with a mind and body that are open, flexible, adaptable, and free.

Please remember as you go forward that if circumstances do not allow you to do the daily sitting meditation practices you have scheduled, you should adjust, adapt, and improvise. Practice walking meditation. Do yoga meditation. Be open-minded and flexible. Bend, stretch, twist, and breathe so that you don't break. This will help you to reach the Promised Land.

***

One final note: If you are an athlete or involved in any kind of physical activity you may want to obtain George Mumford's book, *The Mindful Athlete: Secrets of Pure Performance* (2015). Mumford is the African American sports psychologist who taught meditation to the Chicago Bulls and Los Angeles Lakers basketball teams. As their meditation coach, he helped the Bulls and Lakers win several National Basketball Association championships. Read his book. There is a lot we can learn from Mumford about meditation and life.

TERMINAL: Albany, New York

Harriet Tubman usually headed to Albany with her passengers after leaving New York City. In route, she often visited her friend, the wealthy white social reformer Gerrit Smith, in Peterboro.

Smith, also known as the "Sage of Peterboro," was an Underground Railroad stockholder. He provided generous financial support for antislavery activities and fugitive aid work in the United States and Canada, and gave large tracts of land to black settlers. He helped to finance the largest attempted slave escape in US history, John Brown's raid on the Harpers Ferry Armory, and the purchase of enslaved families that he then set free.

As was the case with her visits to Smith's home, Tubman carefully planned every stop, and every phase of her travels. After all, not only was she a fugitive, her passengers were entrusting her with their freedom and their lives. Thus, she traveled not only on foot but also by train, coach, wagon, and boat, as the situation required.

Often the modes of transportation she used were crewed or captained by African American Underground Railroad agents. But they could be costly. In addition to paying for her passengers' fare, she often had to purchase food and "normal" clothes for them, and pay off fearful and greedy accomplices, while at the same time keeping her eyes open for "false brethren" acting as "watchdogs" for slave catchers.

Tubman had a huge responsibility. And when a problem arose, she couldn't go into denial, have a temper tantrum, or find someone to blame. The lives of men, women, and often their children, were at stake. If a problem arose, she had to be flexible, to adapt, and resolve it. And she had to know where to find help when she needed it. Fortunately, if a problem arose in the vicinity of Albany, she could always obtain help from two African Americans, Stephen and Harriet Myers.

The Myers used their resources for nearly thirty years to operate an Underground Railroad station in Albany. As a result, they helped thousands of fugitives to settle in northern New York or continue on to Canada. They provided them not only with shelter, clothing, food, and care but also with plenty of advice concerning the wisdom of sobriety, thrift, and being industrious. In addition, the Myers published an abolitionist newspaper, the *Northern Star and Freemen's Advocate*. In particular, Stephen Myers spoke at antislavery events, lobbied for voting rights, and helped to establish the Free Colored School, one of the first schools for African American children in that area.

Since the Myers were very interested in black community development, they were more than willing to provide runaways all the help they needed to become economically and politically empowered, especially if they were planning to remain in the city. And they were happy to help Tubman, too. After all, she was someone easy to admire. In fact, their feelings about her were probably the same as those of many abolitionists, including Franklin B. Sanborn, the white New England journalist, who unabashedly wrote:

> I regard her [Tubman] as, on the whole, the most extraordinary person of her race I have ever met.

She is a negro of pure or almost pure blood, can neither read nor write, and has the characteristics of her race and condition. But she has accomplished her purposes with a coolness, foresight, patience, and wisdom, which in a *white man* would have raised him to the highest pitch of reputation.[1]

Indeed, Tubman was extraordinary. She developed a vast network of contacts in the South, North, and Canada. She met with them in the terminals that she and her passengers passed through. This network supplied her with the information and resources she needed to conduct her missions of mercy.

Tubman stayed fully aware that slaveholders were tightening the shackles around the ankles, wrists, and necks of people of African ancestry. She knew that husbands, wives, parents, and children were still being snatched from their families, shoved onto auction blocks, and sold down the river. She knew that black boys and men were still being overworked, beaten, and whipped like animals. She knew that black girls and women were still being sexually molested and raped with impunity.

Tubman stayed aware of what was going on because she kept bringing out enslaved men, women, and children who told their stories. She also received messages through her network from slaves who wanted her to help them flee. One of the slaves who wanted her help was Josiah "Joe" Bailey.

Joe was considered by his owner to be "a good slave." It was for that reason that his owner had hired him out for a period of time to work for a neighbor. At the end of the period, the neighbor was so satisfied with the work Joe had done and his overall attitude that he purchased Joe from his owner. Immediately after the purchase, Joe's new owner came to him and said, "Now, Joe, strip and take a whipping!" Perplexed, Joe tried to remind his new owner that he had been a good slave.

> "Master," said he, "haven't I always been faithful to you? Haven't I worked through sun and rain, early in the morning, and late at night; haven't I saved you an overseer by doing his work; have you anything to complain of against me?"
>
> "No, Joe; I've no complaint to make of you; you're a good nigger, and you've always worked well; but the first lesson my niggers have to learn is that I am master, and that they are not to resist or refuse to obey anything I tell 'em to do. So the first thing they've got to do, is to be whipped; if they resist, they got it all the harder; and so I'll go on, till I kill 'em, but they've got to give up at last, and learn that *I'm master.*"[2]

Joe submitted to being whipped, but later that night, he traveled to Tubman's father's cabin with a message: "Next time Moses comes, let me know."[3] It wasn't long before Tubman came down from the North and took Joe up out of slavery. She also carried out with her two men and a woman from nearby plantations, each with their own story about the horrors they had experienced, while enslaved.

Stephen Myers
Source: Wikipedia

10. Paying Attention

The next morning I was on the deck as soon as the day dawned. I called Fanny to see the sun rise, for the first time in our lives on free soil; for such I then believed it be. We watched the reddening sky, and saw the great orb come up slowly out of the water, as it seemed. Soon the waves began to sparkle, and everything caught the beautiful glow. Before us lay the city of strangers. We looked at each other, and the eyes of both were moistened with tears. We had escaped from slavery....

—Harriet Jacobs, *Incidents in the Life of a Slave Girl*
Former fugitive slave

Slaveholders considered even one escape as a loss of "valuable property." They viewed the flight of thousands of slaves to be a major threat to the institution of slavery. The average price of a slave in the United States was about $400 in 1850, or about $10,000 in today's currency. By 1860, the average price of a slave had increased to about $800, or around $20,000 in current dollars.[1] The value of slaves' labor was much higher.

The slaves valued most highly were young adult males who could work as field laborers; females in their childbearing years; and artisans, cooks, and domestic servants. Unskilled older males, females past their childbearing years, and elderly slaves were less valued. Often, least valued were slaves who could read and write and evidenced the capacity to reason critically and think deeply. These were the ones believed to be most likely to escape or lead a rebellion to overthrow white supremacy.

In an effort to retake runaways, slaveholders distributed "runaway slave" notices with detailed descriptions of the people who fled. The notices also offered large rewards plus expenses to slave catchers for finding and returning runaways (which also added to the cost of their losses). Notices also appeared in newspapers, in store windows and behind counters, on the walls of downtown streets, at railroad stations, on posters near bridges, and on tree trunks in rural areas. In addition to these notices, slaveholders also depended on slave patrols, professional slave hunters, and lawmen. These men often questioned law-abiding citizens and members of the enslaved community in hope of finding a lead that would help them capture the runaways.

In addition, the slaveholders used their political influence to get the US government to enact laws that helped them to get their runaway slaves back, such as the Fugitive Slave Act of 1850. Among other things, this law:

- made it a federal crime to help a runaway slave, and to *not* help return them to their Southern owners;

- created special federal courts with their own commissioners to hear cases involving escaped slaves, and granted incentives to the commissioners who ruled in favor of slaveholders;

- made it easy for slave catchers to apprehend any African American "suspected" of being a slave and denied the apprehended the right to a jury trial and the right to testify on their own behalf;

- imposed huge fines and prison terms on anyone found guilty of violating the law, and allowed the confiscation of all their property.

The Fugitive Slave Act of 1850 became law because the federal government was under the control of politicians from Southern states. They were in control because of what is known as the "Three-Fifths Compromise," a compromise reached by Northern and Southern delegates to the US Constitutional Convention in 1787, when our present form of government was being created. It allowed states to add three-fifths of their slave population to that of the white population in determining the number of representatives each state would have in the House of Representatives.

Since most slaves were located in the South, the compromise gave the South disproportionately greater representation in the House and Electoral College relative to its free population. This advantage, plus proslavery support in the North, gave Southern politicians and slaveholders great influence in the Congress, in the election of the President, and in determining the composition of the President's cabinet and the Supreme Court.

The Fugitive Slave Act of 1850 turned the North into "a hunting field for slaves," according to African American stationmaster Jermain Loguen.[2] It sent a message to fugitive slaves living as free men and women in the North that it was not safe to be black anywhere. It was not even safe for blacks who were born free or were legally freed. Many of them were accused of being runaway slaves and were apprehended.

Thousands of fugitives and free blacks, fearing for their safety, migrated from the United States to Canada. There they made new homes in black settlements, especially in the Canadian West (as the province of Ontario was known). They rebuilt their lives in more than three hundred townships and city wards.[3]

Some of the larger settlements were in Arnherstburg, Chatham, Colchester, Dresden, Galt, Elgin, Gosfield, Hamilton, London, Sandwich, St. Catharines, Toronto, and Windsor.[4] Slightly more than half of the free blacks living in the settlements were from New York, Pennsylvania, and Ohio, with the majority of the fugitives originating in Maryland, Kentucky, and Virginia. Within a few years after passage of the Fugitive Slave Act of 1850, there were as many as forty thousand free blacks and fugitives residing in Ontario.

Most free blacks and fugitives, however, remained in the northern United States because of strong family and community ties, and because they were determined to stand up for their rights. Nevertheless, they were also concerned about their safety and had to give their attention to what was going on around them all the time. Bands of slave catchers prowled through cities and towns all hours of the night and day looking for black men, women, and children they could snatch and sell to slave dealers for shipment down south. These hunters got plenty of help from law-abiding Northerners who felt obligated to let it be known where fugitives resided or were hiding. Many of them didn't like black people anyway, so they were quite happy to turn them in. Besides, they could obtain hefty rewards.

One of the ways free blacks and fugitives resisted the fugitive slave law was by forming vigilance committees. The committees worked to prevent fugitives and free blacks from being apprehended and taken south. Through these committees, people were able to watch out for their own safety and potential threats to others' safety as well.

In Christiana, Pennsylvania, the vigilance committee was chaired by a fugitive from slavery, William Parker, who was ably assisted by his wife, Eliza Ann, also a fugitive. They had been told by a vigilant informant to watch out; trouble was coming their way.

On the morning of September 11, 1851, a US marshal, a slave-holder, his son and nephew, and three other men arrived at the Parker house, and demanded that they be given custody of the slaveholder's slaves, who were believed to be hiding inside. The Parkers, who were armed, refused to hand over any of the occupants in the house. The marshal's party threatened to burn the house to the ground. Still, the Parkers remained defiant. Soon, fifteen men arrived to assist in the apprehension of the slaveholder's "property." The Parkers were ordered again to turn over the occupants of the house or else they both would be killed. However, the Parkers refused to comply.

As tension from the standoff continued to escalate, Eliza Ann blew a horn that signaled to their neighbors that help was urgently needed. Several dozen black neighbors rushed to the Parker house from all directions with guns, clubs and razor-edged corn cutters, and a fight broke out. The slaveholder was killed and his son and nephew were wounded. The US marshal and his men fled for their lives.

The Parkers also fled for their lives. Eliza Ann and her children were secreted away. William and the slaves who were hiding inside the house were swiftly placed on the Underground Railroad to Canada. On the way, they stopped at the terminal in Rochester, where they took refuge in the station operated by Frederick Douglass and his wife. Douglass wrote:

> I could not look upon them as murderers. To me, they were heroic defenders of the just rights of man against man stealers and murderers. So I fed them, and sheltered them in my house. Had they been

pursued then and there, my home would have been stained with blood, for these men who had already tasted blood were well armed and prepared to sell their lives at any expense to the lives and limbs of their probable assailants.[5]

Meanwhile, US President Millard Fillmore dispatched 45 US Marines and 40 Philadelphia police officers to Christiana to arrest those suspected of interfering with the apprehension of the slaves. All were acquitted. In the meantime, Parker, his wife and children reunited in Canada.

What's Going On

Although there are many stories of kidnappings and apprehensions in today's world, the state of constant vigilance that was required of blacks in the Antebellum Period is not needed today. However, this does not mean that as freedom seekers we don't need to "watch it" and "take note." We need to know, to borrow words from the African American singer Marvin Gaye, "What's going on." Knowing what's going on will enable us to continue our journey to freedom.

Without knowing what's going on, our attention can easily be drawn to thoughts, and as a result our attention as well as our minds, and our lives, can become shackled and bound. We can end up in some form of slavery. "Slavery" can be a violent rage, addictions, depression, excessive debt, or even getting caught up in distractions and entertainment, or the activities of "friends" who do not have our best interests at heart. It can be anything that prevents us from uplifting our lives in freedom.

In order to know what's going on, we have to slow down, rest our attention on the breath while observing our posture, movements, sensations, feelings, states of mind, and perceptions. We

ɾinuously, moment to moment, with curiosity
ɾthout judging or wanting to change what we
ɾnd observing. When we do this, we begin to see
ɾer world much more clearly, with a better understanding ɾ ɾ's going on, what is important, and what we need
to do to remain free.

Paying Attention

Let's pay attention to what's going on. Take a seat and for several minutes practice each of the meditation techniques below.

1. Breathe normally. Rest your full attention on your breath and observe it very closely. You may become aware that your breath comes in and goes out and that each "in" and "out" breath has a beginning, middle, and end, and that at the end is a gap. You may even notice that your breath is long or short, even or uneven, rough or smooth, heavy or light, fast or slow, warm or cool, and so forth. Whatever you discover about your breath, observe it very closely without manipulating it.

2. Become aware of your posture and sensations in each part of your body. Begin with the heels, soles and toes of your feet; then slowly move your awareness upward to your ankles, and then slowly through your calves, knees, thighs, pelvis, abdomen, chest, shoulders, back, arms, hands, neck, head, and face. Then reverse this order, slowly moving your awareness through each part of your body from your scalp to the soles of your feet. You may even notice tightness, stiffness, throbbing, soreness, pressure, or an itch. Whatever sensations you become aware of, inside or outside your body, closely observe, without any judgment whatsoever about what you find or experience.

3. How are you feeling? What pleasant and unpleasant feelings are you experiencing right now? Are you feeling joy, satisfaction, love, relaxation, inspiration, gratitude, and confidence, or are you feeling pain, discomfort, nervousness, resentment, annoyance, shame, disappointment, doubt, embarrassment, stress, fatigue, or loneliness. Sights, sounds, smells, tastes, odors, thoughts, things, or people can be the source of our pleasant and unpleasant feelings. Whatever you are feeling, even if it is a neutral or indifferent feeling, just observe the feeling thoroughly, moment to moment, without judging.

4. Become aware of your state of mind. What is it: loving, joyful, caring, alert, compassionate, confident, or patient? Or is it greedy, hateful, jealous, arrogant, sad, indifferent, sleepy, or bored? Are you *tired* of reading this book or are you *curious* and want to read more? Whatever your state of mind, observe it. Don't cling to it because it's pleasant or repress it because it's unpleasant. Don't judge it. Just continually and thoroughly observe your state of mind, with each arising moment.

5. What is arising in your awareness: sights, sounds, scents, smells, sensations, thoughts, feelings, states of mind? Whatever it is—the cry of a baby, the aroma of soul food, the shades of light on the curtains, walls or floors, the rising and falling of your chest as you breath, etc.—observe it. Look at it, listen to it, savor it, smell it, and feel it. Do this thoroughly and precisely, moment to moment, without judgment, while discerning its impermanent, ever changing nature.

Slowing down and resting our attention on the breath—rather than our thoughts—joins our body, breath, and mind. This calms, clears, and focuses our mind, and allows us to become more aware of our bodily sensations, feelings, state of mind, and perceptions.

Paying attention allows us to become more aware of our habitual tendencies, as they arise, linger, and fade. With the discipline to simply *be* and observe, we are then able to make wise choices about how to respond to what's going on, internally and externally, rather than react blindly. This is true while we are sitting in meditation and in our everyday lives. With greater awareness of what's going on, and with wise choices, we can uplift our mind, our existence, our family, and our community.

To reduce the likelihood that your attention will be "apprehended," "snatched," or "pulled away" by thoughts, you will need to be aware of what's going on with you 24/7, while you are at home, at work, on the bus, in the store, in the prison yard, and as you walk through your neighborhood or a park, and at all times—while lying down, standing, sitting, walking, bathing, dressing, cooking, eating, reading, and so forth.

This sounds like it involves a lot, but it doesn't really. Try it the next time you take a shower, get dressed, eat a meal, wash dishes, fold laundry, kiss your lover, prepare for bed, talk with someone, or stand looking at a flowing river. Slow down, maintain an awareness of your breath, and pay very close attention to what's going on: your posture, movements, bodily sensations, feelings, states of mind, and perceptions, moment to moment, without judgment. Take your time and observe thoroughly and precisely what's going on.

When we slow down and pay attention, our ordinary activities become sacred rituals. We move towards wholeness and oneness with reality. We experience the sacredness of our lives, others, and our world.

For example, at mealtime, when you dine alone, instead of rushing to the table and eating, try slowing down. Turn off the television, sound system, cell phone, and video game. Create an environment filled with silence. Find your breath. Then go wash your hands.

Pay very close attention to your posture, movements, sensations, feelings, state of mind, and perceptions as you wash your hands. Be present for these moments of your life. Walk slowly to the table where you will eat. When you arrive, take your time.

Instead of plopping your body in the chair, stand or kneel next to your chair for a few moments. Simply be aware of your posture, movements, bodily sensations, feelings, state of mind, and perceptions as you pause. As you experience what's in your environment—your body, the place setting, utensils, the food on your table, and so forth—be mindful of the interrelated structure of reality. A lot of people have made it possible for everything in your awareness to exist. Acknowledge them with a moment of silence or with a prayer of thanksgiving.

Take a seat. Pay attention to your posture. Look at what is in front of you including space. Slowly reach for a utensil. Allow your fingers to feel the weight, texture, and temperature of the utensil. Slowly place a piece of food in your mouth. Rather than gulping it down, take your time. Slow down. Pay attention to the movement of your jaw, your tongue as well as the salvia and food in your mouth. Chew and savor your food, the taste and texture. Slowly drink and savor your beverage, all the while being mindful of your posture, movements, bodily sensations, and so forth. Instead of racing through your meal, slow down, pay attention, and enjoy and appreciate it.

When you are finished eating, slowly rest your hands in your lap, and just relax there. Take it easy for a few moments. Every moment is a moment of your life—that you don't get back. Appreciate the richness of these moments. Continue being aware of your posture, movements, sensations, feelings, state of mind, and perceptions. After a minute or so rise and just as mindfully remove the items from the table, wash them, and return them to the place where they belong, all the while paying attention to what's going on.

Find other occasions to appreciate your life in this way, such as while you are washing dishes, cleaning the house, taking a shower, folding laundry, getting dressed, or looking at the sun rise or set.

Developing Insight and Wisdom

Going for a walk in nature can be a delightful time to pay attention to what's going on. After all, nature can draw your attention in, focus it, and open you to a greater awareness of yourself and the world. It can also bring you to an awareness of messages that are streaming to you all the time. This is what African American scientist George Washington Carver discovered: "I love to think of nature as an unlimited broadcasting system, through which God speaks to us every hour, if we will only tune in."[6]

What Carver describes is a view that is also held in many sub-Saharan African societies. According to that view, a higher power not only communicates messages through the spirits of our ancestors, but also through the sun, light, moon, darkness, trees, hills, valleys, mountains, rocks, rain, birds, animals, wind, temperature, and coincidence, and when we quiet and still our minds and "tune in," we can receive the messages and use them to bring forth truth, balance, order, and justice to our lives.

Whether you are walking in nature, sitting in your home, relating to people or situations, or kneeling in a church, mosque, synagogue, or temple, by "tuning in" you can receive messages, too.

One of the messages you might receive from tuning in is that everything in our experience is continually changing and has no lasting existence—not our thoughts, feelings, bodies, relationships, beliefs, experiences, buildings, clothes, or seasons. We are actually living in a world of continual change. The life of everything including each of us is fleeting. If you contemplate this you might also begin to see that the habit of dwelling, fixating, or holding tightly on to anything—your thoughts, resentments, good looks, beliefs, ethnicity, or whatever—is ultimately futile. From this realization, a whole new way of relating to yourself and the world can come into being.

Enslavement begins when our attention dwells, fixates, and holds on to our thoughts. Liberation begins when we take our attention off our thoughts and rest it on *what's* going on *while* it's going on—right *here*, right *now*.

***

Meditate. Breathe consciously. Listen. Pay attention. Treasure every moment. Make the connection.[7]

— Oprah Winfrey, African American media proprietor,
   talk show host, actress, producer, and philanthropist

11. Contemplating

I passed the Sunday in solitary reflection in the woods. I was too much engrossed with the multitude of my thoughts within me to return home to dinner, and spent the whole day in secret meditation and prayer, trying to compose myself, and ascertain my true position. It was not difficult to see that my predicament was one of profound ignorance, and that I ought to use every opportunity of enlightening it.

—Josiah Henson, *Truth Stranger Than Fiction*
Former fugitive slave

Slaveholders were not of a mind to let their slaves know what they were planning. Without a moment's notice, a slave—a beloved aunt, son, mother, uncle, sister, father, daughter, brother, or grandparent—could be snatched from his or her family and "sold south" or "sold down the river," never to be seen again by them. Thus, it was standard practice for slaves to listen to their master's every word and to closely observe their every move to gain insight into what they were planning to do. Often they would flee, if it appeared the slaveholder was going to sell them.

Being sold south or down the river referred to a practice in the border states (Kentucky, Missouri, Maryland, and Delaware) and Upper South (Virginia, North Carolina, Tennessee, and Arkansas) of selling slaves for transport to the lower or Deep South (Alabama, Georgia, Louisiana, Mississippi, and South Carolina, as well as Texas and Florida) for enslavement. Although some slaves were transported down the Ohio and Mississippi Rivers or from East Coast ports or shipped on trains to the south, the great majority were transported by forced march on overland routes. It could take months to complete an arduous six hundred mile journey.

As many as one million slaves were caught in this southward migration. Upon reaching southern destinations, they were often detained in warehouses, depots, and pens, all sexes and ages huddled together, until they could be resold at auction for a profit.

The Deep South was where the largest cotton, sugar, and rice plantations were located, and where slaves were treated the worst: overworked, cruelly punished, ill-fed, crudely housed, and left illiterate. It was also where the demand for slaves was the greatest. To satisfy this demand, slave sales were regularly held.

The particulars of the domestic slave trade business varied from one city or town to another, but slaves were usually sold at public auctions, at the center of town, in front of the courthouse or at the town market, inside or on the steps of a hotel or tavern, at a landmark along a certain road or river, or even at a slave owner's home. Slave brokers hired to sell slaves at auction on behalf of slave owners would place "Slaves for sale" advertisements in the local newspapers and posters in store windows, with a description of the slaves—name, gender, age, complexion, skill, and owner—and the location of the auction.

At the appointed date and time, the auctioneer arrived at the site and set up for the event. It was not uncommon for him to send a trustworthy mulatto with an enslaved mind through the streets with a large bell announcing the auction, its location and time. Sellers, buyers, accountants, and other community residents gathered, huddled, mingled, and milled about, and the life of the community proceeded as though nothing shockingly dreadful was about to happen. Common men loudly played cards and drank beer, men of distinction discussed the fine points of politics and religion, lovers sauntered together nearby, women bought fruits and vegetables from market venders, and children ran about and played. Then, the nearby slave warehouse, depot or pen door was swung open, and out stepped the first of many sales of the day. Men were brought out and auctioned first, then women, and, finally, children.

The slaves, who were usually dressed and groomed for the sale by their handlers, were marched from the pen through the excited and unruly crowd and directed to stand facing the crowd on a boulder or platform so they could be seen by interested bidders and spectators. Next, the auctioneer invited prospective buyers to come forward to inspect the slaves if they had not already done so. One slave witness to an auction reported:

> The women would have just a piece around her waist...her breast and thighs would be bare. The seller would have her turn around and plump her to show how fat she was and her general condition. They would also take her by her breast and pull them to show how good she was built for raising children. They would have them examined to show they were in good health.[1]

Buyers would make the men, women and children open their mouths, bend, stoop, turn around, walk back and forth, jump up and down, and they would pinch, poke, and feel them, even in their private places. They would inspect them for flesh scars, which would indicate whether they were compliant, and ask whether they could read or write or had previously escaped.

All who were present at the auction saw and heard everything, especially the weeping, pleading, and anger of slaves, many of whose families were being torn apart—husbands from wives, parents from children, and brothers from sisters. But being blinded by greed, hatred, and indifference, they couldn't see our ancestors' inherent dignity, and they couldn't bring forth their own. They couldn't see that black lives matter. Blinded to the indignity of what they were all participating in, the only thing they could see was the twisted logic that led them to conclude that white people were "superior."

"Sold! Sold! Sold! Sold, to the highest bidder!"

Often the newly purchased slaves were returned to the place of confinement for boarding until the number of slaves needed by their buyer had been acquired. Then the drivers would arrange the entire group in a coffle: first, pairs of men chained together, followed by pairs of roped women; and then, in wagons, naked children along with tents and provisions. The slave drivers, whips in hand, ordered the dejected and grieving bondsmen to "step lively" as the pen door swung open. Out marched the shackled human chattel, onto the public streets of towns and cities, to parade before amused onlookers. They proceeded to the byway or a waiting vessel that would take them to their destination. Former slave Isaac Williams recalled,

> When slaves were sent to Georgia they would go in gangs of five-hundred or more, all handcuffed, two by two, and a long chain running down the middle of the line uniting them as one living snake-shaped mass. None could hope to escape. Women and men, all together, were treated alike. No delicacy was observed, and at night all would lie down together by the roadside and sleep. If any lagged by the way, there were plenty of rough overseers who would lay the lash on unsparingly, and the poor fainting victims would often lie bleeding on the road and die from sheer exhaustion. True, there were wagons for the sick and for children, but this did not

prevent many from giving up and dying by the way-side, where quickly a hole was dug and they were dumped in like dogs.[2]

Insight Out of the Clear Blue Sky

Imagine that you are in the Deep South. How do you move toward freedom in the North? You might escape from a coffle or plantation and flee to a maroon encampment—an isolated forest or swamp populated with a dozen or so runaways—and from there continue overland at night until you reach a port city, such as New Orleans, Memphis, or Louisville, where you could enjoy the anonymity of the urban community inhabited by free black residents; and then, after obtaining relief, you might head for the docks and try to figure out a way to board a steamboat going north.

As you observe the frenzied activity on the dock, you might notice the runaway slave notices posted all along the pier. You might see watchers guarding the gangway to the boats and river authorities stopping free blacks to inspect their free papers. You might also overhear a steamboat captain tell his engineer or steward of a recent escape and instruct them not to hire any more free blacks or slaves for hire as dock workers or cooks.

Meanwhile, in the distance, a slave coffle in heavy loud chains trudges slowly down a gangplank of a boat that is loading bales of cotton. You might also see alert travelers, workers, and cigar-smoking officials ready to do their "civic duty" by reporting any suspicious-looking black person or packages such as crates to the authorities. You might consider mixing with the black dock workers and slipping onto a boat with them. However, after studying them very closely you might sense that even your own people would betray you if they saw you attempting to become free.

You might conclude the situation is just impossible and return sad and depressed to the black district of the city and resign yourself to remaining holed up in the attic or underneath the floorboards of someone's home or a safe house for days, weeks, months, or years until a way is found for you to safely continue your journey to freedom. Or you might relate to the situation as runaway John P. Parker did.

Parker's attention did not move from the question: How do I move toward freedom in the North? These words are what he pondered on the docks of New Orleans. The result: he gained insight.

> As I sauntered along the dock, I came on a steamer which was being loaded with freight. Looking up, I saw a large sign: "For Memphis and Upriver Points."
>
> Out of the clear blue sky there came to me as clearly as though someone had spoken it aloud: "That's your boat." Furthermore it was to leave that night. I had not the least doubt from that time forward I would be safely aboard when she cast off on her trip north. That decision having been made, I went back to the city as contented as though I was to be a first class passenger instead of a stowaway.
>
> As soon as it was good and dark, I went back to my steamer, the *Magnolia*. It was one thing, I discovered, to receive a message from the high heavens, but it was quite another thing to fulfill that message....
>
> Standing in the shadow of a pile of cotton, I watched and wondered how I was to get aboard my steamer. The blazing fire pots [were] at both ends of the gangplank on which the deck hands walked

back and forth. There were cables that tied the steamer to the dock, but I was no tightrope walker, so they were dismissed. There apparently was no means left for one except [to] go up that broad gangplank. If that was my way, it was my way, was my fatalistic conclusion.

Just as I was about to take my fate in my own hands, my way opened up. It was in a narrow gangplank in the bow which the deckhands threw out when they tied up the forward cables. I saw how plainly it was lighted up when the firebox blazed and how much it was in the dark when it faded away. What further gladdened my heart was, there was an open hatch at the end of the board that led to the hull. My lucky star I felt shining as I made my way toward the dock end of the slim and narrow board. When the light in the firebox faded out, I made a run for it, dropped into the hold, just as my enemy the firebox lighted even the hold where I was lying panting with fear. But then I was unseen, safely aboard my steamer bound north. This episode I believe gave me confidence in myself, in my ability to meet any and all situations which might arise to confront me.[3]

Obtaining Insight

The way that Parker gained insight into his situation and acted, without thought at the right moment, shows what happens when we relate to our experiences in an attentive, open, and receptive way. A broader range of perspectives, possibilities, and choices comes into view than we thought existed. We are much more likely to bring forth our inherent goodness, genius, and potential, and go forward confidently and skillfully.

Insight of the sort that aided Parker is available to us every moment of the day. One way we can access it is by practicing *contemplation*.

Contemplation practice is similar to calming meditation, except that instead of resting our attention on the breath, we rest it on *words*. We rest our attention on words to gain insight into the meaning that the words hold for us. Eventually, like a full moon in a night sky appearing from behind moving clouds, the meaning the words have for us appears and illuminates our mind. When it does, we shift our attention from the words and rest it on the meaning. The meaning will then guide us to deeper understanding and insight.

Words to Contemplate

Before you begin this practice, you will need to find words to contemplate.

You can choose to contemplate one of the quotations in this guidebook, or you can contemplate a short passage from a sacred text, a poem, a piece of prose, or a collection of daily meditations. Passages from *Acts of Faith: Meditations for People of Color* by Iyanla Vanzant and *Black Pearls: Daily Meditations, Affirmations, and Inspirations for African-Americans* by Eric V. Copage can be very helpful. Here's a sample passage from *Acts of Faith*:

> The stress began the day you learned you were expected to please other people. Parents wanted you to stay clean and be quiet. Neighbors wanted you to be respectful and helpful. Teachers wanted you to be attentive and alert. Friends wanted you to share and hang out. Whenever you failed to do

exactly what someone expected of you, you weren't good, or good enough. You were bad, or weak or dumb. Unfortunately, you began to believe it. Giving in to the demands, day by day, you lost a little more of yourself and your understanding of the truth. The truth is you are fine, just the way you are! Perfect in your imperfection! You are divine! Growing brighter and more brilliant each day, you can accept the truth of who you are. The next time you want to know who you are, what you are or if something is the right thing to do, don't ask your neighbor—ask the power within ... and pay attention to the response![4]

You may want to contemplate shorter passages, or a small portion of a larger one such as this one. There is no "right" passage to use or "right" source of a passage. Now, after you've found a passage that you feel holds meaning, you're ready to begin the contemplation practice.

Contemplation Practice

1. Take your seat and calm your mind by practicing calming meditation.

2. Slowly read the passage or quotation you've selected, either silently to yourself or out loud.

3. Rest your attention on the words in the passage.

4. If the passage stirs thoughts or feelings, don't allow them to distract you from what you are doing—holding your attention on the words. Gently acknowledge the thoughts

or feelings without judging them. Then return your attention to the words in the passage.

5. Now, find a word or phrase in the passage that seems to have special meaning for you, and make that the object of your contemplation.

6. Rest your attention on the word, phrase, or even image that the word or phrase brings to mind. Relax, and do not move your attention from the word, phrase, or image.

7. Be patient. Eventually, the meaning that the word or phrase has for you—insight—will arise and illuminate your mind. When it does, shift your attention from the word, phrase, or image to the meaning (insight) that has arisen. Rest your attention on that for several minutes. If your attention wanders, gently bring it back.

8. Conclude your contemplation by resuming calming meditation.

You might see where there is a need to take action as a result of the insight you gained through contemplation. Or it might not be necessary to do anything at all. Movement may naturally occur within you, unconsciously. Whatever the case, as was true for John P. Parker, the insight you gain will undoubtedly help you to move forward with your life, in the direction of freedom.

TERMINAL: Syracuse, New York

Harriet Tubman had to be vigilant while traveling from Albany to Syracuse. The US Secretary of State visited Syracuse in May 1851, and he declared that the federal government had every intention of enforcing the Fugitive Slave Act of 1850 in the city. Therefore, as Tubman got closer to the city, she had to be careful.

Upon entering Syracuse, Tubman usually visited Jermain and Caroline Loguen. Jermain Wesley Loguen was born a slave in Tennessee, but escaped to St. Catharines in 1834. In Canada, he worked and taught himself how to read and write. He returned to the United States, graduated from Oneida Institute in Whitestown, NY, and became a circuit preacher for the African Methodist Episcopal Zion (AME Zion) Church.

In the 1840s, after they married, Jermain and Caroline purchased a large house in Syracuse. At that time, the city had a couple hundred black residents and about seven thousand white residents. The couple outfitted the basement of their house with bunks and supplies to accommodate fugitives arriving in the city. Loguen described the fugitive aid work they did:

> The slaves come to us with their frostbitten feet, and then we go to work to get them healed. Sometimes we have to keep them for weeks and months—we

have two mothers, with a child each, to care for with us at present. Their husbands were sold, and they made their escape and came to us some months ago. We have a father that has just got to us with his little daughter about three years old; its mother was taken from it, and the father then ran away with the child, so that man thieves could not get it. We are caring for them too at present. It takes all the time of myself and family to see after their wants; I mean the fugitives. We have so much to do in the night that some nights we get little or no sleep. They often come sick, and must be cared for forthwith.[1]

Loguen eventually took over leadership of fugitive aid work in Syracuse from Samuel J. May, a white clergyman and disciple of William Lloyd Garrison. Working as the full-time general agent of the Syracuse Fugitive Aid Society, Loguen solicited money, food, and clothing from local abolitionists to aid fugitives. He also worked to place new arrivals wanting to settle in the city in employment where they could learn trades.

In addition to being a fugitive aid worker, Loguen was a preacher, an abolitionist lecturer, schoolteacher, and a civic-minded resident who was highly respected by the city's residents. Thus, when the Fugitive Slave Act of 1850 became law, and city residents gathered at city hall to decide what they should do, Loguen urged them to declare the entire city a refuge for people of African ancestry. "The question is with you," he told those assembled. "If you will give us up, say so, and we will shake the dust from our feet and leave you. But we believe better things."[2]

His proposal was approved. The town mobilized to prevent to apprehension of any black person. A year later, in October 1851,

Loguen coordinated the successful rescue of William "Jerry" Henry—a fugitive slave—from US marshals. Although Loguen was arrested and placed on trial, a jury of his peers acquitted him.

Because of the Loguens' anti-slavery work in Syracuse, Tubman was able to feel a bit more secure as she looked for temporary work and donations to help her passengers continue on to Canada. However, some of the people she approached were hesitant to give her money. They knew that she was likely to give their contributions away to anyone who came along and said they needed it. But they also knew that when Tubman received generosity, she always responded with gratitude. For example, once, while escorting four men to freedom, she boarded with them at a station operated by a very poor black family. When she awoke the next morning, she was troubled because she had no money to repay the family's kindness. So she offered what she had: some of her clothing, which they gratefully accepted.

Tubman was a person of great integrity. She never asked for anything for herself. Thus, although people may have hesitated when she asked for their help, she usually obtained what she wanted. Of course, when Tubman couldn't raise all of the funds she needed, she'd simply continue to hire herself out. She washed, cooked, cleaned, ironed, and so forth, until she had enough money to continue her journey.

Upon leaving Syracuse, Tubman returned to a state of high vigilance. She knew that the quickest way to end up in the Deep South was to be identified and pursued by men enforcing slavery laws. Thus, in 1857, when she got a premonition that her parents—free blacks living in Maryland—were in trouble with the law, she asked her higher power what she should do to obtain the money she needed to rescue them. She then went to the New York Anti-Slavery Office:

"What do you want Harriet?" was the first greeting.

"I want some money, sir."

"You do? How much do you want?"

"I want twenty dollars, sir."

"*Twenty dollars?* Who told you to come here for twenty dollars?"

"The Lord told me, sir."

"Well, I guess the Lord's mistaken this time."

"I guess he isn't, sir. Anyhow I'm going to sit here until I get it."[3]

Tubman left the office with sixty dollars and headed to Maryland, arriving at her parents' cabin. Because they were elderly and unable to walk long distances, she made a horse-drawn vehicle out of old boards and wheels from a dilapidated buggy, seated her parents in it, and rode the vehicle to Thomas Garrett's home in Wilmington, Delaware. Garrett remembered the daring rescue:

> She brought away her aged parents in a singular manner. They started with an old horse, fitted out in primitive style with a straw collar, a pair of old chaise wheels, with a board on the axle to sit on, another board swung with ropes, fastened to the axle, to rest their feet on.... [S]he was happy at having arrived safe. Next day, I furnished her with money to take them all to Canada.[4]

It was only afterwards that Tubman was told the details underlying her premonition. Her father had assisted in the escape of several slaves and was subject to being apprehended.

Jermain Wesley Loguen
Source: Onondaga Historical Association

12. Overcoming

Canada was often spoken of as the only sure refuge from pursuit, and that blessed land was now the desire of my longing heart. Infinite toils and perils lay between me and that haven of promise; enough to daunt the stoutest heart; but the fire behind me was too hot and fierce to let me pause to consider them. I knew the North Star—blessed be God for setting it in the heavens! Like the Star of Bethlehem, it announced where my salvation lay. Could I follow it through forest, and stream, and field, it would guide my feet in the way of hope.

—Josiah Henson, *Truth Stranger Than Fiction*
Former fugitive slave

When our ancestors fled from slavery to freedom, they hoped they were leaving all their troubles behind. However, that didn't mean there wasn't going to be trouble up ahead. There were always challenges to be faced and overcome. This certainly is what Henry Bibb discovered.

Bibb, who was born into slavery in Kentucky, saw all six of his younger brothers sold down the river. He escaped from slavery six times, and on several occasions attempted to retrieve his wife and child, only to be apprehended. After fleeing the seventh time, he established himself in Detroit, Michigan, where African Americans William C. Monroe, William Lambert, and James Theodore Holley were the leading abolitionists and stationmasters. Bibb joined the anti-slavery lecture circuit. He then returned to the South for his wife and child, only to discover that his wife had become the mistress of a slaveholder and that his daughter had been sold to another slaveholder for the same purpose.

Bibb overcame his grief by publishing his autobiography, *Narrative of the Life and Adventures of Henry Bibb, An American Slave, Written by Himself,* in 1849. The next year, upon passage of the Fugitive Slave Law, he moved to Windsor, Ontario, Canada with his second wife, Mary C. Miles. Together, they started a black settlement funded by the Refuge Home Society. Mary Bibb established a school for the children of settlers and helped to build a church. Bibb began publishing the *Voice of the Fugitive,* the first black newspaper in Canada.

Sarah H. Bradford, Harriet Tubman's biographer, also wrote about challenges, the ones that had to be overcome by passengers traveling with Tubman. Their challenges were different, of course, as was the "remedy" that was required:

> Sometimes members of her party would become exhausted, foot-sore, and bleeding, and declare they could not go on, they must stay where they dropped down, and die; others would think a voluntary return to slavery better than being overtaken and carried back, and would insist upon returning; then there was no remedy but force; the revolver carried by this bold and daring pioneer would be pointed at their heads...so she compelled them to drag their weary limbs on their northward journey.[1]

Like Bibb and members of Tubman's party, throughout your life, in particular, in your meditation practice, you will encounter challenges. But, with the appropriate remedy, they can be overcome.

Overcoming Challenges in Meditation

In meditation, you overcome challenges by first acknowledging that they exist. This means you'll need to be aware of and observe what's going on. Only *you* know whether you have encountered a challenge to your meditation practice: physical discomfort, drowsiness, or restlessness, or if you lack motivation to practice. When you become aware that you are facing one of these challenges, see if you can apply the appropriate remedy to overcome it. Following are remedies you can use.

Challenge: Physical discomfort—pain, numbness
Remedies you can use to sit without experiencing discomfort:

- Stretch your body or do yoga exercises before sitting.

- Try a different chair or cushion that is comfortable.

- Relate to *mild* pain or discomfort as you would your thoughts. Don't resist; just return your attention to your breath.

- Avoid extreme pain or excessive numbness by assuming a more comfortable posture.

Challenge: Drowsiness—sleepiness, blanking out
Remedies you can use to remain alert:

- Get enough sleep, and eat *after* rather than *before* you meditate.

- Practice in a space where the temperature and humidity are comfortable.

- Practice with your eyes open.

- Place more emphasis on your in-breath than on your out-breath for a few moments.

- Take a break, stretch, and assume a good posture.

Challenge: Restlessness—panic, fantasies
Remedies you can use to maintain composure:

- Meditate in the morning before you get caught up in the activities of the day.

- Do breathing or stretching exercises to relax your body.

- Place more attention on your out-breath than on your in-breath for a few moments. Momentarily close your eyes.

- Observe your thoughts without comment or resistance. Don't judge yourself.

Challenge: Lack of motivation—discouragement, loss of faith in your ability to meditate
Remedies you can use to inspire yourself:

- Establish and maintain a regular time and place to practice.

- Review the meditation instructions.

- Recall the reason you decided to begin this journey in the first place, what initially led you to conclude that meditation is worthwhile, and how meditation has helped you.

- Read the inspirational/motivational writings as well as biographies of fugitives from slavery and other African Americans who have overcome much greater odds than the ones you are facing, yet made it to freedom.

- Decide to meditate, even if you don't feel like it. Exert yourself.

By being aware, acknowledging that you have encountered a challenge, and applying the appropriate remedy, you'll have an easier time continuing or resuming your journey. After a while, your attention will become less distracted and will rest. When your attention rests, you might feel that nothing is happening. You might feel bored and your attention might be drawn away from its place of rest by thoughts about getting something to eat or doing a task. Or you might start daydreaming, become drowsy, or fall asleep. Stay awake and alert.

There is always something arising that can hold your attention captive, that can take control of your mind, body, and life. So continually follow the instructions. Let nothing turn you around. Be *present*. Be *here*. Keep returning to *now*.

Avoiding Aggression

Whatever happens as you meditate, avoid resorting to any kind of aggression to overcome it. As the African American civil rights and labor leader Asa Philip Randolph said, "Violence seldom accomplishes permanent and desired results. Herein lies the futility of war." This applies to meditation, too.

The reason for avoiding warring with the challenges you encounter is that they are not your enemy. All of the challenges that arise on the path of meditation—and in your life—are opportunities for you to become aware of what needs your attention. Moreover, the more you become familiar with your challenges, understand them, and relate to them and yourself with an accepting attitude, and apply the remedy, the less likely they are to prevent you from going forward in your practice and in your life. The more likely they are to actually facilitate your liberation.

Remain awake. Acknowledge your challenges. Calmly and gently apply nonviolent remedies. Find your North Star and rest your attention on it. Keep following it. Don't worry. Keep the faith. You will overcome.

13. Practicing

I'm on my way to Canada,
That cold and dreary land;
The sad effects of slavery,
I can't no longer stand.
I've served my master all my days,
Without a dime's reward;
And now I'm forced to run away,
To flee the lash abroad.
Farewell, ole master, don't think hard of me,
I'll travel on to Canada, where all the slaves are free.

—Harriet Tubman, Former fugitive slave
a favorite song she often sang, quoted in
Scenes in the Life of Harriet Tubman by Sarah H. Bradford

The men and women who fled from slavery knew they were taking a huge risk. Therefore, as they trekked under the stars and moonlight, through forests, up roads, across fields, and along rivers and streams, they were on high alert for slave catchers every step of the way. When the darkness began to yield to the light, it was common practice for them to retreat to safe places—unoccupied buildings, swamps, caves, and woods. There, often alone, they renewed their bodies and minds so that at dusk they could resume their northward journey.

A Place to Practice

As a meditator, you also will need a safe place to which you can retreat, where you can renew your mind and body. This will enable you to relate skillfully to whatever arises as you go through your day.

You can find a safe place anywhere, such as in a room in your home. If you are incarcerated, you might be able to use the jail or prison cell to which you are assigned. You can also use a quiet public place such as a library. Whatever the place, try to find one that is quiet, uncluttered, and uplifting, that has natural light and a comfortable temperature and humidity level.

A Place to Sit

You will need something comfortable to sit on. A chair is ideal. The edge of your bed will do. Anything will work as long as it allows you to sit relaxed in sitting meditation posture with your head and upper body vertically aligned.

Loose-Fitting Clothing

In addition, you will need comfortable, loose-fitting clothing. Ordinary, everyday clothes are usually just fine. If your clothing is tight, consider removing or loosening some articles so you can sit comfortably and breathe freely. If you become chilly while practicing at home, it's okay to wrap yourself with a blanket or sweater.

A Practice Time

You'll also need to decide on a regular time that you'll go to your meditation place to practice. An ideal time, if it works for you, is at dawn. For many meditators this is the time of the day when their biological clock naturally supports their efforts to meditate. This is also the time of day that runaways retreated to hiding places to renew their body and mind.

While many meditators practice in the morning, others practice in the evening. Evening is when many runaways resumed their journey to freedom. This can also be a time for you to resume your journey to a free mind. You can gain a lot of inspiration and support for your practice by starting your daily meditation sessions in the morning or evening.

Of course, you don't have to meditate in the morning and/ or evening. You can meditate at any time during the day that suits you: midmorning, noon, mid-afternoon, evening, or night. Whatever time you choose, initially try to schedule your sessions to last fifteen minutes each day, as suggested by Nelson Mandela. You can gradually extend your sessions as you take on new practices or have more time to practice, such as on weekends and holidays, and during vacations.

Meditation Techniques

Select one or more meditation techniques to practice during your meditation session. Although initially it may be helpful to make calming meditation your main practice, and later add other techniques to your session, which techniques you choose to practice is completely up to you. Your choice may be influenced by what you are interested in doing or the time you have available, and what you choose to do may change over time. Whatever, if you decide on practicing more than one technique, decide on the sequence in which you will do them (which one you'll do first, second, third, and so on). Rather than planning what you *want* to do, plan on doing what you reasonably *can* do and try to stick with it. Write it down.

After you have practiced regularly for a while, think beyond your session to how you can incorporate the techniques you've practiced into other areas of your life. The following sample Daily Practice Schedule is one that might help you to come up with ideas about what you can do. Keep it simple, and feel free to experiment.

A Daily Practice Schedule

1. When you wake up:
   a. Before getting out of bed: clarify in your mind your intention for the day. Perform the restoration technique (step 12 in chapter 9).

181

b. During your meditation session: Acknowledge your ancestors. Begin meditation practice (for example, practice the calming meditation technique). Conclude your session by expressing a heartfelt wish that it will also help others: *Whatever good I have gained from this practice session, I give to others so that they may become free.*

2. As you go through the day:
    a. Ask yourself: What kind of world am I creating for myself and others with my mind? Is it a world in which there is generosity, love, and wisdom or a world where there is greed, hatred, and indifference?
    b. Integrate the meditation techniques you have learned into your daily activities. For example, here are some situations in which you may be able to practice the techniques without calling a lot of attention to yourself:
        i. Calming—when you are anxious or upset, or seated at your workplace or in a waiting area with nothing else to do.
        ii. Walking—when you are walking through your home, down the hallway at work, or waiting at the bus stop.
        iii. Paying attention—while you are taking a shower, getting dressed, cooking, eating a meal, or washing dishes.
        iv. Yoga—when you are taking a break from sitting a long time or preparing to go for a walk or need to stretch.
    c. Rest your attention on your breath, whenever you think of it.

3. Early in the evening, a couple of hours before your bedtime:

a. During your meditation session: Acknowledge your ancestors. Begin meditation practice (for example, practice the calming meditation technique). Conclude your session by expressing a heartfelt wish that it will also help others: *Whatever good I have gained from this practice session, I give to others so that they may become free.*

b. Assess how you did with your meditation and intentions for the day.

4. Before you go to sleep practice the restoration technique.

The main thing to remember is that although initially it may be more helpful to practice only once or twice a day, meditation is an ongoing practice. You can be engaged in meditation any hour or moment of the day.

A Meditation Shrine

Some meditators find it helpful to create a meditation shrine on a table in front of the space where they regularly meditate. A meditation shrine is similar to the table or other surface in our homes on which we display family photos or mementos. You have seen this in homes where family photos are displayed, even photos of Martin Luther King, Jr. and Rosa Parks. The photos and mementos remind the residents of what is important in their lives, and they inspire them. For meditators, meditation shrines do the same thing. They remind and inspire us to retreat and practice.

If you choose to create a meditation shrine, you can place a small lighted candle on it. The candle will help you to create a warm and inviting environment that is conducive to meditating. It can also remind you of the campfires around which our African ancestors sat, gazed, chanted, and danced—the origin of meditation. Or it can remind you of the lantern-lighted spaces that served as a refuge for our ancestors as they moved from station to station on the Underground Railroad. What you place on your shrine is up to you. But don't forget: If you use a lit candle, don't leave it unattended.[1]

Practicing with Family

In addition to bringing to mind your ancestors and parents when you begin a meditation session, you may also find it helpful to bring members of your family or household to your practice session—if you can. After all, if we are going to develop strong families where the inherent goodness, genius, and potential of each member is nurtured and flourishes, we need to make intentional efforts to support the development of each family member. We can do this not only by ensuring that they have protection, food, shelter, clothing, education, and so forth, but also by encouraging them to value and develop their mind.

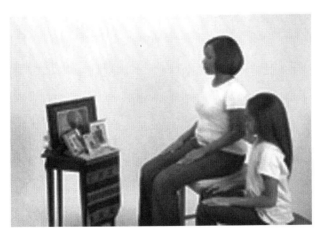

If you feel comfortable doing so, you may want to let family members know that you are practicing meditation and your reasons for doing so, and ask them to support your efforts. For example, you can ask them to remind you when it's time for you to meditate or kindly ask them not to disturb you when you practice. Listen with an open mind to what they may say about your meditation practice. It's okay to share a little bit about your personal experience with meditation.

Family members might respond in any number of ways to you meditating: express misgivings based on what they have heard from others, be happy that you are trying to uplift yourself, give you encouragement, or indicate that they want to learn more. If they want to know more, you can suggest that they visit www.freeyourmindguide.com, share this guidebook with them, or invite them to join you for meditation practice.

What you don't want to do is to try to "sell" them on the idea of practicing meditation. It is not helpful to you or them, and it's not necessary. This applies to children, youth and adults.

That said, given the level of aggression and violence among teenagers and young adults, as well as among spouses, partners, and others who share households, it is clear that meditation can be very helpful. This is because meditation helps us to become more aware of our internal responses to perceived insults and disagreements. Being more aware is important because it is not the insults and disagreements themselves that trigger us to think, say, and do things that are harmful and even violent. It's *dwelling, fixating, and holding on to our thoughts* about the perceived insults and disagreements—and building on them in our minds—that cause us to strike out.

When we meditate, we observe what's going on in our minds. Over time we become more familiar with our thoughts, and our tendency to dwell, fixate, and hold our attention to them. We become more familiar with our feelings of frustration, resentment, anger, and disappointment. We also develop the discipline we need to simply *be* with our thoughts and feelings without surrendering to verbally abusive and physically violent impulses. Doing this helps us to respond to challenges at home, school, work, and in the community with a little more calm, patience, understanding, caring, skill and wisdom.

Practicing with Children

One of the most effective ways we can help our children to develop free minds is to develop a free mind ourselves. When they see us practicing meditation, if we are the kind of parent whom they see as exemplary, they may want to meditate too. If your children want to meditate, create a space next to you where they can sit. Give them meditation instructions that they can understand. But do not expect much discipline from them, especially if they are less than eight years old. They may not always want to practice when you do or be able to sit still and follow the techniques for long. That's OK.

Seeing *you* meditate, knowing there is a quiet time and safe space in the home where they can simply be with you or by themselves, and observing the effects of meditation on your behavior, can impress on them the wisdom of developing their own minds. Moreover, being in a home where they can meditate and learn about African American history and culture will help them to develop an inner core of pride, healthy self-esteem, positive feelings, and strategies for dealing with the challenges they will inevitably encounter in their lives.

Bells, Gongs, or Drums

To support your efforts to focus and give your session a sense of forward progression, you may want to use a sound to signal the beginning and conclusion of each session as well as the start and end of each technique within a session. For example, you may want to *clap* your hands, *ring* a bell, *strike* a gong, or *beat* a drum. You can do any one of these three times to begin your session (symbolizing the keys to your liberation: body, breath, and mind) and to end your session, or you can do it once at the beginning and end of each technique you practice. Just rest your attention on the sound. Remember, this is your practice, to design according to your own wisdom. So, for example, if you choose to, you can begin each technique or session by saying the Swahili word *Harambee* (See "Using Kwanzaa Chants" in chapter 26) and conclude each technique and session with the Yoruba word *Ashe* (See step 6 of the Affirmation Practice in chapter 22).

Practicing Regularly

There may be occasions when it seems as though, in the words of the black nationalist and human rights activist Malcolm X, "in the hectic pace of the world today, there is not time for meditation...."[2] And there may even be occasions when distraction takes you away from meditation practice for an entire day, week, month, or year. Such lapses in meditation practice happen. But, they do not mean you are a failure or that you can't meditate—just as Tubman's unsuccessful first attempt to escape from slavery didn't mean she couldn't become free.

No matter how long your attention is away from your breath—a minute, a day, a month, or a year—as long as you eventually return your attention to the breath—which you can do at any moment of any day—you are still a meditator. You're still on the path to a free mind.

That said, if your practice has lapsed and you want to go forward, it can be helpful to review Part I of this guidebook, especially chapter

2 (Calming), chapter 4 (Breathing), and chapter 12 (Overcoming). You might also find it helpful to reread other chapters that inspire you. Then, take a seat, and find your breath—your North Star.

No one owns you. You don't have to voluntarily place yourself under the authority and control of distracting thoughts—or for that matter, anything, including people, beliefs, and organizations—for days, weeks, months, or years. Reclaim your existence. Keep practicing meditation. This is the only way to reach your destination. Keep going—until you arrive. It's the only way your mind can become free.

Beyond any thoughts that distract you and cloud your mind, you possess everything you need. You have a body, breath, and mind. You have meditation principles and practices. You have African and African American history and culture. You have your ancestors and elders. You have your inherent dignity. You have inherent goodness, genius, and potential. You don't need to wait for a leader or a teacher. You *are* the leader and the teacher. You don't need a government program. You *are* the program, and *are* the program administrator. You have *everything* you need to uplift yourself, and be of help to your family and community.

Just start where you are—right *here*, right *now*—and use what you have, and use it wisely.

Meditate regularly. Use the techniques and principles in this guidebook during your daily meditation session, and as you go through the day. Doing this will dissolve the boundary between your daily meditation session and other aspects of your life. As the boundary dissipates, and meditation becomes less *something you do* and more *who you are*, distracting thoughts will cease being impediments to your freedom, fulfillment and happiness. Then, the inherent goodness, genius, and potential possessed by ten thousand generations of our ancestors will shine through your life for all to view, like the stars in a clear night sky.

PART II:
FREE YOUR HEART

THE FUGITIVE SLAVE'S APOSTROPHE TO THE NORTH STAR

Star of the North! while blazing day
Pours round me its full tide of light,
And hides thy pale but faithful ray,
I, too, lie hid, and long for night:
For night;—I dare not walk at noon,
Nor dare I trust the faithless moon,
Nor faithless man, whose burning lust
For gold hath riveted my chain;
Nor other leader can I trust,
But thee, of even the starry train;
For, all the host around thee burning,
Like faithless man, keep turning, turning.

In the dark top of southern pines
I nestled, when the driver's horn
Called to the field, in lengthening lines,
My fellows at the break of morn.
And there I lay, till thy sweet face
Looked in upon "my hiding-place."

Star of the North!
Thy light that no man deceiveth,
Shall set me free.

By John Pierpont (1785-1866)

[William Wells Brown, quoting from "The Fugitive Slave's Apostrophe to the North Star" by John Pierpont (1785–1866), *Airs of Palestine, and Other Poems*. 1840.—Poems. 1854, in *The Narrative of William W. Brown, A Fugitive Slave* (1848). Reprinted in Barnes and Noble Classics. *The Great Escapes: Four Narratives*. New York: Barnes and Noble, 2007].

TERMINAL: Auburn, New York

Harriet Tubman's route to Canada went through the city of Auburn, which is where many committed abolitionists lived. Among them were white female stationmasters such as Martha Coffin Wright and Frances Miller Seward. Tubman probably fed and housed her passengers at their homes as well as the homes of blacks residing in the city. Meanwhile, she worked temporary jobs and solicited donations to help her passengers continue their journey.

In 1859, Seward's husband, US Senator William Henry Seward (who would become secretary of state in President Lincoln's administration), offered to sell Tubman seven acres of land with buildings on easy terms. Tubman accepted Seward's generous offer and relocated her parents and brother, John Stewart, from Canada to Auburn.

With the acquisition of the Auburn property, Tubman's life became a little more complicated. In addition to supporting her parents and the indigents residing in her house, helping refugees in St. Catharines, and financing her rescue missions, she now had to raise funds for a mortgage.

She talked to her friends about the idea of raising funds by giving public talks. However, they thought the idea was dangerous. After all, Tubman was a notorious fugitive. Her friends had good reason to believe that if she started speaking in public she would be apprehended, brutally punished, or even murdered.

Tubman thought about her friends' concerns. She also thought about the needs of her parents, the indigents living in her home, the fugitives in Canada, and the millions of African Americans in the South who were yearning for deliverance from slavery. Without concern for her own safety, she decided to proceed with her plans for giving public talks.

A white New England journalist, Franklin B. Sanborn, arranged for Tubman to give talks at small private and semipublic gatherings. Many of the educated and wealthy people who came to these events had already heard about Tubman, but they had never seen an image of her. Thus, when Tubman arrived at her venues her modest appearance always prompted murmuring from the audience.

Tubman was barely five feet tall, and dark-skinned. She was missing her upper front teeth but had a winning smile. She dressed in modest but neat apparel. Her demeanor was gracious and self-assured. Her manner of speaking was direct and clear, and as she proceeded to speak in her Southern black dialect, telling stories about her life in slavery, her escape, and her rescues from the South, she revealed a mastery of language, narration, suspense, metaphor, symbol, wit, song, and dramatic gesture that left her audiences spellbound. Her talks were always followed with heartfelt applause. A reporter who heard her speak reported, "The mere words could do no justice to the speaker; and therefore we do not undertake to give them; but we advise all our readers to take the earliest opportunity to see and hear her."[1]

During this period, there were many abolitionists who traveled across the North, giving speeches, sermons, lectures, testimonials, and talks. Among the earliest were Sarah and Angelina

Grimké. Although their Quaker parents owned several hundred slaves and were strong supporters of slavery, the sisters were strongly opposed to it. Therefore, they left their parents in the South and relocated to the North where they became abolitionists. Although they were subject to ridicule, they spoke out in lectures and essays against slavery and the denial of equal rights to women.

By far, the most famous abolitionist speaker in the North was Frederick Douglass, who gave about seventy speeches and lectures each year, not including the ones he routinely gave in his hometown, Rochester. He held the attention of audiences wherever he spoke with his intelligence, wit, and dramatic flair: "I appear before the immense assembly this evening as a thief and a robber," he sometimes began, "I stole this head, these limbs, this body from my master and ran off with them!"[2]

Mary and Emily Edmonson also appeared on the abolitionist lecture circuit. They had been among the slaves involved in the 1848 *Pearl* incident.[3] This was the largest single escape attempt by slaves in US history. It involved slaves who had worked in the homes of the most influential families in Washington, DC. All seventy-seven of the escapees, including Mary and Emily, were retaken on a boat heading down the Chesapeake Bay on its way to Philadelphia.

Upon being apprehended, most of the escapees were sold down the river to New Orleans, including fifteen-year-old Mary and thirteen-year-old Emily. New Orleans was the largest slave market in the nation and was well known for selling African American teenage girls with light complexions as sex slaves. Knowing this, the girls' father, Paul Edmonson, himself a free black, persuaded influential abolitionists to arrange for their return to Virginia. Later, he succeeded in having the girls' freedom purchased.

Afterwards, Mary and Emily traveled throughout the North with their father and other abolitionists, telling their stories about the evils of slavery.

As for Tubman, her speaking tour took her throughout Massachusetts to Concord, Framingham, New Bedford, Worcester, and Boston, where she became a huge sensation. The leading intellectuals of the day, including Henry David Thoreau, Ralph Waldo Emerson, and William Ellery Channing, came out to hear what the great heroine of the age had to say. Undoubtedly the leading African American abolitionists in Boston also came out, such as John S. Rock, a doctor, dentist, lawyer and the first African American admitted to practice law before the US Supreme Court. On many occasions he hosted Tubman in his home. Also among the leading abolitionists in Boston who came to hear Tubman were Lewis and Harriet Hayden.

Lewis Hayden had been enslaved in Kentucky and had obtained freedom for himself, his wife Harriet, and son with help from the white Underground Railroad conductors Calvin Fairbank and Delia Webster, both of whom were later apprehended and imprisoned. Hayden traveled to Boston, where he became a businessman, abolitionist lecturer, and a leading member of the Boston Vigilance Committee.

As a member of the Committee, Hayden used his influence to gain Fairbank's release from prison (Webster had already been released), and to organize the rescue of fugitive Shadrach Minkins from the custody of the US Marshals. The rescue of Minkins was such an affront to the authority of the federal government that President Millard Fillmore called it "a scandalous outrage." However, for the Haydens, it was business as usual.

As leading stationmasters in Boston, the Haydens used their residence to shelter fugitives. As was typical of most female stationmasters, Harriet Hayden ran the household and in this capacity played a critical role in caring for and protecting the fugitives in her charge. One friend observed that

> She had all of a woman's tact, persistence and cleverness, and was conveniently, deaf, dumb, and blind when necessary and hence she was not a popular nor useful aid to U.S. marshals and Southern masters hunting their runaway slaves in [Massachusetts].[4]

Tubman would travel to Boston on other occasions. On one occasion, in 1864, she met a tall, dark-complexioned black older speaker named Sojourner Truth. Like Tubman, Truth had run away from slavery (in New York); changed her name (from Isabella Baumfree); and dedicated her life to the abolition of slavery, fugitive aid work, equal rights for blacks and women, and the eradication of alcohol consumption. She spoke and sang and had, like Tubman, a deep faith that a higher power was guiding and protecting her in all of her activities.

To be on the antislavery speaking circuit, Truth needed faith as well as plenty of courage. This was a time when men and women sat separately for public talks, and women were expected to be "ladylike" and remain silent in public, not challenging men's exclusive right to speak in public. But this did not stop Truth from speaking out against slavery and sexism. That's because she had complete confidence in her inherent dignity—her inherent goodness, genius, and potential. Thus, she fearlessly challenged prevailing notions about black and female inferiority with her forthrightness, wit, and eloquent wisdom.

As for Tubman, she would continue to travel to Boston and other cities throughout the North, attending conventions, lectures, and fairs. Often she would arrive without being recognized. She would take a seat and quickly fall asleep because of her narcoleptic condition. Attendees who had never met her before concluded that she was "nobody." But when she was called on to speak, she would wake up, ascend to the rostrum with great dignity, and captivate her audience. Of her performances, William Wells Brown reported, "Moses had no education, yet the most refined person would listen for hours while she related the intensely interesting incidents of her life, told in the simplest manner, but always seasoned with good sense."[5] This was certainly the case in August 1859, when she spoke at the New England Colored Citizens' Convention in Boston. According to a reporter in the audience:

> Miss Harriet...was introduced as one of the most successful conductors on the Underground Railroad. She denounced the colonization movement and told a story of a man who sowed onions and garlic on his land to increase his dairy production; but he soon found the butter was strong, and would not sell and so he concluded to sow clover instead. But he soon found the wind had blown the onions and garlic all over his field. Just so, she said, the white people had got the [blacks] here to do their drudgery, and now they were trying to root them out and send them to Africa. "But," said she, "they can't do it; we're rooted here, and they can't pull us up."[6]

Sojourner Truth
Source: Library of Congress

Mary and Emily Edmonson
Source: Maryland State Archives

14. Bravery

At last the time for action arrived.

—William Wells Brown,
Narrative of William W. Brown
Former fugitive slave

To discourage the enslaved population from escaping, slave patrols policed plantations and hunted anyone who ran away. The patrols subjected our ancestors to a reign of terror—abducting, whipping, raping, maiming, lynching, burning, shooting, and humiliating. All this was done to teach them that if they wanted to remain alive, they had better keep their mouths shut and stay in their place—on the plantation.

In keeping our ancestors fearful, the slaveholders and slave patrols arrested their development. They caused them to feel insecure and inadequate. Thus, even if our ancestors overcame their fears and took flight in the direction of freedom, fearful thoughts and doubts were still likely to arise and cause them to stop, turn around, and return to bondage.

For example, in September 1849, when Harriet Tubman and her two brothers got up the nerve to run away, they did not get far. Her brothers became frightened of what might happen if they were captured. With Harriet unable to persuade them to keep going, they returned to the plantation.

For Tubman's brothers, fear was like a slave patrol. Without going beyond their fearful thoughts, they could not become free. However, as Frederick Douglass explains, going beyond fearful thoughts was not easy to do:

Whenever we suggested any plan [of escape], there was shrinking—the odds were fearful.... The case sometimes stood thus: At every gate through which we were to pass, we saw watchmen—at every ferry a guard—on every bridge, a sentinel—and in every wood a patrol.... This in itself was sometimes enough to stagger us; but when we permitted ourselves to survey the road, we were frequently appalled. Upon either side we saw grim death, assuming the most horrid shapes. Now it was starvation, causing us to eat our own flesh; now we were contending with the waves, and were drowned;—now we were overtaken, and torn to pieces by the fangs of the terrible bloodhound. We were stung by scorpions, chased by wild beasts, bitten by snakes, and finally, after having nearly reached the desired spot,—after swimming rivers, encountering wild beasts, sleeping in the woods, suffering hunger and nakedness,—we were overtaken by our pursuers, and, in our resistance, we were shot dead upon the spot! I say, this picture sometimes appalled us, and made us "rather bear those ills we had, than fly to others, that we knew not of."[1]

There really is nothing "wrong" with fear. Fear like the kind Douglass experienced kept many would-be fugitives safe and alive. However, when fear arrests our development, instills in us feelings of insecurity, inadequacy, and low self-esteem—paralyzes us—it is not keeping us safe or alive. It is keeping us enslaved and keeping us from fully living. Thus, we need to do something to free ourselves from its grip.

What Douglass did was to rest his attention on a vow he had made to himself to leave the house of bondage. This helped to calm, stabilize, and focus his mind. It allowed him to clearly see that his fearful thoughts about the unpleasant things that might happen, his doubts about his ability to respond to situations that might arise, were merely his thoughts; and that by letting go of them, resting his attention on the North Star, and his vow, he could go beyond his fears to freedom.

Douglass uplifted his mind. Then, with help from Anna Murray, he took a train from Baltimore to Philadelphia disguised as a sailor, with papers that gave him the identity of a free sailor. Upon arriving in the North, he was aided by William Still of Philadelphia and David Ruggles of New York City. With their help, as well as the help of William Lloyd Garrison, he uplifted his personal existence, became a leader in the fight for the abolition of slavery, and in the process became one of the most notable Americans of the nineteenth century.

As a meditator, when it's time for you to practice or when troubling thoughts arise during your session, you might find yourself becoming afraid too. Although your thoughts may not be about wild beasts and slave catchers, they might be accompanied by uneasiness. If this happens, you may find yourself wanting to stop meditating. Try to avoid giving fearful thoughts authority and control over your mind, meditation practice, and life. Whatever fear arises is small compared to what our ancestors experienced— and went beyond.

You can go beyond fear, too. You can sit and meditate without being freaked out and immobilized. Here are some steps you can take while meditating:

- Remind yourself that everyone has fearful thoughts from time to time—they arise, stay awhile, and then fade.

- Avoid dwelling, fixating, or holding on to thoughts. Allow them to arise and fade.

- Return your attention to your breath, your North Star.

- Follow your breath out as it dissolves in the space around you.

- Thoroughly observe the energy of fear in your body with an attitude of acceptance.

- Rest your attention in the *here* and *now*. What do you see, hear, smell, taste, and feel right *here* and right *now*?

- Allow the energy of fear in your body to rise and fade.

- Be loving and kind to yourself.

Relating to fearful thoughts in these ways during your meditation session can help you to weaken the hold that fear has on your mind. They can help you to bravely go forward in to each moment no matter what thoughts arise. These steps can also support your efforts to relate to the fear that arises when you are *not* practicing sitting meditation, as you go through your day.

When it comes to dealing with fear in everyday life, the following suggestions can help:

1. Become aware of your fear.

2. Feel the energy of your fear.

3. Examine your fear.

4. Befriend yourself when you experience fear.

5. Move through your fear.

Become Aware of Your Fear

You can become aware of your fear in various ways, starting with listening to yourself talk about what you don't like, what you're not interested in, what you don't need to prove, what you can't do, won't do, or are too tired or too busy to do. Listen to yourself. Ask yourself: is it possible that you feel this way because there is something that you're afraid of? Notice what makes your heart pound, your stomach tighten, your breathing quicken, your body sweat. These are often signs that something you fear has gotten a hold on your mind.

While you're at it, look at what makes you depressed, irritated, and angry as well as what you might be holding back, guarding, hiding, resisting, avoiding, denying, lying about, trying to control, or refusing to talk about. These can be signs that, on some level, your fight-or-flight response has been activated.

You also can become aware of your fear by looking at how you feel about certain people, activities, circumstances, or experiences. Often we fear what we don't like or don't want to happen. For example, we might not like our boss because we fear he or she will fire us and as a result we will be unable to keep our promises to our children.

One of the best ways to become aware of what you fear is to simply look at where you are stuck in your life. Are there stories you've created over the years to justify living beneath your potential? Don't be afraid to ask yourself tough questions. This exercise won't hurt you. So go ahead. Look through any smoke you've been blowing and into the fire. The truth you discover can set you free.

Through awareness, we begin to see that our mind has many fearful thoughts. We usually can't see them clearly until we calm, stabilize, and clear our mind. For this reason, it is worth our time to meditate. It's worth our effort to rest our attention in the *here* and *now* so we can see our fearful thoughts, give them our non-judgmental attention.

Feel the Energy of Your Fear

You can feel the energy of fear by turning your attention away from what you are thinking about to the way fear expresses itself in the body—in your muscles, heartbeat, and respiration. Notice where you feel tension. Sometimes we clench our jaws or our fists without even being aware of it. Open yourself to the energy of fear. Allow the energy of fear to rise and pass through your body like steam rising from a pot of boiling water. Acknowledge that you are physically experiencing fear. Acknowledge that you are afraid. Go ahead, say it: "I'm afraid"; "I am scared!" People don't often acknowledge fear, but it is much more common than you might think.

Examine Your Fear

Examine your fear. Look for answers to these questions about the content of your fearful thoughts—what you are afraid of:

- Is it true? Is this just a fearful thought or is it wisdom?

- Who says it is true?

- Is it happening right now?

- Is it based on assumptions?

- Is it based on rumors?

- Is it based on prejudices?

- Is it based on beliefs?

- What emotions accompany it?

- What physical sensations accompany it?

- What other thoughts or images accompany it?

- In what ways is it limiting your life?

Examining fear will help you to see that what we are often afraid of is thoughts, our *thoughts* about what we *think* will happen. Since what we think will happen in the future does not actually exist in reality, right now, what we are often actually afraid of is *nothing*. We are afraid of a story we have created about what *might* happen. We are afraid of our thoughts.

If you look into the situation and find that you really are headed in a dangerous direction, you can choose to change course. Sometimes changing course brings up fear as well. If fear does come up, you can work with it along with your initial fear.

Befriend Yourself When You Experience Fear

Be a good friend to yourself. Remind yourself that there is nothing wrong with being afraid. Fear is a human emotion. Give yourself all the love, care, and support that you need. This might be the love, care, and support you didn't receive but always wished you had received from society, parents, siblings, lovers, teachers, and friends. Extend compassion toward the parts of yourself that are scared, anxious, depressed, sad, angry, confused, and uncertain.

What you don't want to do is to tell yourself negative, limiting things that you may have internalized, such as "I'm not capable of doing it." Reset your mind. Take your attention off such thoughts. Return it to your breath, and follow your breath out as it dissolves in the space around you. Remind yourself that the things you are saying to yourself are only thoughts in your mind; they are not reality.

Tell yourself things that are supportive, such as: "I will give it my best shot," "Yes, I can," "I'll try and see what I learn," and "My ancestors have given me what I need to go forward—inherent dignity—and I will honor them by risking failure, disapproval, and embarrassment to bring it forth."

Do what Frederick Douglass did. He entertained only thoughts that led him "away from the house of bondage" and to a "determination to *act*."[2]

Move Through Your Fear

Go beyond fear by taking small steps in the direction of what makes you afraid until you have gone beyond it. It's important to remember, though, that when you take small steps, you are not trying to *get rid* of fear. What you are trying to do is simply *become familiar* with the way fear operates within your mind and body. Be mindful of the energy of fear as it arises, abides, and fades in your body and mind.

Forget about trying to get rid of fear or doing things the "right" way. For now, just take little steps. You have to take little steps before you can take big ones. Little by little, experience your fear. You can do this. Move through your fear a little at a time. Eventually, you'll become so familiar with how fear operates in you that it will no longer freak you out or cause you to become or remain stuck. You may have fear, but it will not be able to hold you back. It will not be able to keep you from bringing forth your inherent goodness, genius, and potential.

Like Douglass and Tubman, you don't have to remain bound by your thoughts about the harm that was caused in the past or your thoughts about the harm that might occur in the future. You can relate to your fearful thoughts in ways that help you to develop the courage you need to risk failure so that you can leave your chains behind.

15. Creating

[I]n every human breast, God has implanted a Principle, which we shall call Love of Freedom; it is impatient of Oppression, and pants for Deliverance; and by the leave of our Modern Egyptians, I will assert, that the same Principle lives in us.

—Phillis Wheatley, Former slave
quoted in *The Collected Works of Phillis Wheatley,*
edited by John Shields

The men and women who ran to freedom had performed various kinds of work during the years they were in slavery. Most worked as field hands, tending sugar, rice, tobacco, cotton, and other crops, depending on the location of the plantation they lived on. They cleared woodlands and fields; planted, weeded, and harvested or picked whatever was grown; and worked with livestock. They worked between ten and fourteen hours each day in heat, rain, and cold. During harvest time, it was not unusual for them to work as many as eighteen hours each day. The laborers often included those who were sick, injured, grieving, or had not recovered from childbirth. They not only had to contend with being overworked, but with being severely beaten with rawhide and hickory rod whips. Many of them retired for the night to windowless shacks with dirt floors, and no furnishings, with only an open door or cracks in the walls for ventilation.

Some of our ancestors worked as house servants. Often residing in their slaveholder's house or mansion or "the big house," they cleaned, washed, and sewed clothes; cooked and served meals; arranged gardens; provided child care and parenting; and drove carriages. They were under the constant supervision of the slaveholder and his family. In addition to being at the family's beck and call every moment of the day and night as personal attendants, they were frequently subjected to insults, rape, and whippings from the slaveholder, the slaveholder's spouse, children, and other family members and their friends.

Others worked as industrial laborers, performing manual and technical work. The men, women and children who did this kind of work were usually slaves who had been hired out by their slaveholders to companies or to government agencies. Often, they were seen working in chain gangs on railroads, bridges, canals, levees, ports, and byways and in mills, mines and forests. For them, whippings were frequent, as one worker recalled:

> I was whipped while there three times. The last whipping I got was very bad, because I did not finish my pit, though, I worked hard to get it done. It is always the way, that if a slave tries ever so hard to finish his task, and tires himself almost to death, he is sure to get a whipping if he leaves only a little piece, or if a few straggling weeds are left, or if it is not done exactly to please the overseer. They tie him up by his hands, and put a pole between his legs to make his skin tight, and give him twenty or thirty lashes. The tighter they stretch him the more the whip gashes. The slaveholders are all the time contriving punishments.[1]

Many slaves died as a result of brutal treatment and dangerous and unsafe work conditions. Knowing this could happen, many slaveholders purchased slave insurance to protect their "investment."

There were a few slaves who worked as artisans. They crafted furniture, metalwork, pottery, and shoes; some did decorative art such as woodcarving. They were also involved in various aspects of building construction as carpenters and brick or stone masons. In these ways, they were involved in the construction of most buildings in the South.

Although artisans were usually granted more autonomy than other slaves and thus had some relief from the capricious behavior of their slaveholders, they nevertheless were subject to whippings from them for "not following instructions." Of course, any act of self-defense—as Solomon Northup learned within an hour of stopping his slaveholder, Tibeats, from whipping him—was an unpardonable offense.

> I tried to beseech my Heavenly Father to sustain me in my sore extremity, but emotions choked my utterance, and I could only bow my head upon my hands and weep. For at least an hour I remained in this situation, finding only relief in tears, when, looking up, I beheld Tibeats, accompanied by two horsemen, coming down the bayou. They rode into the yard, jumped from their horses, and approached me with large whips, one of them also carrying a coil of rope.
>
> "Cross your hands," commanded Tibeats, with the addition of such shuddering expression of blasphemy as is not decorous to repeat.
>
> "You need not bind me, Master Tibeats, I am ready to go with you anywhere," said I.
>
> One of his companions then stepped forward, swearing if I made the least resistance he would

break my head—he would tear me limb from limb—he would cut my black throat—and giving wide scope to other similar expressions. Perceiving any importunity altogether vain, I crossed my hands, submitting humbly to whatever disposition they might please to make of me. Thereupon, Tibeats tied my wrists, drawing the rope around them with his utmost strength. Then he bound my ankles in the same manner. In the meantime the other two had slipped a cord within my elbows, running it across my back, and tying it firmly. It was utterly impossible to move hand and foot. With a remaining piece of rope Tibeats made an awkward noose, and placed it about my neck.

"Now then," inquired one of Tibeats' companions, "where shall we hang the nigger?"[2]

Occasionally, slaveholders allowed their enslaved artisans to keep a small portion of the income their labor generated so they could later purchase their freedom. However, such arrangements were often a trick by slaveholders to keep skilled slaves compliant and income producing. Wages were usually kept very low. As a result, it could take ten, fifteen or twenty years, working day and night, to raise the amount needed to purchase one's freedom or the freedom of family members. Some slaveholders would wait until the agreed-upon amount was raised, take the money, and then refuse to grant their slaves freedom as promised.

Often the work done by our ancestors was accompanied by singing. This was especially true when the work involved wielding an axe, hammer, spade, or hoe; unloading, rowing, sawing, or digging; husking or picking crops; lining railroad tracks; cooking, or rocking babies.

Singing allowed our ancestors to regulate the pace of work, verbally protest against slavery, soothe themselves and each other, and express hope for liberation. Although the structure and tune of the songs sung might have been familiar—they were often a call and response type—the words were usually spontaneous and improvised. They would reflect the mood of the singer or recall a recent event. Or they would simply be words that had no meaning at all but would provide a rhythm or beat for the bodily movements that were needed to perform the work. For example, one abolitionist heard slaves sing:

> William Rino sold Henry Silvers;
> Hilo! Hilo!
> Sold him to de Gorgy trader;
> Hilo! Hilo!
> His wife she cried, and children bawled,
> Hilo! Hilo!
> Sold him to de Gorgy trader;
> Hilo! Hilo![3]

Persons overhearing our ancestors singing as they labored in gangs in forests, on roads, or in plantation fields often commented that the music was "beautiful."

Whether singing or not, our ancestors were usually involved in bringing into existence something that had not previously existed. Their work involved the act of *creating*. But there was one problem with their creative work: they were not creating anything to uplift their own lives or the lives of their people. Rather, all their creative energies and efforts were being used to uplift the lives of the people who were oppressing them: the slaveholders and the slaveholders' wives, husbands, parents, children, families, community, and their descendants.

Slavery was such a perversion, an attempt to dehumanize black people, that many of them simply could not live with it. So they let go of the belief that they were unworthy of a good life and fled to the North to create a new life in freedom. Every step northward can be seen as a creative act that led them closer to that new life, one that could be satisfying and fulfilling.

Like our ancestors who ran for freedom, you may also want to stop pouring your life energy into people, activities, and projects that are keeping you in bondage, in servitude, or otherwise stuck. You may want to start creating a new work of "art": an existence that allows you to enjoy and make the most of your inherent good-ness, genius, and potential. If so, starting your "work of art" may be challenging. After all, as African American poet and novelist Gwendolyn Brooks notes, "Art hurts. Art urges voyages—and it is easier to stay at home."[4]

Indeed, when faced with the opportunity to create a new life, we may want to stay at home, or, as people used to say, "stay on the plantation." We may want to keep right on doing the same old things we've always done. This may be because the thought of actually doing the things we want, or need, to do to improve our lives can make us feel anxious. If you have ever taken a test, had a job interview, or gone on a first date with someone you care for, you know some of the symptoms of anxiety: sweating, dizziness, headache, racing heartbeat, nausea, fidgeting, muscle tension, restlessness, and agitation.

When we feel anxious, we often avoid starting what we want, or planned, to begin, disengage from work we are doing, or, for no apparent reason, fail to complete what we have started. We might even refuse to let go of work that we have completed so that we don't have to move on to another task with which we are not familiar. In such instances, instead of trusting that we possess the resources—inherent goodness, genius and potential—to deal with whatever arises in each moment, we tend to avoid the unknown altogether. Regrettably, when we do this, we allow our uneasiness, apprehension, awkwardness, shyness, and embarrassment to keep us in bondage. We maintain the illusion that we are respectable and competent. We "stay on the plantation." But, by remaining in our comfort zones, we harm ourselves. We never discover, and the world never sees, the full range and depth of our goodness, genius, and potential.

Managing Anxiety

We don't have to relate to anxious thoughts and their symptoms as though we are slaves responding to a slave patrol's command to "Stop, n----r!" We are the "children of the brave." We can create a new life in freedom by managing our anxiety. Following are some strategies you can use:

- **Acknowledge anxiety.** Recognize and acknowledge that nervousness and anxiety are normal human emotions. Everyone, including you, will experience them at one time or another. When this happens, be patient and kind to yourself.

- **Breathe.** In the moment when you notice anxiety, you can practice the calming meditation in chapter 2, one of the breathing exercises in chapter 4, or one of the walking meditations in chapter 8. All of these techniques can help you to access the resources needed to respond to the situation you are anxious about.

- **Relax.** Try the following progressive relaxation; it's an exercise that can have an anti-anxiety effect. Relax your forehead, then the area around your eyes. Next, relax the corners of your mouth. Now listen to sounds around you without concentrating on them. Gradually bring your awareness into your arms and legs. Wherever there is tension, imagine that it flows out of your body through your fingertips and toes. Slowly lift your chin and smile.

- **Chant or pray.** Chant a word or phrase using rapid repetitions, or say a prayer asking your higher power to support you. This will help you to interrupt the stream of fearful thoughts and induce mental calm. Here are a few words you can chant out loud or whisper: "relax," "peace," "ease," "free."

- **Rehearse.** Raise your confidence level by rehearsing and preparing for the event that you are nervous about. If there is something you'll need to say, practice saying it repeatedly. If there is something you'll need to do, practice doing it repeatedly. Visualize yourself in the situation you will be entering, exactly as you want to appear. Use your imagination to familiarize yourself with the situation you'll enter.

- **Examine.** Put your nervousness and anxiety in perspective. What are you afraid of? Apply the questions in the previous chapter for "Examining Your Fear" to your anxiety. Is there a good reason to be anxious?

- **Eat well.** Maintain good nutrition. Avoid foods that induce anxiety, such as caffeine, sugar, and processed foods. Eat food such as whole-grain breads and pastas, proteins, legumes, fruits, and vegetables. Avoid alcohol and drink plenty of water.

- **Meditate.** Maintain a regular sitting meditation practice. It will help you to induce the mental calm you need to see your situation and choices clearly. Allow the energy of anxiety to naturally arise and fade. Follow the North Star.

- **Exercise.** Practice yoga, dance, jogging, or other types of movement. This can causes the brain to release *endorphins* from the pituitary gland into the blood and spinal cord. These powerful chemicals are very effective in producing a feeling of well-being. Any kind of physical exercise will help to ward off anxiety and nervousness.

- **Create.** Engage in creative activities such as gardening, cooking, modeling, singing, acting, photography, golfing, collecting shells or rocks, jewelry making, dancing, painting, or drawing. Such activities can be very helpful, as they allow you to rest and focus your attention on something other than your anxious thoughts. They can help you to gain a fresh perspective.

African Mask-Drawing Practice

Let's create something. Get a pencil, crayon, or marker, and a blank sheet of paper. In this particular practice, you will draw the African mask shown below. As you draw, place your attention on the line you are creating, just as you place it on your breath during calming meditation.

When you become aware that your attention is on your thoughts about what you are doing—doubts, uncertainties, confusion, judgments—recognize that they are simply thoughts, label them "thoughts" without judging them and return your attention to drawing your line. Don't worry about drawing the mask perfectly; you can't. You may have to "take a leap" and get off a line or go in an opposite direction in order to accomplish your objective. When thoughts arise, simply note them and the way they make you feel, let them go, return your attention to what you are doing and keep drawing your line.

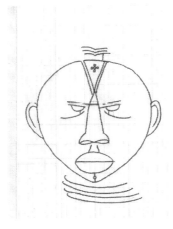

The thoughts and feelings that arise while drawing this mask are likely to be similar to the ones that will arise when you're doing *any* creative act, whether it's a work of art in the usual sense or taking the steps to find a job, apply to college, take a test, clean your home or car, or help a friend. Acknowledge them as "thoughts" without giving them any more of your attention and continue drawing your line. We have to be willing to work creatively with what arises in our mind and life just as our ancestors did as they uplifted themselves in freedom.

When you have finished drawing your mask, look at what you have created. You may want to color it or hang it on a wall in your home as a reminder of what you can do, if you stay with it. You may want to repeat this exercise at other times using other materials. Most important, apply the lessons you learned from drawing your mask—working through subtle uncertainties, doubts, anxieties, and hesitations—to the art of creating a beautiful life. Remember what African American publisher and entrepreneur John H. Johnson said: "To succeed, one must be creative and persistent."[5]

Stay awake and continue drawing your line, whatever forms it takes. Trust in your ability to respond appropriately to any situation that makes you feel anxious. Don't worry about making "mistakes" or "messing up." View all your so-called "mistakes" and "mess-ups" as opportunities to learn and grow so that you can continue creating the life you want. View "mistakes" and "mess-ups" as the unavoidable part of bringing forth your inherent goodness, genius, and potential.

No matter what thoughts arise in your mind, let them go; remain present in each moment. Keep drawing your line. Little by little place yourself in situations where you can develop and bring forth more of your inherent goodness, genius and potential. Your life can be a beautiful work of art, so please stay with it.

16. Developing Helpful Mindsets and Habits

When I left the house of bondage, I left everything behind.

—Sojourner Truth, Former fugitive slave
quoted in *Sojourner Truth: Slave, Prophet, Legend*
by Carleton Mabee and Susan Mabee Newhouse

During the Antebellum Period, most whites in the United States believed in white supremacy rather than racial equality. Thus, while they may have differed among themselves on the subject of slavery, most of them shared the mindset that black people—freemen, fugitives, and the enslaved—were inferior and thus a threat to American civilization.

So, in 1816, prominent slaveholders and non-slaveholders came together to form the American Colonization Society. Some members of the Society favored having the US government purchase and deport the enslaved blacks to Africa, along with any free blacks willing to emigrate. Other members wanted only to get the free blacks out of the country. It was felt that free blacks were the greatest threat—inciting slaves to rebel, aiding runaways who escaped, demanding the same rights as white people, and refuting in words and deeds the deeply embedded belief that whites are superior.

The Society secured funds from the US Congress, and Northern and Southern states, to purchase slaves and send them, along with free blacks, to Liberia. Although several thousand free blacks and slaves emigrated, the Society's colonization scheme didn't work. It was simply not practical. Not even the US government had the resources to purchase and deport millions of slaves. It didn't even have the resources to deport a couple hundred thousand free blacks.

More importantly, the Society's plan didn't work because it was unacceptable to most free blacks. Many of them had initially supported a colonization plan by African American merchant Paul Cuffee to establish a trading colony in Liberia. However, when it became apparent that colonization was being seriously considered by influential whites as a way to get all free blacks out of the country, most free blacks withdrew their support of colonization. They decided that they weren't going anywhere. "We will never separate ourselves voluntarily from the slave population in this country," exclaimed Richard Allen, the founder of the first national black church in the United States. "They are our brethren by the ties of consanguinity."[1]

One consequence of the increasing free black population and their rejection of colonization was that whites with racist mindsets developed some very racist habits. They got into the habit of taking actions that subordinated free blacks in society.

Northern whites prohibited blacks from voting, testifying in court, and serving as jurors. They restricted the size of free blacks' gatherings, denied state aid for the education of black children, prohibited free blacks from bearing arms and selling or purchasing alcohol, required free blacks to carry identification papers, and allowed free blacks convicted of crimes to be sold into slavery. They discriminated against them in bank lending and employment and segregated them in public places including housing, restaurants, hotels, theaters, churches, and public transportation. The mechanisms for subordinating free blacks varied widely from state to state, and changed often.

Most Northerners were OK with these racist anti-black practices, especially ones that restricted the ability of free blacks to compete with the arriving European immigrants for jobs. Many were also OK with the expansion of slavery into the unsettled western territories.

In fact, there was a lot of support in the North for slavery—that is, until the Southern states began to use their power in the federal government to pass slavery laws that directly threatened Northerners' sovereignty and freedom. It was only then that large numbers of Northerners began joining the abolitionists, free blacks, fugitives, and slaves in fighting to destroy the source of Southern states' power: slavery.

Still their belief that blacks were inherently inferior to whites did not change much. This belief was deeply embedded, fixed, and set in their minds. (For many it still is.) Therefore, as a matter of habit, they avoided taking actions that would change the laws and practices that subordinated blacks. They did not make it a habit of acting to give blacks equality.

Runaways arriving in the North discovered that it was not the Promised Land they had envisioned. The stench of racism was everywhere; it did not cease to exist simply because they were free. In the racist environment of the North, the Northern black community was like a breath of fresh air. It welcomed runaways to freedom, provided them with protection, temporary shelter, clothing, food, medical care, employment, job referrals, education, spiritual nurturing, and help with locating family members who had escaped to the North or Canada.

Even with all this help, new arrivals needed something else to uplift themselves in freedom: they needed to let go of *unhelpful mindsets* they carried with them from their years in slavery. They needed to let go of many of the beliefs that they held about the world and their place in it.

Here are some unhelpful mindsets that new arrivals had to let go of:

- We are not as intelligent, capable, worthy or beautiful as other people.

- We will never be allowed to get ahead and excel in society.

- We are not supposed to nurture strong relationships with our parents, spouses, and children.

- We can't work collectively as a people to improve our conditions.

While such mindsets might have helped them survive under slavery, they would not help them survive as free men and women in the North. They needed new mindsets. Some of the *helpful* mindsets they needed to develop were:

- We are as intelligent, capable, worthy and beautiful as other human beings.

- We must obtain an education and strive to excel in everything we do.

- We are worthy and capable of building lasting, healthy relationships with our parents, spouses, and children.

- We can work collectively to improve conditions in our community.

New arrivals developing helpful mindsets such as these were able to uplift themselves in freedom. They got into the habit of learning reading, writing, and math. They got into the habit of looking for work and learning vocational trades. They got into the habit of supporting their families and providing good parenting to their children. They got into the habit of being industrious, frugal, civic-minded, law-abiding citizens. In the process, they contributed to the development of important institutions in the black community:[2]

- The black family, which supported the needs of both immediate and extended family members.

- Businesses in the service industry and craft trades, as well as in manufacturing and merchandising.

- Churches such as the Abyssinian Baptist Church, African Methodist Episcopal Church, African Baptist Church, and First Colored Presbyterian Church.

- Newspapers such as the *Mirror of Liberty, Freedom's Journal, North Star, Provincial Freeman, National Era,* and *Brooklyn Daily Eagle.*

- Political organizations such as the New York Vigilance Society and State Central Committee of Colored People of Ohio.

- Schools such as the African Education Society, the New England Union Academy, and Phoenix High School.

- Social welfare groups such as the African Educational and Benevolent Society, the Philadelphia Library Company of Colored Persons, the Garrison Literary and Benevolent Society of New York, the Philadelphia Female Anti-Slavery Society, and Prince Hall Masonry.

By developing helpful mindsets and habits, new arrivals to the North were able to bring forth their inherent goodness, genius, and potential. They proved themselves capable of achievements far beyond what white Americans wanted them to believe were possible. Against so many odds, they revealed the greatness of their inherent dignity.

Developing Helpful Mindsets

After experiencing repeated defeats, rejections, and setbacks, it is easy for us to develop the mindset that our abilities and our situation are set in stone, with no possibility of improvement. In reality, though, nothing is fixed or permanent. Nothing is set in stone. To see this, all we have to do is to review the biographies of phenomenal African Americans who had humble beginnings and went on to do great things. Look at the news and weather. Change is everywhere. Just when we think we've seen it all, something new occurs. That's because anything is possible.

In order to create a more uplifted life, we need to have this mindset: "Anything is possible for me." The mindsets that we often carry around with us—"I can't do this," "They won't allow me to do that," "This is who I am, period," or "They are never going to allow us to get ahead" are unhelpful. What we need is a mindset that recognizes that we possess unlimited, inherent goodness, genius, and potential, a mindset that says, "Yes, I can create the life I want."

We are developing such a liberating mindset by meditating. We are creating a new mindset by refraining from fixating on negative thoughts. We are resetting our mind by letting go of negative thoughts and returning our attention to the breath and following it out as it dissipates in space. As we do this, our mind becomes more open, and we are better able to see. And what we eventually come to see is that—like nature, the weather, the news, and many notable African Americans—our personal traits, qualities, and station in life are not set in stone. They may seem to be, if we are dwelling, fixating, holding on to our limiting thoughts about our capabilities and situation. In actuality, however, whether we are rich or poor, an A student or F student, are praised or condemned, we still can learn, grow, and make our situation whatever we want it to be.

Please don't buy into anyone's suggestion that you can't bring forth the fullness of your goodness, genius, and potential. That is an unhelpful mindset, one that will surely keep you shackled and bound. Don't be a slave to such negative thinking. You *always* possess the capacity to change your situation for the better. This is the mindset you need to escape enslavement and uplift yourself.

Developing Helpful Habits

You can also change your situation for the better by letting go of habits that hold you down and developing habits that lift you up. For this, the following exercise can help.

1. Find a place where you can sit uninterrupted. Ask yourself a couple of questions: How am I moving through life? Is the way I am moving through life helping to uplift me or hold me down? Without judging yourself or comparing yourself with others, examine your mindsets and behaviors, with regard to money, food, family, drugs, relationships, charitable causes, children, education, health, work, religion, disagreements, housekeeping, driving, voting, etc.

2. Ask yourself a few questions: What habits do I have that are unhelpful, which are holding me down? What habits do I have that are helpful, which help me to lift my life up? Is the way I do things in one area of my life the same way I do things in other areas of my life? Simply reflect on the process and patterns that you use as you move through your life.

3. On a piece of paper, list five habits you have that are helpful. On a separate piece of paper, write five habits you have that are unhelpful.

4. Next, reflect on the two lists of habits. What mindsets do you have that support these habits? See if you can hear

the habitual thoughts, beliefs and attitudes behind these habitual behaviors.

5. For each unhelpful habit you have written, identify a new habit that is the opposite of the unhelpful one, which can help you to uplift yourself. Add the new habits to the list of helpful habits.

6. File away your list of unhelpful habits, so you can periodically review it as a reminder and acknowledgment of how far you've come. Place your list of helpful habits where you can see and review them regularly.

7. Pay attention to your behavior as you go through each day. Look for opportunities to let go of unhelpful habits and engage in helpful ones—and do just that when you are able.

Relating to unhelpful and helpful habits does not mean you need to become ambitious. Just be aware of how you are moving through your days so that you can take actions that are helpful.

Here are sample lists of unhelpful and helpful habits; some of these items may or may not appear on your lists.

Unhelpful Habits (that keep me down)

- Procrastinating.

- Spending all my free time hanging out with friends who do not have my best interests at heart.

- Eating food that causes me to gain weight.

- Going into debt for things I don't need.

- Tossing my trash on the ground as I travel through my neighborhood.

<u>Helpful Habits</u> (that lift me up)

- Each week develop a plan with goals and tasks, and do one task each day that moves me closer to my goals.

- Spend an hour each day with myself in solitude, contemplation, or meditation.

- Consume more vegetables, fruits, and nuts, water, and less meat, starch, fat, and sugar.

- Purchase only what I can afford to pay for with my own money.

- Place trash such as paper, cans, and bottles in the trash can.

Everyone's lists of unhelpful and helpful habits are going to look different, so don't try to make yours look like the ones above. Just be aware of your habits. Awareness will help you to grow, to live your life more fully. It will help you to "do the right thing."

Respect Yourself

Treating everyone respectfully is another habit you want to develop in your efforts to uplift yourself.

Begin by regularly commemorating the lives of preceding generations of your people. After all, they are your *ancestors*. You are related to them. They are how you got here. Many of them stayed up late at night for you. They suffered great indignities for you. They cried for you, and they prayed for you. Some of them died for you. Certainly when it comes to respect, you don't want to forget them. Your life did not begin with you. You are part of a continuum.

Make time to reflect on your ancestors and on what their lives might have been like. This will help you to appreciate their exemplary qualities and contributions. This will help you to remember who you are and your calling.

Also, strengthen the habit of respecting your *elders*. Although there may be aspects of their lives indicating that the legacy of slavery has been too great a burden for them to overcome, there is never a reason to disrespect them. You are not superior to anyone. Elders can provide you with advice and perspectives from their life experiences. This is true whether their life has been marked by failure or success. Seek guidance from them.

Let go of the mindset that you can figure out how to live life on your own, and that there is nothing that old folks can teach you. If you respect your elders and listen with an open mind to what they have to say, you will always learn something. But you need to listen—very deeply. When you do this, you'll discover that you don't have to keep stumbling and falling and getting stuck on the road of life. You have wise and caring elders in your family and community who can help you.

This doesn't mean that you should stop listening to "the sound of the genuine" within yourself. For as African American theologian Howard Thurman observed, "if you cannot hear it, you will never find whatever it is for which you are searching and.... you will all of your life spend your days on the ends of strings that somebody else pulls."[3] You don't want that to happen. So, yes, seek the counsel of your elders. But don't forget, this is your life. You need to make the decisions. Make smart decisions and take smart actions and assume responsibility for them.

You also want to develop the habit of respecting your *descendants* including the ones who have not been born yet. We are their roots. We can't just live our lives in any old way. We can't allow ourselves to become so distracted and overwhelmed that we place the destiny of our people in others' hands. We are responsible for transmitting the wisdom of our ancestors to our children and youths. Our duty is to interact with them in ways that help them to grow and blossom. This will enable them to fulfill the charge they received before their birth and enable them to prepare the way for succeeding generations of our people.

Lastly, we want to make a habit out of being respectful to *everyone*. Although we may think we are separate individuals or a separate group, that's really an illusion. In actuality, all of us—black, white, Hispanic, Asian, etc.—are interconnected, descendants of the "mitochondrial Eve," sons and daughters, brothers and sisters, caretakers for the next human generation. We are members of the same family.

So, in brief, when we develop helpful mindsets and habits, and respect everyone, we uplift ourselves and human dignity.

17. Affecting Life

[T]hey forget that God rules in the armies of heaven and among the inhabitants of the earth, having his ears continually open to the cries, tears, and groans of his oppressed people; and being a just and holy Being will at one day appear fully in behalf of the oppressed, and arrest the progress of the avaricious oppressors.

—David Walker, *Walker's Appeal*
African American antislavery activist

Through a series of compromises, the leaders of the United States violated the sacred principle on which the nation was founded—that all people are created equal. They made laws and decisions such as the ones below which cemented in American life the reprehensible idea that white people were superior and black people were inferior.

- The Compromise of 1787 [1]

- The Compromise of 1793 [2]

- The Compromise of 1820 [3]

- The Compromise of 1850 [4]

- The Compromise of 1854 [5]

- The Dred Scott Decision of 1857 [6]

Interrelated Lives

When our nation's leaders made these laws, they ignored the "cries, tears, and groans" of our ancestors. But "a just and holy Being" appeared "in behalf of the oppressed" and arrested their progress. A civil war commenced that nearly destroyed the nation. By the time the war was over, hundreds of thousands of men were dead.

One of the lessons we can learn from the actions of our nation's leaders is that our actions have effects. They affect people.

When our minds are clouded by greed, hatred, and indifference—as was the case with our nation's leaders—our actions tend to be violent, hateful, greedy, inconsiderate, harsh, dishonest, envious, resentful, and so forth, and everyone connected to our actions is harmed. When our minds shine with generosity, compassion, and wisdom—as was often the case with our ancestors—our actions tend to be peaceful, generous, loving, caring, kind, gentle, truthful, joyful, and so forth, and everyone connected to our actions is helped. We may not always see the ways in which others are affected by the actions we take. But the people who are connected to our actions experience their effects.

"We are all caught in an inescapable network of mutuality, tied in a single garment of destiny. Whatever affects one directly, affects all indirectly," Martin Luther King, Jr. said. King referred to this as "the interrelated structure of reality."[7]

Knowing that interrelatedness (and implicitly interdependence, cause and effect, and impermanence) is the nature of reality, and that everything we think, say and do connects in some way to others, we quite naturally want to act in ways that help rather than harm, especially in our relations with neighbors, coworkers, friends, and loved ones. After all, everything is interrelated. When we help others, we help ourselves. When we harm others, we harm ourselves. When we have a genuine desire to help, and act from that motivation, we uplift our lives and the lives of others.

So to uplift ourselves and others, we don't want to do what our nation's antebellum leaders did—ignore what's going on. We want to pay attention. When we pay attention, we can more clearly see what we are doing, the effects our actions are having, and what we and others really need. We can then skillfully act in ways that help rather than harm.

The following exercise is one you can use to help you to act in ways that are helpful.

1. When you feel the impulse to engage in an unhelpful action (violence, harshness, greed, etc.), let go of the thoughts you are dwelling on, and bring your attention to your breath—your North Star—and then into your body.

2. Observe in your body the emotional energy, tightness, or hardness that accompanies the impulse you have detected. Hold your attention in your body. Breathe.

3. Be completely present with the impulse rather than drawn back into your thoughts about the situation.

    What beneficial would be accomplished if you actually said or did what the impulse is compelling you to do? How would the person and his or her loved ones be affected? How would you and the people you care about be affected? What about the next day? The next year? Is it really worth it?

4. Instead of engaging in an unhelpful action, see if you can respond with a helpful action—for example, one that is peaceful, loving, kind, caring, or gentle. So, for instance, if a person has said something to you that you strongly disagree with, instead of harshly criticizing, come back to the present, right *here*, right *now*. Then try to respond in a way that is genuine, kind, and expresses your truth.

5. Pay attention. Remain mindful. Observe what happens next.

6. Repeat the steps above whenever the impulse to engage in an unhelpful action arises.

None of us has a "right" to behave in ways that are offensive, abusive or harmful to other people—not even you, no matter how right you think you are. Each of us is part of a continuum with responsibilities to act with dignity (not like a rude and hostile slaveholder). It is doubtful that ten thousand generations of our ancestors lived and died so we could live our lives in an undignified manner. That's not why we are here. But if you behave in undignified ways, continue to work with this exercise.

On the other hand, if you are a victim of others' rude, abusive, hostile, or violent behavior the sooner you put some distance between yourself and them, the better off both you and they will be. Pulling away can help you to remain on the path to a free mind, and it can give your adversary the space and time they need to discover that they are going in the wrong direction, away from freedom.

Repairing Harm Caused

African American poet Countee Cullen once wrote, "We must be one thing or the other, an asset or a liability...."[8] This is so applicable to our discussion. For we must be one thing or the other, attentive or inattentive, helpful or harmful.

Being inattentive, as we learn from our nation's leaders, can make us a liability. It can cause us to act in ways that have harmful effects. But, let's face it, none of us is perfect. All of us are capable of thinking, saying, and doing things that cause harm. But when you cause harm to yourself or others, please refrain from beating up on yourself. Our ancestors have been stripped, tied, and whipped enough. You don't need to pour salt in your wounds, place forty-pound weights on your legs, or wear a multipronged iron collar around your neck with a bell.

Whatever you habitually use to punish yourself—self-effacing and self-defeating thoughts, comments, and actions; or escapist behaviors like drug and alcohol use, sex, or violence—put it down. As Martin Luther King, Jr., said, "boldly throw off the manacles of self-abnegation."[9]

Instead of renouncing yourself and taking on the attributes of a slaveholder in relation to yourself, let go. Just let go. Let go of the thoughts that are keeping you down. Return your attention to your breath. Follow your breath out as it dissolves in the space around you. Return to attentiveness. Be fully present with whatever you are experiencing, while you are experiencing it, moment to moment, without rendering any judgment.

From this point forward, here are five things you can do:

1. Recognize the actions you took that caused harm.

2. Acknowledge with heartfelt regret the harm your actions caused.

3. Identify lessons that you can learn from the situation.

4. Vow to yourself that you will try not to do what you've done again.

5. Take a positive action toward repairing the damage, if that is possible, or an action that lays ground for more positive action in the days and years to come.

What all this means is that if you want to become free, sometimes you will have to let go of your expectations of yourself as well as others' expectations of you. As the African American rapper and actor Tupac Shakur said, "You can spend minutes, hours, days, weeks, or even months overanalyzing a situation, trying to put the pieces together, justifying what could've, would've happened, or you can just leave the pieces on the floor and move the fuck on."[10]

Let it go. Come out of your head. Return your attention to the North Star. Like the fugitive standing on the bank of the fast moving Ohio River, be completely present where you are. Pay attention. Wade in the water. Be with the flow. Feel amazing grace. Enter the Promised Land.

TERMINAL: Rochester, New York

Many of the leading abolitionists did not approve of the actions of Northerners who went into the South to entice or escort slaves away from their owners. They felt such ventures endangered the lives of everyone involved, and could provoke violent retaliations from slaveholders. Harriet Tubman didn't worry about these concerns. She continued making trips into the South to bring her people to freedom.

When questioned about the dangers she faced, Tubman responded:

> I started with this idea in my head, "There are two things I've got a right to, and they are, Death or Liberty—one or the other I mean to have. No one will take me back alive; I shall fight for my liberty, and when the time has come for me to go, the Lord will let them kill me."[1]

Gradually, stories about Tubman and her rescue missions began to circulate in towns and cities throughout the North. Eventually, they found their way across the Atlantic Ocean to Europe. As her reputation spread, she became more than a celebrity. She became a living legend: the "Moses of her people."

To religious educator Samuel Miles Hopkins, Tubman was an example of "what a lofty martyr spirit may accomplish, struggling against overwhelming obstacles."[2] To social reformer Gerrit Smith, "she had a rare discernment, and a deep and sublime philanthropy."[3] To journalist Franklin B. Sanborn, "she was too *real* a person, not to be true."[4] To writer Sarah H. Bradford, "Harriet's charity for all the human race is unbounded."[5] William Seward, the former governor and US senator of New York, who would serve as secretary of state in President Lincoln's administration, described her this way: "I have known her long, and a nobler, higher spirit, or a truer, seldom dwells in the human form."[6]

William Wells Brown describes what African Americans thought of Tubman:

> While in Canada in 1860, we met several whom this woman had brought from the land of bondage, and they all believed that she had supernatural power. Of one man we inquired, "Were you afraid of being caught?"
>
> "O, no," said he, "Moses has got the charm."
>
> "What do you mean?" we asked.
>
> He replied, "The whites can't catch Moses, 'cause she's born with the charm.
>
> The Lord has given Moses the power."[7]

As Tubman's legend spread, it energized abolitionists, generated support for her rescue missions, emboldened slaves to escape, and earned her the hatred of Southerners. Some sources report that Southerners posted substantial rewards for her apprehension—dead or alive—twelve thousand dollars and forty thousand dollars. No matter what amount may have been offered for her capture, it made no difference to Tubman. She would be the last person on Earth to allow a reward to deter her from what she believed was her God-given duty. Thus, she continued to go into the South and come away with more people.

During some of her trips out of the South, on the way to Canada, Tubman visited the home of Anna and Frederick Douglass in Rochester, and probably housed her passengers there.

Anna Murray Douglass must have admired Tubman for the selfless work she was doing. After all, Anna had had a long involvement with the Underground Railroad herself. She was the railroad agent who had enabled Frederick Douglass to escape from slavery in 1838, and after they married, enabled him to pursue his abolitionist activities. After living in New Bedford, Massachusetts for several years, they relocated to Rochester in 1847. In Rochester, they established an Underground Railroad station in their home. There, while raising children, they provided temporary shelter to many fugitives.

In writing about their Underground Railroad activities, Douglass recalled that,

> On one occasion I had eleven fugitives at the same time under my roof, and it was necessary for them to remain with me until I could collect sufficient money to get them on to Canada. It was the largest number I ever had at any one time, and I had some difficulty in providing so many with food and shelter, but as may well be imagined, they were not very fastidious in either direction and were well content with very plain food, and a strip of carpet on the floor for a bed, or a place on the straw in the barnloft.[8]

One of the reasons the Douglasses were in Rochester was that Frederick wanted to do more for the abolitionist cause. In the years after his escape from slavery, he became one of the leading anti-slavery lecturers in the North, wrote his highly acclaimed slave narrative, and toured Europe as an abolitionist lecturer (during which time two Englishwomen successfully led an effort to purchase his official freedom from slavery). Then, upon his return to the United States as a free man, he announced to his friends in Massachusetts that he planned to publish an abolitionist paper.

Douglass's plan was met with disapproval by many of his friends. They told him that he should stick with lecturing; couldn't add anything new to what was already being published in the *Liberator* and *Anti-Slavery Standard*; lacked the education and experience needed to succeed as a newspaper publisher; and was arrogant to think—being just a few years out of slavery—that he could instruct white people on democratic ideas. Douglass felt that their comments were genuine and well-intentioned. But the more he listened, what he *heard* them expressing was their low estimate of black people. This made him all the more determined to go forward with his plans. Thus, he moved with his family to Rochester where, with the help of supportive friends, he started publishing the *North Star*.

The *North Star* (which was later renamed *Frederick Douglass's Paper* because competing newspapers tried to cut in on the success of his paper by adding "*Star*" to their names) was published weekly from 1848 through 1860. The newspaper bore the mark of excellence. It became a strong voice for the abolition of slavery and a valuable source for African American news and opinion.

In one of the first issues of the newspaper, Douglass responded to friends who had opposed his decision to start the paper:

It is neither a reflection on the fidelity, nor a disparagement of the ability of our friends and fellow-laborers, to assert what "common sense affirms and only folly denies," that the man who has suffered the wrong is the man to demand redress,—that the man STRUCK is the man to CRY OUT—and that he who has endured the cruel pangs of Slavery is the man to advocate Liberty. It is evident we must be our own representatives and advocates, not exclusively, but peculiarly—not distinct from, but in connection with our white friends. In the grand struggle for liberty and equality now waging, it is right and essential that there should arise in our ranks authors and editors, as well as orators, for it is in these capacities that the most permanent good can be rendered to our cause.[9]

Douglass began to abandon long-held abolitionist views that he had shared with his mentor, William Lloyd Garrison. Garrison had argued that the US Constitution was a slavery document, that the US Government was a slaveholder's government, and that abolitionists should boycott the government by refraining from voting and other political activities. However, the messages that began crying out from the *North Star* expressed the view that the Constitution was an *anti*-slavery document, the US Government was not committed to slavery, and that in order to abolish slavery, what was needed was political action such as voting, rather than merely moral appeals. The newspaper also called for equal rights for blacks and women.

Anna Murray-Douglass
Source: Library of Congress

18. Forgiving

Yes, God, I'll love everybody and the white people too.

—Sojourner Truth, Former fugitive slave
quoted in *Sojourner Truth: Slave, Prophet, Legend* by
Carleton Mabee and Susan Mabee Newhouse

The life of a slave was filled not only with long hours of hard physical labor. It was also a life lived in terror and heartbreak. Understandably, these emotional injuries—inflicted over years and decades—deeply affected our enslaved ancestors. Some of them wished or prayed that their slaveholders would die. They wanted their slaveholders to die because they were harming them, and so that they could no longer harm black people.

Josiah Henson not only wanted his slaveholder to die, he wanted to have the pleasure of killing him. He got within one swing of delivering an axe into the skull of his sleeping slave-holder; then, as he writes,

> ...all at once, the truth burst upon me that it was a crime. I was going to kill a young man who had done nothing to injure me, but was only obeying commands which he could not resist; I was about to lose the fruit of all my efforts at self-improvement, the character I had acquired, and the peace of mind that have never deserted me. All this came upon me instantly...I shrunk back, laid down the axe.[1]

Harriet Tubman became so angry with her slaveholder, and afraid he would sell her sibling, that she prayed for his death.

> I prayed all night long for master, till the first of March; and all the time he was bringing people to look at me, and trying to sell me. Then we heard that some of us was going to be sold to go with the chain gang down to the cotton and rice fields, and they said I was going, and my brothers and sisters. Then I changed my prayer. First of March I began to pray, "Oh Lord, if you ain't never going to change that man's heart, kill him, Lord, and take him out of my way."
>
> Next thing I heard old master was dead, and he died just as he lived. Oh, then, it appeared like I'd have given all the gold in the world, if I had it, to bring that poor soul back.[2]

Sojourner Truth prayed for all white people to be killed. But like Henson and Tubman, she eventually decided to forgive. Each of them seemed to come to the realization that the acts of individual slaveholders were the result of larger forces in society. For instance, Tubman observed:

> They don't know any better, it's the way they were brought up. "Make the little slaves mind you, or flog them," was what they said to their children, and they were brought up with the whip in their hands.[3]

In the explanation for his change of heart towards his former slaveholder, Frederick Douglass also recognized that there are other forces at work influencing human behavior:

I regard him as I did myself, a victim of circumstances of birth, education, law, and custom. Our
courses had been determined for us, not by us. We
had been flung, by powers that did not ask our consent, upon a mighty current of life, which we could
neither resist nor control. By this current he was a
master, and I was a slave; but now our lives were
verging towards a point where differences disappear, where even the constancy of hate breaks
down, where the clouds of pride, passion, and selfishness vanish before the brightness of infinite
light.[4]

Indeed, our behavior, as Douglass notes, is often determined
by factors far beyond our ability to see, resist or control. This is one
of the reasons we frequently need a lot of time to understand why
people behave as they do before we can forgive them. However,
even with the passage of time, we still may not be able to sort out
all the factors and details in a way that enables us to understand.
We are complex. Although we may have a lot in common, we each
still experience the world differently and act and live in different
realities.

This was certainly true for enslaved men and women on the
plantation—such as Margaret and Robert Garner. Although both
were enslaved, their lives were different. Unlike Robert and other
men who were expected to increase the wealth of the slaveholder
solely through labor, women such as Margaret were expected to
accomplish that end through their labor and by bearing children.
As mothers, they naturally made the well-being of their children
their priority. However, their efforts to protect their children had
a downside. Under the slaveholder's threat to harm or sell their

children, mothers were often coerced into a sexual relationship with their slaveholder.

A significant percentage of black women and girls were raped during the Antebellum Period. The rapists were politicians, judges, clergymen, soldiers, planters, overseers, and even husbands whose wives did nothing to stop them. It's no accident that in 1860, 30 percent of the free blacks in the North were mulattoes, 40 percent of the free blacks in the South were mulattoes, and 10 percent of the slaves in the United States were mulattoes.

On one hand, there was the reality of the woman traumatized by being raped and impregnated, and having to endure either a painful abortion or a full-term pregnancy with the child conceived in that trauma. And there was the trauma experienced by her husband, who had to stand down, humiliated and powerless to do anything to protect his wife and their family. The two were on the same plantation, but lived and acted in two different realities, two different circumstances that tested the meaning of "true love." For, on "the morning after," and each morning for the rest of their lives, they still had to go on. At the sound of the horn, they still had to rise in their cabin and file out to the field of labor. They still had to live together and help raise the children, as long as they were not separated by being sold to a slaveholder on another plantation.

What enabled them to go on with each other? It was *forgiveness*. The woman had to let go of any thought that her husband could help to protect her, and her husband had to let go of any thought that she had a choice. They each had to let go of their thoughts and forgive each other in order to keep going. What enabled each individual to do this is the awareness that they too had, on many occasions, been flung by powers that did not ask their consent, which they "could neither resist nor control."

The Mirror

One way we can begin to understand other people so that we can move forward with our own lives is to reflect on actions we have taken. Perhaps we had sex with someone outside of our marriage or committed relationship, physically assaulted someone, used illicit drugs, or neglected our health. Perhaps we have taken something that did not belong to us. Perhaps we have nurtured negative thoughts such as prejudice, resentment, or hatred toward a person or group, or chosen to remain ignorant or indifferent to the needs of others. Perhaps we have spoken harshly or abusively, or lied, gossiped, or disrespected people in need of love and understanding.

When we reflect on our own actions, we may recall situations where we also "had been flung, by powers that did not ask our consent...which we could neither resist nor control." We might also see where we acted out of greed, hatred, and indifference. We might even see where we have some things in common with those we consider our enemies.

Fortunately, though, by asking for forgiveness and giving forgiveness, we can free ourselves from the constancy of hate, pride, passion, and selfishness that can keep our minds in bondage. We can embody the wisdom of African American educator Booker T. Washington, who said: "I will let no man drag me down so low as to make me hate him."

The following forgiveness practice is one that you can use to help you refrain from hating—yourself or others. It can keep you from getting stuck, so that you can keep moving forward. Please note, though, that this practice is done by *you*. Depending on the situation, it may or may not be wise or even possible to actually say to someone that you forgive him or her or to ask the person for forgiveness. For example, if they have not even acknowledged that they caused you pain, they may not really appreciate or feel a need for your forgiveness. Sometimes you may find it helpful to forgive or ask for forgiveness from someone who is long gone from your life. Forgiveness primarily heals your heart, and helps you to move on in your life.

Forgiveness Practice

1. Take a seat. Practice calming meditation for a few minutes.

2. Recall a time when you behaved in a way that may have been harmful to a family member, a friend, or a stranger. This could also include groups of people, such as those of different races, ethnicities, sexual orientations, religions, nationalities, ages, physical or mental abilities, and so forth, as well as "outsiders" who are not a part of your group of friends.

    a. Bring to mind whomever you may have harmed; the harmful action of body, breath, or mind; and the situation.

    b. Reflect on what was going through your mind: the ways in which ignorance, desire, and hatred or pride, passion and selfishness may have contributed to your behavior.

    c. Recall the effects that your actions may have caused.

3. Now, bring to mind the person or persons you harmed, state what you did to harm them, and ask them to forgive you. Adapt the following words as appropriate to your situation:

    a. "[Name of the person or group], I understand how my actions [state what they were] caused you harm. I promise to be careful not to cause you harm in the future. Please forgive me for the harm I have caused."

    b. "[Name of the person or group], please forgive me for the harm I have caused."

    c. Repeat, slowly: "[Name of the person or group], please forgive me for the harm I have caused."

4. Practice calming meditation for several minutes.

5. Now, recall a time when you were harmed. This may have been by an individual or a group.

    a. Bring to mind the person or persons who harmed you; the harmful actions they took with their body, breath, or mind; and the situation.

    b. Reflect on what might have been going through their mind; the ways in which ignorance, desire, and hatred or pride, passion, and selfishness may have contributed to their conduct.

    c. Recall the harm that was caused.

6. Allow yourself to feel any hardness, uneasiness, heaviness, constriction in your body, any pain that remains with you because of what they did or didn't do. Then, to the extent that is possible, dissolve the hardness in your heart by extending forgiveness to them. Call them by name and adapt the following words to your situation:

    a. "[Name of the person or group], you have hurt me [state what they did and how you were harmed]. I understand from personal experience how we all act in ways that are harmful to others. For this reason, I am not going to carry hatred in my heart for you. It does not help me, and it does not help you. I offer my heartfelt forgiveness for the harm you caused me and hope that you will never cause harm like this [state the harm they caused] to others." I choose to forgive you because I am ready to move on.

b. "[Name of the person or group], I unconditionally forgive you."

c. Repeat, slowly: "[Name of the person or group], I unconditionally forgive you."

7. Practice calming meditation for several minutes. Then move on. Resume your regular meditation practice or mindfully proceed to your other activities.

At different times, you may want to do the first part of this practice—asking for forgiveness—and at other times, the "forgiving" part. If you find when doing this practice that you are not ready to forgive, that's OK. Be kind to yourself. Repeated practice over time can help you to eventually forgive.

You will be able to forgive because you are capable of letting go. You have been *practicing* letting go, letting go thoughts about yourself, others, and the world you live in.

When you let go of your thoughts, allowing them to rise, abide, and fade, and return your attention to right *here*, right *now*, "clouds of pride, passion and selfishness vanish," and "the constancy of hate breaks down." Often, we find that all that remains are "circumstances of birth, education, laws and customs... upon a mighty current of life." In other words, all that remains are powers which do not ask our consent: impermanence, interdependence, causes, conditions, effects, and (depending on whether you dwell, fixate, and hold or let go) suffering or liberation, "the brightness of infinite light."

This does not mean that you should associate with people whom your wisdom tells you not to trust. And it does not mean that you (or anyone) should deny or ignore or forget what happened. But what it does mean is that when you harm someone or are harmed, you *can* free your heart and mind of aggression so that the wounds you or the other received do not keep you shackled or cause you to create even more pain for yourself or others.

In *No Future Without Forgiveness,* Archbishop Desmond Tutu, who led South Africa's Truth and Reconciliation Commission after apartheid ended there, writes insightfully that "because of forgiveness there is a future."[5] This is a truth that Henson, Douglass, Truth, and Tubman understood. They acknowledged the past, recognized that countless forces and conditions brought it into existence, and let go. They forgave and used what they learned about the past to inform them as they went forward. Like them, if you want to go forward and reveal your inherent goodness, genius, and potential, you will have to eventually forgive, and let go.

19. Caring

One night I made an incursion into the enemy's country. When I came back to the river my companion failed to appear with my boat. I secured a smaller one, loaded my crowd, and found I had one too many for my craft. The man left onshore was the husband of one of the women in the boat. We were being pursued and had no time to argue the point.

As I hesitated, one of the men in the boat walked ashore to make room for the husband. While this act was contrary to the eternal law of self-preservation, this ignorant slave sacrificed his freedom, without a moment's hesitation. Unfortunately, he was captured before we got across the river, a heroic victim of his own unselfishness.

So I could go on and write about instances of courage and sacrifice that these runaways showed and endured in their determined effort to break away from slavery.

—John P. Parker, *His Promised Land:
The Autobiography of John P. Parker*
Former fugitive slave

Much of the suffering our ancestors experienced was a direct result of slavery. They suffered when they had to endure their owner's whippings; when they had to bear the slave master's child; and when they returned from the field of labor to find their parent, spouse, or child had been sold and was gone, forever.

They also experienced suffering that had nothing to do with slavery, things that were an inescapable part of life. For example, just like us, they suffered when things changed, when pleasures came to an end, when they injured themselves or became ill, when loved ones died, and as they grew old.

Whatever suffering our ancestors experienced, they had ways of coping with it. One way they coped was by laying down their distressful and painful thoughts and *caring* for the well-being of *others*. They took their attention off thoughts about themselves and placed it on thoughts that wished *well-being* (happiness, good health, and prosperity) for others—such as slaves on the plantation who had escaped, been sold away, raped, or brutally punished. This helped to lessen our ancestors' suffering, gave them a greater appreciation of the suffering that others were experiencing, and made them more inclined to help others who were in difficult situations. In this way, caring helped to lessen everyone's suffering and foster healing. It fostered understanding, communication, and community.

Like our ancestors, we can also cope with suffering, and foster community, by taking our attention off worrisome thoughts about ourselves and placing it on thoughts that wish well-being for others. We can do this by practicing caring meditation.

In caring meditation, we bring to mind an ever-widening circle of people who may be suffering and extend a wish for their well-being. We not only extend a mental wish, we also arouse within ourselves caring feelings and extend them, too. Let's explore this.

In Caring Meditation #1, you are going to start by extending caring to yourself. Next, you are going to open your heart a little wider, by extending caring to a friend. Then, you are going to continue opening your heart by extending caring to a neutral person, then to a person with whom you have difficulty, then to descendants of Africans who were enslaved, and finally to everyone in the world. Caring Meditation #2 provides another version of this technique.

Caring Meditation #1

1. Take a seat and practice calming meditation for several minutes.

2. Bring to mind an area of your life in which you are suffering and in need of caring. Say the following caring wishes aloud or silently. As you say each line, arouse and extend heartfelt caring to yourself.

May I reach the Promised Land.
May all my troubles go away.
May I enjoy worldly and spiritual blessings.
May I be at peace and free.

Say these caring wishes two more times.

3. While maintaining a connection to the feeling of caring, bring to mind a friend who may be suffering. Form a visual image of the person in your mind. Say the following caring wishes, aloud or silently. As you say each line, extend heartfelt caring to your friend.

May [his or her name] reach the Promised Land.
May all [his or her name]'s troubles go away.
May [his or her name] enjoy worldly and spiritual blessings.
May [his or her name] be at peace and free.

Say these caring wishes two more times.

4. Now, maintaining a connection to the feeling of caring, bring to mind a person toward whom you have neutral feelings who may be suffering. For example, this person could be a bus driver, waitress, cashier, receptionist, or sanitation worker. Form a visual image of the person in your mind. Say the following caring wishes, aloud or silently. As you say each line, extend heartfelt caring to the neutral person.

May [name or description of the person] reach the Promised Land.
May all [his or her]'s troubles go away.
May [he or she] enjoy worldly and spiritual blessings.
May [he or she] be at peace and free.

Say these caring wishes two more times.

5. Next, while maintaining a connection to the feeling of caring, bring to mind a person with whom you are having difficulty who may be suffering, even if only from their own confusion. Say the following caring wishes, aloud or silently. As you say each line, extend heartfelt caring to the person. Note: If you find that you can't do this, return to step 2 and extend caring to yourself. You can always return to step 5 when you are ready. Whatever you decide, go on to step 6 below.

May [his or her name] reach the Promised Land.
May all [his or her]'s troubles go away.
May [he or she] enjoy worldly and spiritual blessings.
May [he or she] be at peace and free.

Say these caring wishes two more times.

6. Now, while maintaining a connection to the feeling of caring, bring to mind people of African ancestry, whose ancestors were targets of the chattel-slave system in the United States. Hold an image of them in your mind. Say the following caring wishes, aloud or silently. As you say each line, extend heartfelt caring to them.

May all the descendants of African slaves reach the Promised Land.
May all their troubles go away.
May they enjoy worldly and spiritual blessings.
May they be at peace and free.

Say these caring wishes two more times. Of course, you can also do this step of the practice to extend caring to the descendants of other people who were oppressed because of their race, ethnicity, religion, sex, or sexual orientation.

7. Finally, while maintaining a connection to the feeling of caring, bring to mind the people of all backgrounds in your home, neighborhood, workplace, city, region, state, country, and other countries, and other beings who may be suffering. Say the following caring wishes, aloud or silently. As you say each line, extend heartfelt caring to an ever-widening circle of people, until your heartfelt caring includes everyone in the world.

May everyone reach the Promised Land.
May everyone's troubles go away.
May everyone enjoy worldly and spiritual blessings.
May everyone be at peace and free.

Say these caring wishes two more times.

8. Conclude by practicing calming meditation.

You can include this technique in your daily meditation session. Or you can practice it in everyday situations where you or others are suffering. Notice what happens to your own outlook, and your heart, when you practice in this way.

Caring Meditation #2

1. Take several minutes to calm your mind by practicing calming meditation. Then, read the following passage.

On March 2–3, 1859, the largest single sale of human beings in US history occurred on the Ten Broeck Race Course on the outskirts of Savannah, Georgia. The event would become known as "The Weeping Time." The Pierce M. Butler family, which had a holding of more than nine hundred slaves, whose families had lived on their rice and cotton plantations for over six generations, took the people they enslaved to auction in order to pay debts.

In the days before the auction began, the Butler slaves were brought up from the plantations in groups by steamboat and rail. A reporter described them as dressed in clothing made from coarse fabric, with men wearing hats and women wearing colorful turbans fashioned out of handkerchiefs. They were housed in unfurnished sheds built for horses and carriages at the racetrack with nothing but their baggage. Meanwhile, slave buyers and speculators from across the country filled Savannah hotels and rushed to the racetrack to "inspect" the humans for sale. Over four days, our ancestors are poked, pinched, and fondled, and even compelled to expose themselves to full scrutiny of buyers.

Here is the scene: All of the slaves, exhausted, have been moved to a large room under the grandstand (a makeshift slave pen). There are vacant stares, rocking back and forth, and weeping. The room in which they are corralled connects to another room (the showroom), also under the grandstand, where the sale will take place. The showroom is crowded with rowdy, profane, rough young and old-silver haired men. It is loud, smoky, and wet from a downpour of rain. Pierce Butler arrives. The auctioneer and clerk take their place on a two-and-half-foot-high auction stand. Butler makes his way through the crowd and, after greeting acquaintances, sits down. The auction overseer rises, eventually quiets the crowd, and announces to the buyers the terms of payment. The auction begins.

The enslaved men, women and children are led out of the slave pens and paraded into the showroom, through the crowd of buyers and spectators, and up onto the auction stand for all to view. Bidding is now underway. A succession of low bids and then high bids are heard. *"Sold!"* shouts the auctioneer. Ties between husbands, wives, parents and children, sisters and brothers, lovers and friends are forever severed as 436 slaves are auctioned. *Sold!* There are pleas, shrieks and cries, weeping and lamenting, and hopeless grief. *Sold!* The faces of our ancestors bear agonized expressions, crushed hopes, broken hearts, as they take one last glance into the eyes of their beloved, which hold their anguished reflection. *Sold!*

The auction netted for the Butler family an amount that is equivalent to about $6.7 million today, and brought the people who were sold

unfathomable grief and suffering which has continued for their descendants to the present day.

2. Form a mental image of the enslaved people mentioned
   above, or at least one of them. As you breathe, arouse and
   extend genuine, heartfelt, unconditional caring to them.

3. After you have extended caring to people who were sold at
   this slave auction, see if you can arouse and extend genuine,
   heartfelt, unconditional caring to the other people present,
   even those whose actions were deplorable: members of the
   Butler family; the auctioneers; the slave sellers and buyers; the bookkeepers and Negro drivers; the amused and
   indifferent spectators. What about the people living today
   who are their descendants? Can you see that many of them
   are suffering too? Can you forgive? Can you let go? Can
   you move on with a heart that cares for everyone? Can you
   let go of your thoughts and return your attention to the
   breath, to right *here*, right *now*? Can you see, as Tubman
   noted, "They don't know any better, it's the way they were
   brought up." What thoughts arise in your mind? Can you
   see "the brightness of infinite light?"

4. Conclude by practicing calming meditation.

To become free, we have to let go. But letting go does not mean
forgetting our past, and the crimes that made our ancestors weep.
We have to retain that knowledge. It can help us to chart our way
forward and enable us to open our hearts to the suffering of others. This is what our ancestors did. As a result, they were able to
cope. They were able to keep going, and become free.

20. Helping

I have heard their groans and sighs, and seen their tears, and
I would give every drop of blood in my veins to free them.

Harriet Tubman, Former fugitive slave
quoted in *Scenes in the Life of Harriet Tubman*
by Sarah H. Bradford

Upon arriving in the Promised Land, runaways experienced their initial moments in freedom in different ways. Josiah Henson recalled, "I threw myself on the ground, rolled in the sand, seized handfuls of it and kissed them, and danced round till, in the eyes of several who were present, I passed for a madman."[1] William Wells Brown recalled, "I wanted to see my mother and sister, that I might tell them 'I was free!' I wanted to see my fellow-slaves in St. Louis, and let them know that the chains were no longer on my limbs."[2] Frederick Douglass also experienced great joy, but it did not last. He recalled,

> I felt like one who had escaped a den of hungry lions. This state of mind, however, very soon subsided; and I was again seized with a feeling of great insecurity and loneliness. I was yet liable to be taken back, and subjected to all the tortures of slavery. This in itself was enough to damp the ardor of my enthusiasm. But the loneliness overcame me. There I was in the midst of thousands, and yet a perfect stranger; without home and without friends, in the midst of thousands of my own brethren—children of a common Father, and yet I dared not to unfold to anyone of them my sad condition. I was afraid to

speak to any one for fear of speaking to the wrong one, and thereby falling into the hands of money-loving kidnappers, whose business it was to lie in wait for the panting fugitive, as the ferocious beasts of the forest lie in wait for their prey.[3]

Harriet Tubman was also lonely upon reaching the Promised Land, and she wanted to go back into the South to get loved ones she had left behind.

> I had crossed that line. I was free. But there was no one to welcome me to the land of freedom. I was a stranger in a strange land; and my home, after all, was down in Maryland; because my father, my mother, my brothers, and sisters, and friends were there. But I was free, and they should be free. I would make a home in the North and bring them there, God helping me.[4]

However, before Tubman and other fugitives could do anything to help their loved ones, they had to uplift themselves. Instead of giving in to the impulse to "tell everybody" or "do something," they had to allow these impulses to rise and fade, and give their attention to the situation right in front of them, to what they needed to do right then. Instead of heading south, they had to withdraw so that they could complete the final phase of their transformation into free men and women. Only afterwards could they reemerge.

That's what Tubman did. She removed the apparel of slavery from her body, dressed herself in an uplifted way, found a job, and a place to live. She became self-sufficient and frugal. She forged relationships with positive role models. And while she was creating her new life, she learned everything she could about the Underground Railroad. She stayed informed about current events in her hometown, including slave sale ads, with the help of friends who read the newspapers. And she continued to nurture her heartfelt longing to rescue her people by repeatedly saying to herself, "My people must go free."

Longing to Help

As you practice meditation, there will be occasions when you will feel just like Douglass and Tubman—alone, and a stranger in the world. Although you may want to share your experiences with others, you may recognize that much of what you want to share is simply inexpressible. Even if you could find words to express it, who would listen, and if people listened, who would understand? Who could ever really understand *your* experience?

Your feeling of aloneness, wish to connect with others, might give rise to the impulse to run off and help loved ones, friends, acquaintances, and strangers whose minds you know are shackled and bound. Although you may want to "say something" or "do something," often the wisest thing you can do is to simply *be* with your feeling of aloneness and to continue working on freeing your mind. After all, you are "yet liable to be taken back, and subjected to all the tortures" of an enslaved mind.

This does not mean that you need to abandon your desire to connect with and help others. Rather, you can speed up the arrival of the day when you can *truly* help, by following Tubman's example. She continued to free her mind of mindsets and habits that could hold her down and developed ones that could lift her up. Do those two things first. Undoubtedly, she also thought about her family and friends. In fact, the recurring thought that "they should be free" is probably what motivated her to keep uplifting herself so that one day she could free them. Likewise, while you are working to transform your mind, and thinking about loved ones who are still shacked and bound, you can do what Tubman did: keep telling yourself "My people must go free."

"My people must go free." Repeat the phrase to yourself. "My people must go free." Connect with your heartfelt empathy and caring for the people you want to help, "My people must go free." Say the phrase when you get up in the morning, as you go through the day, when you turn in at night. "My people must go free." You don't have to be embarrassed about saying this. Repeating this phrase will help you to remember that you have a sacred charge to keep, and that your ability to fulfill that charge depends on you uplifting yourself in freedom.

"My people must go free." Repeating this phrase will also help to ensure that you do not forget where you came from, what you had to go through to get to where you are, and the difficulties you overcame. "My people must go free." It will help to ensure that you do not forget that there are people experiencing the same challenges you overcame or are trying to overcome. Some of them may have dropped out of high school or college, become teenage or single parents, become homeless; some may have an addiction problem, be mentally ill or physically disabled or be serving time in jail or prison. Even those who look as if "they have it made" may be suffering from anxiety, loneliness, depression, or worse. "My people must go free." It will also help you to remember the many people who helped you.

"My people must go free." While you are saying this phrase, you will have to accept the fact that although you may want to help or are able to make some helpful gestures, you may not be able to do anything whatsoever to actually change anyone's situation for the better—at this time. But what you *can* do is to continually nurture your longing to help so that you will help if a situation arises in which you actually can.

"My people must go free." Repeat the phrase to yourself when you meet someone who is suffering: a person who is homeless, a rude or disrespectful person, a perpetrator or victim of a crime, a drug addict, anyone who is struggling to fulfill their potential. "My people must go free." Say it with genuine, heartfelt, unconditional caring. "My people must go free."

By meditating regularly, uplifting our personal situation, and repeating the phrase, we can free our minds of our "issues" and our preoccupation with ourselves, and can allow our hearts to continue to grow. This can help to ensure that our "good intentions" and concern for ourselves does not become an obstacle to the happiness of others when we do begin to act for their benefit.

Acts of Kindness

Another thing we can do to develop our capacity to help others is to perform small acts of kindness. There were many instances of Underground Railroad agents, and even those who remained in slavery, doing this. Performing small, kind acts helps us to:

- let go of our preoccupations with ourselves, our hopes and fears;

- overcome the hesitation to help;

- clear our minds;

- open and lighten up our hearts;

- develop a caring attitude toward others;

- get in the habit of helping others; and

- strengthen and make irreversible the inclination to help.

Often, we think that being kind to someone means that they "owe" us something in return. Or if someone is kind to us, we "owe" them something. While this is sometimes the case, such as in economic transactions, that is not the idea in this practice.

The idea behind performing small acts of kindness is to act with genuine, heartfelt, unconditional kindness, without any concern for outcome or benefit to ourselves. It is not to gain approval, applause, or recognition—just simply to be helpful. One way to perform acts of kindness is by viewing the object of our kindness—the other person—as though he or she once saved our life or took great care of us. Another way to look at it is to recognize that walking in our midst each day are men, women, and children who do not receive kindness, and who do not receive caring and respect.

All you have to do is to look at the faces of the people with whom you reside, work, shop, and ride each day to see that people need kindness—genuine, heartfelt, unconditional kindness. Perhaps the people closest to them have closed their hearts and presently are not able to provide them with the kindness they need. But guess what? You can. You can give it to them unconditionally, without wanting, seeking, expecting, or accepting anything in return.

Please don't underestimate the importance of the kind actions you take: what they mean to other people. Just as a single harsh or cruel comment from your mouth can devastate and shake the confidence of a child or adult for the rest of their life, the smallest kind act from you can transform someone's life for better. Can you recall some of the kind acts directed to you that have positively affected your life?

Kindness Practices

Here are a few acts of kindness you can do:

- Give someone you meet a heartfelt smile.

- Allow a bus passenger to have your seat.

- Hold the door for the person behind you so he or she can enter first.

- Encourage a friend with a project he or she is undertaking.

- Help an elderly neighbor with yardwork.

- Speak to a child on his or her own terms.

African American educator Booker T. Washington once wrote, "I have learned that the best way to lift one's self up is to help someone else."[5] Like Washington, you can lift yourself up (and others, too) by performing simple acts of kindness. It doesn't cost you a cent or take more than a few seconds of your time to be kind.

You will have no problem finding acts of kindness to perform. Every day we are presented with opportunities to act kindly. You will have to pay attention to recognize many of those opportunities, though. Just as you are with someone you care a great deal for—your parents or your child—stay alert to opportunities to be kind. That's what Tubman did.

Although Tubman had no children of her own, she treated everyone lovingly as though they were her parent or child. The kindness that she displayed throughout her life was evident when her friend, former Secretary of State William Seward, died. As reported by Sarah H. Bradford:

The great man lay in his coffin. Friends, children, and admirers were gathered there. Everything that love and money could do had been done; around him were floral emblems of every possible shape and design, that human ingenuity could suggest, or money could purchase. Just before the coffin was to be closed, a woman black as night stole quietly in, and laying a wreath of field flowers *on his feet*, as quietly glided out again. This was the simple tribute of our sable friend, and her last token of love and gratitude to her kind benefactor. I think he would have said, "This woman hath done more than ye all."[6]

Indeed, Tubman *had* done more. She had uplifted her mind, uplifted her existence, and performed many acts—small and large—of genuine, heartfelt, unconditional kindness, all while repeating to herself a simple phrase: "My people must go free." This is how she became—with her enlightened heart—the Moses of her people.

TERMINAL: Buffalo, New York

Harriet Tubman may have traveled to Buffalo on occasion to lose pursuers on her trail. No one knows for sure. If she did, she would have sheltered her passengers there in an agent's home or in a church, perhaps the famous Michigan Street Baptist Church, until she could arrange for them to be ferried across the Niagara River into Canada. It's hard to know what she actually did. That's because, to protect her passengers, much of her work was done in secret. Often she would not be heard from for weeks and months. During that time she'd be secretly reentering the South, escorting passengers to the North, through Pennsylvania and New York, and on to Canada.

William Wells Brown was one of many people who admired Tubman. He made his home in Buffalo after escaping from his slaveholder in Cincinnati, Ohio, in 1834. He found work on Lake Erie steamboats, which he used as Underground Railroad stations. He hid runaways on board so they could be transported to Canada. In this way, he helped many fugitives make it to freedom.

However, moving runaways through Buffalo, to the ferry, was never easy, as this account from Brown makes clear:

> We started, and when about a mile below the city, the sheriff and his men came upon us, and surrounded us. The slaves were in a carriage, and the

horses were soon stopped, and we found it advis-
able to take them out of the carriage, and we did
so. The sheriff came forward.... His men rushed
upon us with their clubs and stones and a general
fight ensued. Our company had surrounded the
slaves, and had succeeded in keeping the sheriff
and his men off. We fought, and at the same time
kept pushing on towards the ferry.... After a hard-
fought battle, of nearly two hours, we arrived at the
ferry, the slaves still in our possession. On arriving at the ferry, we found that some of the sheriff's
gang had taken possession of the ferry-boat. Here
another battle was to be fought, before the slaves
could reach Canada.[1]

The flight of men, women, children to freedom and the efforts
of their helpers to aid them always involved a struggle. In an
1857 address on West India Emancipation, Frederick Douglass
explained why a struggle was necessary, and why people in bondage must never give up.

The whole history of the progress of human liberty
shows that all concessions yet made to her august
claims, have been born of earnest struggle.... If there
is no struggle there is no progress.... Find out just what
any people will quietly submit to and you have found
out the exact measure of injustice and wrong which
will be imposed upon them, and these will continue
till they are resisted with either words or blows, or
with both. The limits of tyrants are prescribed by the
endurance of those whom they oppress.[2]

Tubman knew this. It is not surprising, then, that while traveling through Troy, New York, in the spring of 1860, when she discovered that a fugitive named Charles Nalle had been apprehended and was likely to be returned to the South, she exerted herself on his behalf.

Nalle's attorney, Martin Townsend, gave the following account of what happened that day as US marshals began to move his client.

> Harriet Tubman, who had been standing with the excited crowd, rushed amongst the foremost to Nalle, and running one of her arms around his manacled arm, held on to him without ever loosening her hold through the more than half-hour's struggle to Judge Gould's office, and from Judge Gould's office to the dock, where Nalle's liberation was accomplished. In the melee, she was repeatedly beaten over the head with policemen's clubs, but she never for a moment released her hold, but cheered Nalle and his friends with her voice, and struggled with the officers until they were literally worn out with their exertions, and Nalle was separated from them.[3]

Tubman exerted herself to free Nalle because she knew something that many of her accomplices did not know. She knew from her lived experience that, as she put it, "Slavery is the next thing to hell."[4]

William Wells Brown understood what Tubman meant. After passage of the Fugitive Slave Act of 1850, he fled to England with his daughters to avoid being captured. While there, he wrote a novel about hellish aspects of slavery experienced by mulatto women. His book, *Clotel: Or, The President's Daughter,* 1853, was the first novel published by an African American.

While Brown was in England, a British couple purchased his freedom. He then returned to the United States as a free man.

William Wells Brown
Source: Massachusetts Historical Society

21. Dressing

Their yearly clothing consisted of two coarse linen shirts, one pair of linen trousers, like the shirts, one jacket, one pair of trousers for winter, made of coarse negro cloth, one pair of stockings, and one pair of shoes....

—Frederick Douglass,
Narrative of the Life of Frederick Douglass
Former fugitive slave

Throughout all sub-Saharan African societies, the black skin of African people, the shape of their head, their hair, eyes, nose, lips, chin, arms, breasts, hips, buttocks, legs, feet, and gait were considered to be expressions of divine beauty. However, during the Antebellum Period, the US slaveholding society had a different view. It viewed black men, women, and children as ugly and held that their physical characteristics indicated that they were inferior to white people.

Slaveholders stripped our ancestors naked, and exposed the nude bodies of men, women, and children to the general public. This was done to administer punishments during whippings, for inspections at slave auctions, and for the white public's amusement.

When slaveholders did allow our ancestors to wear clothing, they usually prohibited them from wearing ordinary clothing. They issued them "negro clothes." Negro clothes were made from what was called negro cloth, a cheap, coarse fabric. Wearing the clothes made our ancestors feel uncomfortable and self-conscious, insecure, and out of place, especially around whites, in part because often no provisions were made for their clothes to be cleaned or for them to maintain good hygiene.

The overall effect of these practices was to debase our ancestors and destroy their sense of personal worth, and reinforce the prevailing belief that black people were powerless and inferior.

Fugitives arriving in the North knew that negro clothes conveyed an unhelpful message. They knew that if they continued to wear the clothes, their appearance would put them at risk of being caught by slave catchers, reinforce Northern racist attitudes, and hinder their own efforts to create a new life in freedom. Therefore, they discarded the apparel of slavery.

Our newly liberated ancestors then dressed themselves in uplifting apparel that was clean, in good repair, well-fitted, coordinated, and fashionable. They refrained from dressing in ways that were unattractive, inappropriate, distracting, or offensive. Thus, they were able to connect more deeply with, and bring forth the powers of, their inherent dignity.

To see what they looked like, and to gain insight into how ordinary clothes may have made them feel, take a few minutes to examine the images of the men and women in this guidebook. You might even be able to feel the force of their presence as their contemporaries did.

After growing up in slavery, wearing negro clothes, dressing in a more uplifted way may have felt a little uncomfortable to them at first. However, over time, the clothes empowered them and allowed them to move with greater ease in society as free men and women.

Like the fugitives who fled slavery to create a life in freedom, you can also decide what message you want your personal appearance to convey. When you go out in public, your personal appearance can convey the magnificence of your inherent dignity—your inherent goodness, genius, and potential—or it can hide these qualities in you and thus convey a lack of dignity. Your appearance can convey the message, "I am worthy of respect," or it can say the opposite.

Effects of Poor Appearance

When our personal appearance is poor or sloppy, we tend to:

- think more negatively about ourselves, our situation, and others;

- feel more anxious and less confident and capable;

- act less at ease, less competent;

- perform at a lower level, be less productive; and

- keep others from seeing our positive traits and give them reason (justified or not) to regard us unfavorably.

It is worth considering why people regard us unfavorably when we dress poorly and, further, whether we really want to dress in a way that encourages them to view us that way. We may want to think about whether our appearance is helping us, and whether it is helping those we care about—our spouse, siblings, children, friends, and other African Americans—to rise above the legacy of slavery. We certainly don't want to model poor appearance. We want to be a shining example.

Effects of Uplifted Appearance

When our personal appearance is uplifted, we tend to:

- think more positively about ourselves, our situation, and others;

- feel less anxious and more confident and capable;

- act more at ease, more competently;

- perform better and be more productive; and

- enable others to see our positive traits and to regard us more favorably.

When you go out in public, you can see people who have good personal appearance who are regarded favorably by the people around them. How does it make you feel when you see African American men, women, or youth dressed in an uplifted and dignified way? Do they make you proud that you are an African American? Does it make you proud to see our people carrying themselves that way? Again, consider the implications for yourself and how others feel when they see you.

With good personal appearance, you can move in the world more freely. Other people will tend to respond more positively to you when your hygiene is good and your hair and nails are neatly groomed; your clothes and shoes are clean and in good repair, fit and are worn properly; you sit, stand, and walk with good posture; and you have a manner of speaking that is clear, direct, and positive.

When you uplift your appearance, you naturally uplift your self-esteem, self-respect, and self-confidence as well as your capabilities and credibility. You enhance your ability to influence the opinions and actions of others in your home, school, church, workplace, and community. You are better able to fulfill your aspirations. All this happens because when you uplift your appearance, you uplift your mind. And when you uplift your mind, you eventually uplift your appearance and the way in which you move in the world.

Being Authentic

Maintaining an uplifted, dignified appearance can be challenging. Popular culture is potent; it can persuade us to buy things we don't need, eat food that's not good for us, and wear fashions that affect us just as negro clothes affected our ancestors. Moreover, popular culture gives rise to a "mass consciousness" that influences our outlook and makes it difficult for us to see, and question, what the culture (its artifacts, stories, histories, myths, legends, rituals, celebrations, heroes, symbols, beliefs, assumptions, attitudes, rules, norms, ethical codes, and values) is compelling us to think, say, and do. Whatever "everyone" is doing seems to be "normal." But what we have to remember is that doing what is viewed as normal by the larger society is not always in our best interest.

Buying into the dominant culture can be a problem, whether we're consuming unhealthy food, wearing degrading clothing, participating in entertainment that dulls or agitates our minds, or adopting prevailing notions about our people and issues facing our community. Whether you are rich, poor, or somewhere in between, you've probably also noticed that keeping up with popular culture can be costly as well.

For example, if you allow what you are doing to jeopardize your financial well-being or the well-being of your family, you may find that you don't have the resources and networks that are needed to recover. Many people have found themselves in this situation. So it is important for you to be aware of *your* reality and not be persuaded to think, say, or do things that are not in your best interest, that keep you and your people down.

The sooner we realize that everything others do is not necessarily good for us to do, the sooner we'll stop following "the crowd" or doing what is "in vogue," and start following our own good example, and the good examples in our community. After all, the only way to really be normal is to be authentic—who and what you really are. That is what you become when you bring forth your inherent goodness, genius, and potential.

At no time in our history have our ancestors urged us to limit ourselves by being like everyone else. We were not told to allow our limitations, other people's low expectations of us, or what is "normal" to be our standard. We are children of the brave and devout. We were told to set higher standards and expectations for ourselves. We were told to always elevate ourselves, and to go further and elevate our families, our community, our society, and all of humanity. Our charge is not to conform to this world, but to transform and transcend it.

So then, how do you keep yourself from following the crowd down a path that is not helpful, a path that can actually keep you from bringing forth your inherent goodness, genius and potential? How can you avoid being hoodwinked and manipulated (by advertising and product endorsements) into becoming a mere imitation or fabrication of someone else's alien, confused, or degrading image of what you should look and act like? As a person of African ancestry, how do you become part of the solution rather than part of the problems facing our people?

Obviously, when it comes to your personal appearance, the first thing you need to do is to find out who you really are. Do some reading. Then, taking the following steps will help you to dress authentically.

1. *Be attentive.* Pay attention to your personal appearance.

2. *Be reflective.* For example, ask yourself: Do the clothes I'm wearing express who I really am? Does my personal appearance convey my inherent dignity? Does my appearance convey my inherent goodness, my inherent genius, and my inherent potential? Is the way I'm dressed helping me? Is the way I'm groomed and dressed helping to uplift others? Am I setting a good example for youth and

children to follow? Is the way I'm groomed and dressed communicating a positive message about my people to the larger society?

3. *Be gently corrective.* If the answer to any of the above questions is "No," see if there is something you can change, even gradually. See how it feels to experiment with small changes to your personal appearance. Whatever you do, see if you can avoid molding yourself into the image created by people who don't have your best interests at heart.

We can use this approach—being attentive, reflective, and gently corrective—with everything we do: dressing as well as parenting, talking, housekeeping, studying, driving, eating, shopping, leading, and so forth. Why would we want to use this approach? Because everything we do fashions our mind. We are either developing habits that will cloud our mind or clear it up, habits that will keep us down or lift us up. Is what you're doing uplifted? Is what you're doing a true expression of who you are? Is what you're doing part of the solution? If the answer to these questions is "No," explore why this is so and what you can do to start making small changes.

The best way to become authentically who you are—and in the process to uplift yourself—is by regularly meditating. Let go of all the titles, labels, roles, descriptions, and categories that you and others use to define who you are. Take a break from them because, in the absolute sense, they are not you anyway. They are just thoughts, concepts, and labels, some helpful, some not.

Reset your mind. Just simply *be*. It's actually cool to have a mind that is free. So keep your life fresh and real. See how refreshing authenticity feels. Let go, and allow your inherent goodness, genius and potential to come forth and shine through. You can do this. And, as you do, you'll reveal the true you.

***

I find in being black, a thing of beauty: a joy, a strength; a secret cup of gladness, a native land in neither time nor space, a native land in every Negro face! Be loyal to yourselves: your skin, your hair, your lips, your Southern speech, your laughing kindness, your Negro kingdoms, vast as any other.

—Ossie Davis, African American playwright, actor, and director[1]

22. Affirming

The dawning of this, another year, awakened me from my temporary slumber, and roused into life my latent but long-cherished aspirations for freedom. I was now not only ashamed to be contented in slavery, but ashamed to seem to be contented.... I now drove from me all thoughts of making the best of my lot, and welcomed only such thoughts as led me away from the house of bondage....The intensity of my desire to be free...brought me to the determination to act as well as think and speak.

—Frederick Douglass,
Life and Times of Frederick Douglass
Former fugitive slave

One night in 1857, while Tubman was staying in the home of the African American radical abolitionist and black-nationalist Henry Highland Garnet, she went to bed and while asleep received a powerful vision. The next morning when she came downstairs for breakfast, she shared her vision: "My people are free! My people are free!"[1]

Mr. Garnet, who did not believe that the slaves would be freed anytime soon, responded, "Oh, Harriet! Harriet! You've come to torment us before the time; do cease this noise! My grandchildren may see the day of the emancipation of our people, but you and I will never see it."[2] Tubman replied, "I tell you, sir, you'll see it, and you'll see it soon."[3]

Garnet's response helps to explain why it was often helpful for free blacks and fugitive slaves to rest their attention on anything other than their thoughts: many of their thoughts were negative. If they could just let go of these thoughts, they could go beyond negativity, and see other possibilities.

As meditators, we are also afflicted with negative thoughts, such as "I can't," "I'm not good enough," "I wish I looked like *that* person," "People don't like me," "I am worthless," or "There is no use trying." Such thoughts are like shackles and chains on the mind. They keep us down, shackled and bound. They are the result of a lifetime of social conditioning. They convince us that we either don't deserve to have fulfilling lives or are not capable of attaining them. As long as we give our attention to negative thoughts, we will have a reason to believe we are not good enough; we will have a reason to believe we cannot bring forth our inherent goodness, genius, and potential. We will unwittingly be helping to keep alive notions of white superiority.

Let's take an inventory of some of the negative thoughts to which we give our attention. In the course of one day, write down or at least notice every time you have a negative thought about yourself. At the end of the day, reflect for a few minutes on the following questions:

- How many negative thoughts about yourself did you have today?

- How many of these negative thoughts have been with you for a long time?

- How many of these thoughts are keeping you from doing what you want to do?

For many people, the answer to each question is "A lot!" This is regrettable because our life tends to conform to the thoughts to which we give our attention, especially negative thoughts, such as the thought that we are inferior. Since such thoughts are deeply ingrained in our mind, we need to work with gentle persistence to displace them. One way we can overcome them is by using affirmations.

An affirmation is a positive statement about us and our capabilities that we repeatedly say to ourselves. It is a statement that what we want for ourselves—what we truly want, not just another consumer item—already exists in reality. Such positive statements displace negative thoughts, remind us of our natural strengths, and alter our self-concept and outlook. They positively influence our attitudes and what we think, do, and say.

The effectiveness of affirmations is not only in the positive statements but also in the repetition of them. To appreciate the effect of repetition, consider what happens in our everyday lives when we receive repeated messages. We all know what happens when we hear the same rumor about a person from different sources—we begin to believe it. Furthermore, we know what happens when we are repeatedly exposed to certain brands—we begin to believe the advertising, even to the point of spending money on things we may not really want or need. And we know what happens when we repeatedly receive messages from our family, church, school, employer, and media that say, in effect, that we are not capable and worthy. We begin to believe it.

We also begin to believe the positive things we are repeatedly told, or tell ourselves, about our worth and capabilities. As African American neurosurgeon Ben Carson said, "If you hear how wonderful you are often enough, you begin to believe it, no matter how you try to resist it."[4]

Creating Affirmations

Let's develop an affirmation.

Write a statement about what you want to exist in reality. Make your statement (1) about *you*, (2) positive, (3) in the present tense, (4) very specific and (5) very brief. For example, if you are a boxer, you wouldn't write "I will not lose any fights" as your affirmation. That statement contains a negative word, *not*. Similarly, you wouldn't use "I will become a champion." That statement is in the future tense, not the present. Here is the well-crafted affirmation developed by Muhammad Ali:

"I am the greatest!"

Muhammad Ali's affirmation was a complete repudiation of established thought about the nature of reality—white superiority. It was not egocentric because, although Ali wanted to win fights, he also wanted to inspire African Americans and other people of color to have confidence in themselves. He wanted to help undo the damage that had been done to their self-esteem by racism.

Why did this affirmation work for Ali? He explained it this way: "I am the greatest. I said that even before I knew I was. It's the repetition of affirmations that leads to belief. And once that belief becomes a deep conviction, things begin to happen."[5]

For Ali, repetition of this affirmation not only shifted his view of himself, it also shifted others' view of him. Thus, he said, "I figured that if I said it enough, I would convince the world that I really was the greatest."[6] In other words, Ali recognized that no one was going to believe in him until he believed in himself. And once he believed in himself, he could *act* courageously with faith that he actually was the greatest heavyweight boxer of all time and was capable of winning his fights. After all, as Ali has noted, "It's the lack of faith that makes people afraid of meeting challenges."[7] Similarly, if you believe you possess inherent dignity, and have confidence in your inherent goodness, genius, and potential, your possibilities expand, and you naturally begin to engage with the world more freely.

Like Ali, you don't have to live enslaved to negative thoughts. You can live as a person who is completely liberated. Every time you use affirmations to displace negative or limiting thoughts and *take steps* to bring what you have affirmed into reality, you proclaim your greatness as well as the greatness of our people. You also deliver justice to our ancestors—those men, women and children—who were brutalized, debased, oppressed, terrorized, humiliated, and murdered, simply because they sought to create an uplifted life in freedom. For them, you ensure that justice never sleeps, because you are continually awake, right *here*, right *now*, affirming with your life's blood that you possess inherent dignity.

Your inherent dignity is what makes you great. However, possessing inherent dignity is not enough. You must bring it forth. Our people want you to bring it forth. And that is what you'll be doing when you use affirmations.

Affirmation Practice

1. Develop an affirmation.

2. Develop a plan of action—three steps you need to take during a calendar week to bring your affirmation to fruition. In this plan, identify any obstacles that might come up, and actions you can take to overcome them.

3. Start taking steps to bring your affirmation to fruition.

4. During the week, as you take actions to bring your affirmation to fruition, recite your affirmation. Repeatedly recite your affirmation, aloud or silently, in a heartfelt way, with a strong belief and conviction. You can do this during your daily meditation sessions or as you go through each day.

5. When doubtful, anxious, or fearful thoughts arise to distract your attention from your affirmation, acknowledge your thoughts by labeling them as "thoughts." Then let them go. Return your attention to your breath and your

affirmation. (By noticing and letting go of your established conditioning, you can begin to change your situation and further your efforts to bring your affirmation to fruition.)

6. Conclude the repetitions of your affirmation with the Yoruba word *Ashe* [ah-SHAY], which is translated as "So be it," "So it is," "It definitely shall be so" and "Make it so," or you can use another personal expression, to strengthen your resolve to bring your affirmation into existence.

7. Update your action plan every seven days with additional steps you need to take to bring your affirmation to fruition, and continue to follow it and repeat your affirmation.

When you have brought one affirmation to fruition, replace it with another one and develop an action plan. But remember, you are not using affirmations just for yourself. If you bring forth your inherent goodness, genius and potential, one day you can inspire or help others to bring forth theirs, too.

Yes, You Can!

[I]n the unlikely story that is America, there has never been anything false about hope. For when we have faced down impossible odds; when we've been told that we're not ready, or that we shouldn't try, or that we can't, generations of Americans have responded with a simple creed that sums up the spirit of a people.

Yes we can....

Yes we can....

Yes we can.[8]

Barack Obama used the affirmation "Yes We Can" when he was first running for president during the 2008 campaign. He used it to help free an uncertain electorate from limiting thoughts about his electability. When the clouds of doubtful thoughts that had been created by generations of racism, apathy, and despair were displaced, people ceased to be blind to what was possible. They regained their vision.

Just as Ali and Obama used affirmations to write a whole new chapter in US history, you can use affirmations to write a new chapter in your life. But remember: Nothing is more affirming than the actions you take to bring what you affirm into reality. It was not enough for Ali to say, "I am the greatest." He had to do the hard work that was needed to prepare for and win his fights—and overcome defeats and setbacks—before the World Boxing Association and World Boxing Council could affirm that he was indeed the undisputed boxing heavyweight champion of the world.

Similarly, it was not enough for Barack Obama to say, "Yes we can." He had to work hard to build the most sophisticated national presidential campaign that had ever existed and effectively communicate his message of change to the electorate—despite efforts to paint him as "un-American"—before he could be selected as the Democratic Party presidential nominee, win the US presidential election, and get the US electoral college to affirm that "yes we can" elect an African American as president of the United States of America.

The election of Barack Obama, with the help of Michelle, should be a reminder to you that there is nothing you can't do—if you free your mind. Let go of thoughts that hold you down, return your attention to the breath, to right *here*, right *now*, and repeatedly state your affirmation. Of course, you also must take action. Otherwise, your affirmation is "all talk."

Likewise, our criticism of elected officials and government is all talk, unless we remember the brave people who fought and died for the right to vote and honor them by staying informed of the issues and casting our votes at the polls on Election Day.

Providing Encouragement

While you are taking affirming actions, pay attention to the brothers and sisters you meet in the course of your day. Most of them are restoring our people in big and small ways. Some are representing us in elected office, teaching in school, leading a congregation, or directing a stop-the-violence or voter education campaign. Others are policing our neighborhoods, searching for a job, doing homework after school, selling bean pies at the intersection, picking up litter off the street, depositing money in their savings account, coaching a little league team, or giving up their seat on the bus for an elderly person, and so forth. Restoration is not merely the result of big things but also countless little things that happen in many places over time. When you see brothers and sisters doing things that help to restore our community—big and small—give them thanks and encouragement.

It only takes a few seconds to give thanks and encouragement, and it doesn't cost a cent. If each of us made a practice of giving thanks and encouragement to five black people each day, in their lives and our own it would make a huge difference. So practice doing it. See what happens.

Undoubtedly, you will meet some people who have doubts about their inherent dignity. Don't look down on them. Are you your brother's and sister's keeper? Do what you are able to do to help them get up. For example, in your own words, you can simply remind them that every person of African ancestry in the United States is a vital part of the African American community. Whether they live in the White House or in the streets, our community needs them.

When we give help and encouragement, we are not trying to take over anyone's life, assume responsibility for their decisions, or shield them from the consequences of their choices. If we do this, then our actions may be detrimental rather than helpful. When we give help and encouragement, what we are doing is reminding our brothers and sisters that they possess inherent goodness, genius, and potential. We are reminding them that they can bring it forth— if they so choose. This is what our community needs everyone in it to do: bring forth their inherent goodness, genius, and potential. Of course, one way we can do this is by practicing meditation.

Helping youth, in particular, stay on a good path in life is what we are doing when we encourage them to continue their education. At one time African Americans had to get a good education so that they could compete with white Americans for employment. Given institutional racism, finding a good-paying job was, and still is, difficult, even with a college degree. However, obtaining and keeping a good-paying job is becoming more challenging because we are in a global economy. We now must also compete with job applicants from countries all over the world, those who immigrate to this country as well as those who compete for American jobs in their native lands.

In this global economy, the good-paying jobs will go to individuals who are highly proficient in math, science, reading, and writing. Unfortunately, these are the very areas where educational performance among African Americans is falling behind. This is in part because we have bought into the mindset that these are areas where black people can't excel—even though black people obtain advanced degrees in math, science, and literature every year from ivy league colleges and universities. Each of us possesses the same inherent capabilities that they do.

Regrettably, at the very time in history when we should be developing proficiency in these key areas, many of our youth and young adults lack this insight, and are dropping out of high school and college, taking extremely low-paying jobs, or even putting themselves into situations that will lead them to jail, prison, and nowhere. These developments say a lot about the society we live in. But they also raise the question: to what extent are our youth, young adults, and ourselves under the authority and control of thoughts, mindsets, and habits that have been passed down generation after generation from the days of slavery? We can find some answers to this question by reading: Joy DeGruy, Ph.D., *Post Traumatic Slave Syndrome: America's Legacy of Enduring Injury and Healing* (Portland, OR: Joy Degruy Publications, Inc., 2005). This book is essential reading that will help us to free our minds.

We must take seriously the fact that we are in a rapidly changing economy, and prepare our children so they can prosper. If we don't do this, it will have long-term political, economic, and social implications for the well-being of the African American community. It will ensure unemployment, low incomes, more single-parent households, less home ownership, fewer black-owned businesses, less political influence on issues that are important to us, the reemergence of racial stigmas, racial barriers, and notions of white superiority, and ultimately the loss of freedom. This is not a legacy we want to leave our children.

We need to encourage our children, youth, and young adults to complete their vocational training, high school, and college education, and let them know that this will increase their chances of having a satisfying life and helping their community. But we also need to let them know that a formal education alone will not free their minds. After all, the institution of slavery, Jim Crow, and many of the racial barriers that continue to exist today were created and are maintained by highly educated people.

We can even find educated people in the news every day who have said or done things that indicate they have lost control of their minds—to thoughts born of greed, hatred, or indifference. We may even have family or church members, friends, coworkers, teachers, or neighbors with diplomas, degrees, certificates, and doctorates who are like this.

More than a formal education is needed to keep us from wasting our mind. More than a GED, diploma, degree, or doctorate is needed to keep our minds from becoming shackled and bound. More is needed in order to extinguish greed, hatred, and indifference. What is also needed—as Nelson Mandela suggested—is meditation. This is undoubtedly one of the reasons Malcolm X, in talking about his prison experience, suggested that meditation can provide us with the best education we can get, second to a college education.[9]

Let's encourage our people—youth and adults—to complete their education and to meditate. If we can do this, we won't have to watch them go "down the river." Instead, we will be able to rejoice as they align their steps and vision with the North Star. Yes, we can do this.

***

One of the processes of your life is to constantly break down that inferiority, to constantly reaffirm that I Am Somebody.

—Alvin Ailey, African American dancer and choreographer, and founder of the Alvin Ailey American Dance Theater

23. Imagining

We are going home, we have visions bright
Of that holy land, that world of light
Where the long dark night is past,
And the morning of eternity has come at last,
Where the weary saints no more shall roam,
But dwell in a sunny, and peaceful home.
Where the brow, celestial gems shall crown
And waves of bliss are dashing round.

Oh! that beautiful home—oh! that beautiful world.

> — Sojourner Truth, Former fugitive slave
> a song she often sang quoted in
> *Sojourner Truth: Slave, Prophet, Legend*
> by Carleton Mabee and Susan Mabee Newhouse

Freedom—in fact almost everything—starts with a mental image. This was certainly true for Harriet Tubman. For example, she recalled that during the period before her escape, she held in her mind images of her flight to freedom:

> All that time, in my dreams and visions, I seemed to see a line, and on the other side of that line were green fields, and lovely flowers, and beautiful white ladies, who stretched out their arms to me over the line, but I couldn't reach them nohow. I always fell before I got to the line.[1]

Images such as this one eventually led Tubman to the place she had longed for—freedom, the Promised Land.

The Power of Images

Like Tubman, we often imagine what we want or need. We hold a mental image of it in our mind. When we do this, our mind views what we imagine as actually existing. We then think, speak, and act in accordance with what we imagined or in ways that bring what we imagined into reality.

Let's explore this. Pause for a few minutes. Take a few deep breaths. Relax your body. Bring to mind the image of a table with a white porcelain surface, on which are a clear glass of water and a juicy yellow lemon that has been sliced in half. Hold the image of these objects in your mind.

Now imagine that you open your mouth and squeeze half of the lemon onto your tongue, until the last drop of juice falls in your mouth. Next, imagine you pick up the other half and squeeze it in the same way onto your tongue, until the last drop falls on your tongue. If your mouth is beginning to fill with saliva or you want a drink of water, then you now have an experience of the power of images. The mental image of the water and lemon cause your mind and body to react as though the image were real.

What we *imagine*, a part of our mind accepts as existing in *reality*. This is true for both negative and positive images. Thus, images that depict and portray us negatively—as incompetent, lazy, greedy, irresponsible, criminal, untrustworthy, stupid, ugly, violent, promiscuous and so forth—affect what we think about ourselves. They have a disabling effect on our minds and personalities—especially if we are exposed to them repeatedly, such as through advertisements, movies, and music videos. They convey the message that we are inferior, unworthy of participating fully in all areas of society and incapable of having a fulfilling life. Such images and their messages disable us because they easily become embedded in our psyche. The outcome is clear, as African American historian Carter G. Woodson has noted:

If you can control a man's thinking you do not have to worry about his actions. When you determine what a man shall think you do not have to concern yourself about what he will do. If you make a man feel that he is inferior, you do not have to compel him to accept an inferior status, for he will seek it himself. If you make a man think he is just an outcast, you do not have to order him to the back door. He will go without being told; and if there is no back door, his very nature will demand one.[2]

Using Positive Images

We need to displace limiting images that we have internalized from a society in which racism is embedded. We need to replace such images with positive, uplifting ones that help us realize our potential. We need to bring into our lives images that empower us, images of what we want and what we can do to fulfill the purpose of our lives.

Here are two simple strategies that you can use to remind yourself that you possess inherent goodness, genius, and potential in a society that often tells you otherwise. First, place positive, affirming images of African Americans and others in the African Diaspora in your environment. Second, create in your mind a detailed image of a positive outcome you want for yourself, exactly as you want it to exist. Bring your image to mind often. Develop a plan and take action to bring whatever you envision into reality.

By forming an image of a desired reality and bringing that image to mind again and again, you can begin to relate to yourself and your environment in an empowered rather than disempowered way. You can begin to awaken and open to previously unseen alternatives, possibilities, and opportunities. As a result, you can begin to think, speak, and act in ways that gradually lead you into the very reality that you imagined.

Even seeing other possibilities can displace our limiting internal images. For example, in *Chains and Images of Psychological Slavery*, African American clinical psychologist Dr. Na'im Akbar recalls a college track and field athlete who set a triple jump record in his region. Then, despite his best efforts, the athlete couldn't surpass the record he had set. This was, in part, because he had no greater image of what was attainable than his own record. Then one day he participated in a national track meet, where he witnessed other athletes surpassing his record. The image that he held in his mind of his record being surpassed expanded the young man's sense of what was possible and expanded his sense of his own capabilities. As a result, he soon broke his own record and did so repeatedly.[3]

This story points to why it is important for us to go beyond social and cultural isolation by exposing ourselves to a broader range of experiences and positive role models. Such influences expand our sense of what is possible, our imagination, and the sense of what we are capable of doing. This happens as long as we don't allow their positive effects to be neutralized by the negative experiences and negative role models that we sometimes allow in our lives.

Of course, when you attempt to apply what you have learned from positive experiences and role models by going beyond what you have been accustomed to doing, at some point you're probably going to experience difficulty. You might fail. Like a toddler taking its first steps, you might fall down. If you do, don't allow that to stop you. Learn as much as you can from your failures, especially from the feedback and criticism you receive. Like a toddler, get back up. Try again. And remember this advice from First Lady Michelle Obama:

When something doesn't go your way, you've just got to adjust. You've got to dig deep and work like crazy, and that's when you'll find out what you're really made of during those hard times. But you can only do that if you're willing to put yourself in a position where you might fail, and that's why so often failure is the key to success.[4]

Failure does not need to be feared. Failure can be the key to success, if you are willing to step back and honestly study and understand the reasons you failed and apply what you learn to help you go forward. Failure is an opportunity for you to learn what you need to know so you can bring forth your inherent goodness, genius and potential. If you don't try, and learn, and keep trying, and keep learning, there's no way you can succeed.

Don't allow positive or negative criticism to distract and deter you. Use them to help you bring forth what you have envisioned. Listen to criticism as well as your own inner wisdom. Learn as much as you can. Honor the voice of the genuine in you. Adjust, adapt, be flexible. Keep moving in the direction of what you have envisioned. Keep your "eyes on the prize." Be steady, gentle and tough. You can fulfill your aspirations. Yes, you can.

Imagination

Empowering images and role models can not merely help us go beyond a sense of limitation. They can help us bring forth the personal qualities—power, skill, courage, wisdom, love, intelligence, grace, integrity, patience, determination, purpose, joy, and so forth—that we need to fulfill our aspirations. These are some of the qualities that we can bring forth within ourselves by creating mental images such as the ones we will create below.

In each instruction below, the image you will create is not real. It is just an image. It is insubstantial, like a rainbow. We are simply creating the image in our mind to loosen our attachment to limiting images and notions that we have of ourselves and our world. Loosening our attachment to them will help us to bring forth the splendid qualities of our own mind.

Don't worry if you cannot hold the details of the images in your mind. Over time, as you practice, this will become easier to do.

Imagining Practice

Take your seat, and practice calming meditation for about fifteen minutes.

Next, bring to mind an ancestor—woman or man of African ancestry—whom you revere. This should be someone in whom you have complete faith, confidence, and respect, someone whom you trust, who possesses qualities that you want to embody.

Now, for each step below, (a) slowly read the instruction—a couple of times if necessary, (b) close your eyes and create the image in your mind, (c) relax and gently hold the image in your mind for a few moments, and (d) open your eyes and proceed to the next instruction. Repeat these steps for each "Imagine" instruction that follows. If you wish, you can record all of the instructions and play them back as needed.

1. Imagine that your revered ancestor is seated on an African throne, on sacred ground, in the wilderness, about twenty feet in front of you, slightly above the level of your forehead. It's just before twilight.

2. Imagine that on the tops of the two posts supporting the backrest of the throne are a splendid *phoenix* bird (on the

right) and a beautiful *sankofa* bird (on the left), and that from each post hangs a beautiful traditional African mask.

3. Imagine that your ancestor is wearing the following items which have been carefully crafted by African shamans: elegant kente cloth apparel; a necklace made from ivory and gold, from which hangs a golden *ankh*; a wrist bracelet made with blue beads and cowrie shells; and a giraffe-skin leather belt around the waist with a gold pyramid-shaped buckle engraved with the image of a sphinx.

4. Imagine that a bronze rattle staff—the symbol of African ancestral authority, engraved with precious symbols of every African tribe—is held in your ancestor's left hand. And in front, below his or her hand, is a *djembe* drum. Leaning against your ancestor's right knee is a striped red, black, and green enamel shield in the shape of the African continent, with a shiny gold trim.

5. Imagine that up above the throne, in the night sky, are the Big Dipper and the Little Dipper, with the North Star directly over your ancestor's head shining brightly.

6. Imagine that your ancestor sits relaxed on the throne, and that he or she emanates the qualities you want to emulate. Consider for a moment what those are, for you, today.

7. Imagine that one foot behind your revered ancestor's throne, equally distributed to the right and the left, stand one hundred notable people of African ancestry who embody and exemplify all the qualities that have enabled people of African ancestry to progress in the United States.[5]

8. Imagine that standing behind the notable people, as far as you can see, are ten thousand generations of your ancestors, including the martyrs. They are softly chanting "Avenge for us the crimes that made us weep, not with the sword, but with your strength—your worth," and are waiting with longing for you to bring forth your inherent goodness, genius and potential.

9. Imagine that three feet in front and three feet to the *right* of your revered ancestor stands Frederick Douglass, exquisite and dignified, next to a wooden lectern, on top on which are his three great autobiographies and a lighted Kwanzaa kinara. In his right hand he holds a handwritten copy of one of his many famous speeches.

10. Imagine that three feet in front and three feet to the *left* of your revered ancestor stands Harriet Tubman, gentle and tough. She wears an elegant headscarf and a satchel. In her left hand, she holds up a rod. In her right hand she holds up in front of her, with extended arm, a lit lantern.

11. Imagine that the lantern and kinara luminate the faces of everyone in front of you—Tubman, Douglass, your revered ancestor, and all of the people of African ancestry—revealing their dignified presence as well as the unsurpassable joy and love they feel for you because you have chosen to bring them to mind, recognize them as helpful agents, and are willing to follow their example.

12. Imagine that in one magnificent, merciful gesture, your revered ancestor—your conductor— leans forward, looks in your eyes, and extends his or her right hand for you to

grasp, so he or she, along with everyone present, can conduct you to the Promised Land.

13. Now, holding in your mind the details of the image you have created, do the following with your eyes closed:

    a. First, acknowledge your revered ancestor, Tubman and Douglass, the notable people of African ancestry, and the multitude behind them.

    b. Second, express heartfelt thanks to your revered ancestor and all people of African ancestry assembled. Offer an aspiration for the well-being of all living beings and things.

    c. Third, repeat the following phrase for each time Harriet Tubman returned to the South to bring slaves to freedom (nineteen) or the number of people she helped conduct to freedom (three hundred) or the number of people she helped to emancipate (one thousand). Repeat this phrase softly with heartfelt longing:

    MY PEOPLE MUST GO FREE

    (For this you can substitute the Swahili version of a Kwanzaa principle and/or use beads to keep count—this will be discussed in chapter 26.) After you are finished chanting this phrase, open your eyes; and for several minutes, just sit reverently, meditatively, in silence, in the presence of your ancestors. Continue to hold the image.

    d. Fourth, in a heartfelt way say aloud:

    I see the trouble that holding on to thoughts can cause. I renounce all forms of slavery. There is nothing wrong with me. I possess inherent, unlimited, goodness, genius, and potential. Bringing these qualities forth is my sacred responsibility.

I am worthy and ready to journey to the Promised Land. This I gladly do for myself and the benefit of all people.

14. Imagine that the lantern and lectern, Tubman and Douglass, the notables and other people of African ancestry behind them instantly transform into a luminous mist that enters your revered ancestor, who now sits in perfect serenity, infinitely more resplendent, magnificent, glorious, and imbued with the inherent goodness, genius and potential of ten thousand generations of people of African ancestry. About him or her is a brilliant blue glow.

15. Imagine that an enlarged North Star now descends to a place directly behind your revered ancestor's throne, and that your revered ancestor and the throne, staff, shield, drum, masks, and the birds instantly transform into a luminous mist that enters the North Star.

16. Imagine that the North Star is eight feet in front of you, slightly above the level of your forehead, about 10 inches in diameter, and that it is the pure essence of the universe, containing everything conceivable and everything inconceivable that you need.

17. Imagine that the North Star begins moving closer to your head, and that as it does it becomes more luminous and smaller, the size of a precious gem, and that it enters the top of your head, descends slowly down the center of your torso, and from there continually radiates soothing, warm, purifying, and healing energy throughout your body, reaching

every single limb, bone, ligament, muscle, vessel, nerve, organ, pore, cell, atom, and gene—and you actually feel it.

18. Imagine that the soothing light and energy of the North Star thoroughly dissipates all limiting thoughts, negative self-images, fears, anxieties, doubts, worries, heartbreak, shame, resentments, jealousies, pride, physical tension, and ailments, and that it completely purifies and heals your entire mind, body, and breath.

19. Imagine that family, friends, neighbors, coworkers, and all the people in the United States and the world wake up and see your light shining, that it is radiating from every pore in your body, that you are a light in the world, and that they feel its healing warmth and are delighted that you are uplifting your mind and personal situation. They cry with inexpressible joy and begin radiating light, too.

20. Imagine that, looking up to the night sky, you glimpse the farthest reaches of the known and unknown universe, and that the remaining stars in the celestial sphere descend like a heavy shower of sparkling diamonds, signaling that you are now, at last, nearing the longed-for Promised Land.

21. Imagine that you hear the Niagara Falls thunder in the distance like African drums, and that you hear several ceremonial blasts from African trumpets heralding your arrival. Suddenly, as if a veil were lifted from your eyes, the night fades, and the brilliant light of unobstructed awareness dawns.

22. Imagine that you: see the sun accompanied by a splendid array of colors rising on the horizon and a rainbow

crowning the falls; feel the cool mist and dew on the grass; smell the fragrant air and various species of flowers; hear birds of various kinds singing and a soft breeze moving through the leaves of trees having a variety of sweet fruit that you can taste; and that you receive essential messages from all of nature.

23. Imagine that you are in a world completely at peace, and that all around you are beautiful mountains, waterfalls, streams; plants, animals, birds, fish, meadows, butterflies; neighborhoods in cities filled with people of all races, ethnicities, nationalities, classes, cultures, religious and political affiliations, educational attainment, ages, genders, sexual orientations, and abilities—all working with good intention, as best they can, in their own way, given their unique realities—to create an uplifted mind, personal existence, family, and community. You clearly, unmistakably, see your inherent dignity—your inherent goodness, your genius, and your potential. You see the inherent dignity of all beings and nature, all things and situations, and you have complete trust and confidence in it.

24. Imagine that you now possess everything you need and, yes, you *are* capable of fulfilling your highest hopes and dreams, which is also the hope and dream of your ancestors.

25. Sit relaxed and practice calming or awakening meditation for several minutes with your eyes open. Then stop labeling thoughts. Stop returning your attention to the breath. Instead just continue to sit in your meditation posture and experience the quiet and peaceful space of your awareness. Relax. When thoughts and perceptions arise, experience them not as distractions but as fresh

reminders to continue resting your mind in the open space of your environment. Be present, right *here*, right *now,* joyful and grateful.

26. Taste the sweetness of your precious life. Appreciate each fleeting moment while it lasts.

27. Conclude this practice by rising slowly, remembering the sacred charge you received before your birth, and walking with dignity—as so many have before you—as a free person in the Promised Land.

As you go through your day, use your connection to your revered ancestor and other people of African ancestry to help you embody the excellent qualities you need. After all, the excellent qualities that were possessed by all of your ancestors—revered, notable, and less notable—are the same ones in your own mind. You simply need to bring them forth.

This does not mean that you should go around looking, speaking, or acting like your ancestors. That certainly wouldn't be an authentic or genuine thing to do. What we are talking about is embodying your ancestors' *understanding* in what you think, say, and do. In this way, their wisdom and the wisdom of your mothers and fathers become a living presence in your life—loving, protecting, guiding, and uplifting you as you go forward.

In order to invoke their presence and wisdom, in addition to meditation, one of the things you'll need to do is to learn as much as you can about them. Open your mind to their writings as well as biographies and other accounts of their lives. Discern what they understood. Bring that wisdom into your life.

But don't forget, using images such as the ones above that incorporate our ancestors without taking action to bring your aspirations into reality is like daydreaming. Tubman understood this. She understood that dreams and visions are only the first step to becoming free. What is also needed is *action*.

What Makes Success Possible

When your actions succeed, please remember that many people have enabled you to succeed. You really don't ever accomplish much on your own. In one way or another, others have paved the way or contributed. A few of them you may know, and some of them you may have forgotten. Many of them you may know but are unaware of the ways in which they have contributed. Most of them you may never know. Whether you are graduating from college or drinking a cup of coffee at your kitchen table, many people of all backgrounds have enabled that to occur.

For example, if you go to school, many people have enabled that to happen. Some of them had the door slammed in their faces, were cursed, spat on, assaulted, jailed, and murdered, or in other ways they devoted their lives to ensuring you would have equal educational opportunities. As a result of their sacrifices, there you are sitting in the classroom with an opportunity to get an education so you can uplift yourself and your people. How do you honor the sacrifices that were made? What would you do?

Okay, you're an adult. You have registered to vote, and can cast your ballot in the upcoming election. People enabled that to happen. Do you really know what they went through? How do you honor the sacrifices that were made so you could vote? Do you exercise your hard-earned right to vote, your freedom, by voting or by not voting?

And, what about the job you have? How many of our people protested, filed lawsuits, filled out job applications, got fired and had to struggle to keep food on the table for their children, and made extraordinary efforts to be exemplary employees so that you could enjoy equal employment opportunities? So what do you do? Do you relate to the people you meet on your job—blacks and whites—disrespectfully, like our ancestors were treated before we were allowed to work in your job position or do you uphold the dignity of the people who paved the way for you to have your job?

Many of the opportunities we have and much of what we do are the result of the contributions and sacrifices of others. This even includes the ordinary things such as the food we ate this morning. Who raised or grew it? Who inspected and transported it? Who placed it in the store or the restaurant for you to purchase? There really is no separate *you* in the world. Everything is interconnected. Everything is interrelated. "[B]efore you finish eating breakfast in the morning," Martin Luther King, Jr. said, "you've depended on more than half the world. This is the way our universe is structured, this is its interrelated quality."[6]

Given the interrelated structure of reality, no matter what you accomplish or do, please remember to acknowledge that actually many people helped to make it possible. Be grateful. This will help you to go forward with humility. Humility will help you to remain attentive to your actions and how others' lives are being affected by what you think, say, and do. It will help you to be in harmony with what your ancestors imagined.

24. Drawing Near

[God] is a great ocean of love, and we live and move in Him as the fishes in the sea.

—Sojourner Truth, Former fugitive slave
quoted in *Sojourner Truth: Slave, Prophet, Legend*
by Carleton Mabee and Susan Mabee Newhouse

Observation upon what passes without, and reflection upon what passes within a man's heart, will give him a larger growth in grace than is imagined by the devoted adherents of creeds.

—Josiah Henson, *Truth Stranger Than Fiction*
Former fugitive slave

Many of the people who were enslaved in Africa and brought to the Americas were from regions in Africa where Islam was practiced. Thus, in the US slave population there were Muslims.

Some of our enslaved ancestors were Christians. They practiced a form of Christianity that shared elements of African traditional religion—a single creator God, symbolic death, water as a spiritual symbol, prayer, song, dance, and belief in an afterlife. However, most slaves knew nothing about Christianity. They were illiterate, prohibited from possessing a Bible, and without access to missionaries and preachers. Many of them practiced some vestige of traditional African religion. In that religion, Lawrence W. Levine notes:

> Man was part of, not alien to, the Natural Order of things, attached to the Oneness that bound all matter, animate and inanimate, all spirits, visible or not.

It was crucially necessary to understand the world because one was part of it, inexorably linked to it. Survival and happiness and health depended upon being able to read signs that existed everywhere, to understand the visions that recurrently visited one, to commune with the spirits that filled the world: the spirit of the Supreme Being who could be approached only though the spirits of the pantheon of the intermediary deities; the spirits of all the matter that filled the universe—trees, animals, rivers, the very utensils and weapons upon which Man was dependent; the spirits of contemporary human beings; the spirits of ancestors who linked the living world with the unseen world.[1]

Whatever their beliefs, if there is one belief that all our ancestors shared, it was this: in order to accomplish anything worthwhile, it is necessary to have the guidance and protection of a higher power. This certainly is what Harriet Tubman believed. She believed that her higher power was everywhere, always present, and always available. But in order to receive guidance and protection, she had to be so close that she could feel her higher power's presence. Then she could make requests and discern what she needed to do. As her biographer, Sarah H. Bradford, notes:

She seemed ever to feel the Divine Presence near, and she talked with God "as a man talketh with his friend." Hers was not the religion of a morning and evening prayer at stated times, but when she felt a need, she simply told God of it, and trusted Him to set the matter right.[2]

One of the ways Tubman stayed near to her higher power was through solitude, which she had plenty of during her wilderness treks in and out of the South. She also found solitude in everyday situations. For example, one winter, Tubman didn't have money for food to feed the many poor people living in her crowded and noisy house. She arose, went into a small closet, and closed the door. She stayed in the closet for quite a while.

When she came out, she told Catherine, her brother's wife, to place a pot on the stove. When Catherine replied that they had no food to put in the pot, Tubman told her to go ahead and heat the water, for there would be food to eat later that day. Tubman got dressed and, with an empty basket on her arm, walked outside into the wintery cold, and headed to the market. When she arrived, the vendors saw her carrying the empty basket, and started filling it with meat, produce, and vegetables. Years later, in reflecting on that day, Tubman commented that she "had not 'gone into her closet and shut the door' for nothing."[3]

Like Tubman, you can also use solitude to move closer to your higher power, close enough to feel its presence, talk, and discern what you need to do. You can do this with the drawing near technique below. But before you begin to practice it, there are a couple of things you'll need to do.

First, identify your higher power. This should be what you believe is an unsurpassable source of guidance and protection that you love and trust completely. Second, choose a special word that symbolizes your intention to be present with your higher power. The word you choose can be the name of your higher power or it can be a word such as "mercy," "peace," "yes," "help," or "now." Whatever word or name you choose, use it throughout this technique.

Now, let's draw near.

Drawing Near Practice

1. Take a seat in a quiet space where you can be alone without being interrupted. Practice calming meditation for several minutes.

2. After your mind is calm, slowly and softly say the special word or name that is the expression of your intention to be present with your higher power. Repeat your special word or name slowly and softly. Your eyes can be open or closed.

3. If you become distracted by thoughts, sensations, and emotions, avoid judging or analyzing them. Remain present, and continue to softly say your special word or name to reaffirm your genuine intention to be present with your higher power.

4. Continue to repeat your special word or name softly as you open more and more to your higher power's presence.

5. When you *feel* your higher power's presence, be completely present with your entire being—your body, breath, and mind. Appreciate the presence—the glory, magnificence, and splendor. Continue to be in this way as long as you want, while continuing to repeat your special word or name.

6. Near the end of the time allotted for this practice, just sit in silence for a few minutes. At this time, you may want to make a request for guidance or protection.

7. Conclude with the Yoruba word *Ashe* (See step 6 of the Affirmation Practice in chapter 22) or another personal concluding expression. As you arise, continue to feel your

higher power's presence. Remain in your higher power's presence as you continue with your day.

Keep your higher power near. By opening to the presence, you can obtain the guidance and protection that you need to uplift yourself and become a way to freedom for your people.

25. Praying

If there is anything which tends to buoy the spirit of the slave, under pressure of his severe toils, more than another, it is the hope of future freedom: by this his heart is cheered and his soul is lighted up in the midst of the fearful scenes of agony and suffering which he has to endure. Occasionally, as some event approaches from which he can calculate on relaxation of his sufferings, his hope burns with a bright blaze; but more generally the mind of the slave is filled with gloomy apprehension of a still harder fate.

—Henry "Box" Brown,
Narrative of the Life of Henry Box Brown
Former fugitive slave

There is, however, great consolation in knowing that God is just, and will not let the oppressor of the weak, and the spoiler of the virtuous, to escape unpunished here and hereafter.

—William Craft,
Running a Thousand Miles to Freedom
Former fugitive slave

In 1831, a Virginia-born slave named Dred Scott was purchased by an army doctor in Missouri. In Missouri and Virginia slavery was legal. The army doctor took Scott with him to Illinois and later to Wisconsin Territory. In this state and territory, slavery was illegal, and any enslaved person entering was considered to be legally free. Scott and his wife, Harriet Robinson, traveled with the doctor as he moved between states where slavery was legal and illegal. In 1843, the doctor died. "Ownership" of the Scotts passed to the doctor's widow. When the widow attempted to hire the Scotts out, they protested and took action to establish that they were free. The widow's brother, John F.A. Sanford, became her attorney.

In 1845, the Scotts petitioned the Missouri state court for their freedom based on their residence in Illinois and in the Wisconsin Territory. However, their actions failed. Undeterred, in 1854, Dred Scott petitioned the federal court for his freedom. When his petition was rejected, he petitioned the US Supreme Court.

In February and December of 1856, the Supreme Court heard arguments in the case *Dred Scott v. John F. A. Sandford* [sic]. On March 6, 1857, it reached a landmark decision. In explaining the court's decision, Chief Justice Roger B. Taney wrote that people of African ancestry, those who were free or enslaved,

> ...had always been, regarded as beings of an inferior order and altogether unfit to associate with the white race, either in social or political relations; and so far inferior, that they had no rights which the white man was bound to respect; and that the negro might justly and lawfully be reduced to slavery for his benefit. He was bought and sold, and treated as an ordinary article of merchandise and traffic, whenever a profit could be made by it. This opinion was at that time fixed and universal in the civilized portion of the white race. It was regarded as an axiom in morals as well as in politics, which no one thought of disputing, or supposed to be open to dispute; and men in every grade and position in society daily and habitually acted upon it in their private pursuits, as well as in matters of public

concern; without doubting for a moment the correctness of this opinion.[1]

The Court did not doubt the correctness of the "fixed and
universal" opinion. It was the Justices' opinion too. Thus, the
Court rejected Scott's appeal. It held that black people—free or
enslaved—had no rights whatsoever under the US Constitution.

Although the Supreme Court decision was a cause for celebration among slavery supporters, it was a source of outrage and
revulsion among abolitionists. Fortunately, while the court was
considering the case, the doctor's widow had married an abolitionist who was unaware that she owned the most famous slave in
the country. He encouraged her to sell the Scott family to another
abolitionist. Within three months after the court ruling, Scott
and his family were set free.

Ironically, decisions of the justices on the Supreme Court,
as well as the compromises of senators and representatives in
Congress and the presidents in the White House, acting on behalf
of the American people, should serve as eternal reminders that
white people are not superior to anyone. They may appear to be
"superior" or even think they are "superior" if they are ignorant
of the historical, institutional, and intergenerational privileges
they enjoy as a result of slavery and racism in America. You might
even think they are "superior" if you, after a lifetime of social conditioning in America, have developed a very low self-esteem and
have no confidence in the inherent goodness, genius, and potential of your own people. In actuality, though, white people possess
the same inherent dignity as people who are black, brown, red,
and yellow. No more, no less. White people and people of color are
equal. They possess the same inherent capabilities.

The enslaved population knew this; they never had any doubt in their hearts. Thus, the Supreme Court decision did not stop them from taking their petitions to an even higher court—their higher power.

Often, instead of dwelling and fixating on thoughts about the unjust treatment to which they were subjected, our ancestors would offer their higher power heartfelt praise and make requests for intervention. They did this in faith that their petitions would be heard, mercifully considered, and justly resolved—sooner or later.

Sometimes their prayers were answered promptly. This was certainly true for Henry "Box" Brown:

> One day, while I was at work, and my thoughts were eagerly feasting upon the idea of freedom, I felt my soul called out to heaven to breathe a prayer to Almighty God. I prayed fervently that he who seeth in secret and knew the inmost desires of my heart, would lend me his aid in bursting my fetters asunder, and in restoring me to the possession of those rights, of which men had robbed me; when the idea suddenly flashed across my mind of shutting myself up in a box, and getting myself conveyed as dry goods to a free state.
>
> Being now satisfied that this was the plan for me, I went to my friend Dr. Smith and, having acquainted him with it, we agreed to have it put at once into execution.... [2]

Tubman was also known to have her petitions answered soon after they were made. One day, when she attempted to purchase tickets so she and her passengers could board a boat, the clerk refused to issue her tickets. Concerned about the safety of her passengers and the success of her mission, she walked away. She explained what happened next:

> I drew in my breath, and I sent it out to the Lord, and I said, Oh Lord! You know who I am, and where I am, and what I want; and that was all I could say; and again I drew in my breath and I sent it out to the Lord, but that was all I could say; and then again the third time, and just then I felt a touch on my shoulder, and looked round, and the clerk said, "Here's your tickets."[3]

In some instances, however, weeks, months, years, nearly a lifetime would pass before an answer to prayers would come. For example, Tubman recalled meeting an emancipated slave during the Civil War, who told her:

> I've been here seventy-three years, working for my master without even a dime in wages. I've worked rain-wet sun dry. I've worked with my mouth full of dust, but could not stop to get a drink of water. I've been whipped, and starved, and I was always praying, 'Oh! Lord, come and deliver us!' All that time the birds had been flying, and the ravens had been crying, and the fish had been swimming in the waters... I've prayed seventy-three years, and now he's come and we're all free.[4]

Taking their attention off limiting thoughts and placing it on their higher power through prayer, and allowing it to rest there, helped our ancestors get through some very tough times. It calmed and opened their minds, and enabled them to see a little more clearly. With the fresh outlook they gained, they were able to then relate to their situation with the wisdom and skill that was needed to go forward with their lives.

You can benefit in a similar way from prayer, especially if your prayer has elements such as these:

- *Praise:* Recognize and laud the greatness of your higher power.

- *Devotion:* Express a deep love for your higher power, a longing to unite, and a determination to live according to higher principles.

- *Gratitude:* Express heartfelt gratitude for what you have that you attribute to your higher power (if you're stuck, think of things we often take for granted, such as health, food to eat, friends, etc.).

- *Petition:* Ask your higher power for what you or others need.

- *Resolve:* Express an intention to embody faithfully what your higher power represents in what you think, say, and do while awaiting a response to your prayer.

Prayer is a personal experience, but these elements are part of many common prayers. They are defined here very simply, but if these elements or any of the following steps do not fit in with your understanding or relationship to prayer or your higher power, do not try to force them. Whatever your approach to prayer, joining it to meditation, as is done in the practice below, can be helpful. So follow the instructions as appropriate for you.

Prayer Meditation

1. Take a seat in solitude. Clear and calm your mind by practicing calming meditation for a few minutes.

2. Be completely present in the *here* and *now.*

3. Draw near to your higher power, as explained in chapter 24.

4. As you open to the presence of your higher power, place your hands together in a praying position, as shown on the cover of this guidebook. Say a prayer, softly but audibly, *for yourself.* Pray sincerely, using elements of prayer.

5. End the prayer by placing your palms gently on your thighs and sitting in silence.

6. Draw nearer to your higher power's presence.

7. As you continue to open to your higher power's presence, again place your hands together in a praying position and say a prayer, softly but audibly, *for family members and friends.* Pray sincerely, using elements of prayer.

8. End the prayer by placing your palms gently on your thighs and sitting in silence.

9. Draw even closer to your higher power's presence.

10. As you open even further, once more place your hands together in a praying position, and say a prayer *for everyone in the world.* Pray sincerely, using elements of prayer.

11. End the prayer by placing your palms gently on your thighs or lap and sit still in the presence, in the profound silence. Let go of attachment to any outcome. Have faith.

12. Conclude prayer meditation with the Yoruba word *Ashe* (See step 6 of the Affirmation Practice in chapter 22) or another personal concluding expression, and go forward with a mind that is open and receptive to what your higher power brings.

You can pray anytime or anywhere. That's what Tubman did. Even before she left her chains, she was continually in prayer:

> I prayed all the time about my work, everywhere, I prayed and I groaned to the Lord. When I went to the horse-trough to wash my face, I took up the water in my hand and I said, "Oh Lord, wash me, make me clean!" Then I take up something to wipe my face, and I say, "Oh Lord, wipe away all my sin!" When I took the broom and began to sweep, I groaned, "Oh Lord, what so ever sin there be in my heart, sweep it out, Lord, clear and clean!"[5]

Through prayer we "sweep" greed, hatred, and indifference from our mind. We make our mind "clear and clean" so that it is open and receptive to blessings from our higher power. After all, blessings come in all forms including premonition, understanding, insight, and visions. When our minds are open and receptive to them, we can then use them to become the means by which our prayers are answered. This is what Marcus Garvey may have meant when he said, "We must give up with the silly idea of folding our hands and waiting on God to do everything for us. If God had intended for that, then he would not have given us a mind."[6] This is what Russell Simmons, the African American business magnate, may have been alluding to this when he observed "The old truth is still true today, 'God helps those who help themselves.' My advice? Meditate."[7]

After we pray, we must keep an open mind so that we can discern what we need to do to bring what we prayed for to fruition.

PART III:
FREE YOUR BODY

STILL I RISE

You may write me down in history
With your bitter, twisted lies,
You may trod me in the very dirt
But still, like dust, I'll rise.

Does my sassiness upset you?
Why are you beset with gloom?
'Cause I walk like I've got oil wells
Pumping in my living room.

Just like moons and like suns,
With the certainty of tides,
Just like hopes springing high,
Still I'll rise.

Did you want to see me broken?
Bowed head and lowered eyes?
Shoulders falling down like teardrops.
Weakened by my soulful cries.

Does my haughtiness offend you?
Don't you take it awful hard
'Cause I laugh like I've got gold mines
Diggin' in my own backyard.

You may shoot me with your words,
You may cut me with your eyes,
You may kill me with your hatefulness,
But still, like air, I'll rise.

FREE YOUR MIND

Does my sexiness upset you?
Does it come as a surprise
That I dance like I've got diamonds
At the meeting of my thighs?

Out of the huts of history's shame
I rise
Up from a past that's rooted in pain
I rise
I'm a black ocean, leaping and wide,
Welling and swelling I bear in the tide.
Leaving behind nights of terror and fear
I rise
Into a daybreak that's wondrously clear
I rise
Bringing the gifts that my ancestors gave,
I am the dream and the hope of the slave.
I rise
I rise
I rise.

By Maya Angelou (1928-2014)

TERMINAL: Niagara Falls, New York

Harriet Tubman used the Suspension Bridge in Niagara Falls, New York, to cross over into Canada with her passengers. There were other places from which she could have crossed, such as Buffalo and Lewiston, New York. However, the Niagara Falls crossing is the one she probably used most often. Tubman's biographer, Sarah H. Bradford, provides this account of one of her trips across the bridge:

> There was now but "one wide river to cross," and the cars rolled on to the bridge. In the distance was heard the roar of the mighty cataract, and now as they neared the center of the bridge, the falls might be clearly seen. Harriet was anxious to have her companions see this wonderful sight, and succeeded in bringing all to the windows, except Joe. But Joe still sat with his head on his hands, and not even the wonders of Niagara could draw him from his melancholy musings. At length as Harriet knew by the rise of the center of the bridge, and the descent immediately after, the line of danger was passed; she sprang across to Joe's side of the car, and shook him almost out of his seat, as she

shouted, "Joe! You've shook the lion's paw!" This was her phrase for having entered the dominions of England. But Joe did not understand this figurative expression. Then she shook him again, and put it more plainly, "Joe, you're in Queen Victoria's dominion! You're a free man!"

Then Joe arose, his head went up, he raised his hands on high, and his eyes, streaming with tears, to heaven, and then he began to sing and shout.[1]

In addition to recent runaways like Joe, fugitives who had lived in the North for many years fled to Canada to avoid apprehension after the Fugitive Slave Act of 1850 became law. Also fleeing were many free blacks who feared they'd be mistaken for fugitives and sent south. A number of African American leaders also moved to Canada—these people were not in danger of arrest, but they wanted to assess the conditions under which the refugees were living so they could offer help. One such individual was the poet Frances Ellen Watkins Harper. "Well, I have gazed for the first time upon Free Land," she wrote to William Still,

and, would you believe it, tears sprang to my eyes, and I wept. Oh, it was a glorious site to gaze for the first time on a land where a poor slave flying from our glorious land of liberty would in a moment find his fetters broken, his shackles loosened.... [2]

Mary Ann Shadd Cary also joined the exodus. She was a teacher by training who believed that racial integration and self-sufficiency were the keys to real freedom. But upon settling in

Canada, she found black children in segregated schools who were receiving inadequate support from the Ontario government.

Like Tubman, Harper, and Sojourner Truth, Cary wasted no time engaging in "ladylike" behavior. She spoke her mind and did what she felt was needed to bring about improvements for her people. She organized and agitated and, in 1854, helped found the militant *Provincial Freeman*, the first newspaper in North America with a woman publisher and editor.

Cary's paper addressed education, housing, health, and welfare issues, and the overall state of the black settlements in Canada. She accused Harim Wilson, a missionary in St. Catharines, of favoritism in the distribution of food and clothing to refugees. She criticized Josiah Henson, the founder of the Dawn settlement, for subserviently doing whatever his white financial backers told him to do. She claimed that Henry Bibb, a Refuge Home Society settlement founder, begged for money and ran his settlement like a plantation. And she criticized "this disgusting, repulsive surveillance, this despotic, dictatorial, snobbish air of superiority of white people over the fugitives."[3]

As Cary, Wilson, Henson, Bibb, and others contributed their efforts, and their individual styles, toward creating a strong community for African Americans in Canada, Tubman continued her own efforts to bring her people out of slavery and across the Suspension Bridge. One of the people whom she most wanted to make this crossing was Rachel, her youngest sister.

Tubman had already made two trips to Maryland to bring Rachel out. However, on each occasion her sister's children were on another plantation and Rachel refused to leave them behind. Tubman attempted to reassure her sister that she'd return for the children, but Rachel refused to leave without them. So Tubman told her that she would make another trip for her and that when she arrived Rachel had better be ready to go.

After raising funds from abolitionists to support her rescue mission, Tubman returned to Maryland for Rachel, but found that she had died a few days earlier. Heartbroken, Tubman hurried to a secret place where she was supposed to rendezvous with her sister's children. She waited for her niece and nephew to arrive. But they did not show up. In the meantime, a major snow storm with high winds moved into the area. Tubman took shelter behind a tree.

Somehow, the Ennals family—Stephen and his wife Maria, their two young daughters and infant—and a man named John crossed Tubman's path. They explained to her that they had run away but were lost and that slave catchers were rapidly closing in on them. They asked Tubman to help them find their way north.

Tubman let go of her plan to rescue her sister's children, and brought her attention back to what was happening in front of her, right *here*, right *now*. She gave the baby a sedative to keep it quiet. Then, as she had done for many other men, women and children, she led the Ennals family and John northward.

Traveling mostly at night, Tubman searched for the North Star. She stayed off the main roads. She trekked through the countryside forests and along the waterways now covered with snow. She foraged for food. At various places along the route, Tubman and her party would halt, and she would use owl hoots, hand signals, secret knocks, and other methods to get the attention of Underground Railroad agents. From the agents she obtained shelter, food, and guidance, as she kept moving, from station to station, winding her way northward through the cold. The trek, however, was not without incident. At one point she and her passengers had to hastily hide in a swamp to avoid detection by slave catchers.

Ultimately, the journey was simply too much for the mother and her children. Tubman left them at an Underground Railroad station, assuring them that she would soon return. Then, she kept going, moving forward, conducting the two men on the perilous journey northwards.

On December 1, 1860, Thomas Garrett wrote to William Still about Tubman's arrival in the vicinity of Wilmington:

> Respected Friend:—William Still:—I write to let thee know that Harriet Tubman is again in these parts. She arrived last evening from one of her trips of mercy to God's poor, bringing two men with her as far as Newcastle. I agreed to pay a man last evening, to pilot them on their way to Chester County; the wife of one of the men, with two or three children, was left some thirty miles below, and I gave Harriet ten dollars, to hire a man with a carriage, to take them to Chester County. She said a man had offered her that sum, to bring them on. I shall be very uneasy about them, till I hear they are safe. There is now much more risk on the road, till they arrive here, than there has been for several months, as we find that some poor, worthless wretches are constantly on the look out on two roads, that they cannot well avoid more especially with carriage, yet, as it is Harriet who seems to have a special angel to guard her on her journey of mercy, I have hope.[4]

With fidelity, Tubman succeeded in getting the entire Ennals family and their friend out of the South, and transported to Philadelphia, and across the Suspension Bridge into Canada.

Mary Ann Shadd Cary
Source: Library and Archives of Canada
C-029977

26. Chanting

I did not, when a slave, understand the deep meaning of those rude and apparently incoherent songs.... They told a tale of woe which was then altogether beyond my feeble comprehension; they were tones loud, long, and deep; they breathed the prayer and complaint of souls boiling over with the bitterest anguish. Every tone was a testimony against slavery, and a prayer to God for deliverance from chains.

—Frederick Douglass,
Narrative of the Life of Frederick Douglass
Former fugitive slave

For our ancestors on the plantations, prayers were often expressed by chanting. One of the ways in which chanting was done was in a "ring shout." A ring shout is an ecstatic ritual that originated in Africa. In their ring shout, the participants left the conventional world and entered a transcendent world, beyond thoughts:

> The men and women arranged themselves in a ring. The music started, perhaps with a Spiritual, and the ring began to move, at first slowly, then with quickening pace. The same musical phrase was repeated over and over for hours. This produced an ecstatic state. Women screamed and fell. Men, exhausted, dropped out of the ring.[1]

It was also common for runaways to chant, while making their journey to freedom. Chanting would perk them up, as runaway Isaac D. Williams explains:

Poor Banks was troubled with great fits of depression, and no wonder, after what he had passed through, and at best our outlook was by no means cheerful. What trackless wastes and swamps lay between us and liberty, with no compass or means to guide ourselves correctly. I was naturally of a more cheerful disposition, generally buoyant and light-hearted, and now and then would try to sing a little, in a low, subdued voice, a sort of monotone chant that slaves would often indulge in. I don't think it was calculated to liven Banks' spirits, [but] after he joined me in a few verses we would soon come to a full stop and get to talking again.[2]

What Chanting Is

Chanting is the rhythmic or repeated speaking or singing of syllables, words, or phrases in one or two notes or pitches. It can be done in various ways:

- Aloud, as a cry, a call, a moan, a holler, a shout, or a song.

- Silently, with a whisper.

- To the accompaniment of dancing, foot stomping, hand clapping, or musical instruments.

- Alone or in a group.

In meditation, when we chant, we use *sound* as the object of our attention. We rest our attention on the *sound* of words or syllables as they vibrate through our body—our throat, head, chest, and abdomen—and as they resonate through space. Attending to sound enables us to:

- calm and focus our mind;

- free our mind from thoughts and emotions;

- be present with our higher power, if that is what we wish to do;

- be attentive to what is going on, opportunities, and blessings; and

- do what we need to do to uplift ourselves and help our people.

If our attention wanders while chanting, we simply recognize our distracting thoughts, without dwelling, fixating, or holding on to them, and label them "thoughts." Then we gently return our attention to the sound of the words we are chanting.

The best way to understand chanting is to do it yourself. The following chanting exercise will help you get started.

1. First, sit up straight so your lungs can expand and contract as you breathe. Place your hand on your belly. As you inhale, allow your belly to expand. As you exhale, allow your belly to contract. Inhale into your abdomen, and exhale from your abdomen. Practice breathing deeply from your abdomen so that your chanting will have more strength behind it and so that you are engaging more of your body in this practice.

2. Second, say a word aloud, repeatedly using one note for each syllable. For example: "chant-ing, chant-ing, chant-ing," etc.

3. Third, sing a string of notes for each of the vowels *a, e, i, o, u*, and do it in one note. For example: "a-a-a-a-a-a-a-a" and "e-e-e-e-e-e-e-e," "i-i-i-i-i-i-i-i," and so forth. As you

sing each vowel, make subtle changes in your jaw, lips, and tongue to alter the pitch and sound. Play with this. See if you can make the sound vibrate in different areas of your body, such as your abdomen, chest, throat, and head. Can you hear the sound in space?

In chanting, you can use syllables, words, and phrases from any tradition—or no tradition at all. You can improvise, varying the tempo and pace of your chant. Just remember that different syllables, words, and phrases when pronounced in different ways produce different sounds or vibrations that have different effects on your mind and body. Just as the sounds of wind rustling through leaves of trees, water flowing in a stream, and thunder rumbling during a storm all have different effects on your mind and body, so do different words when chanted. By being open-minded and exploring different chants, you'll find ones that help you.

Following are a few syllables, words, and phrases commonly chanted in communities that practice some type of meditation. All of these chants can be potent and can uplift your mind and body. You may want to use one or more of them, after you have researched their pronunciation and meaning.

- "Hal-le-lu-jah"

- *Allāhu Ak-bar*

- *Ankh Ud-ja Se-neb*

- *Nam-myo-ho-ren-ge-kyo*

- *Om*

- *Om Ma-ni Pad-me Hum*

Using Kwanzaa Chants

There are also Kwanzaa chants you can use to uplift your mind. Kwanzaa, which means "first fruits," is the annual celebration of African American history and culture that takes place from December 26 through January 1. The celebration was started by Dr. Maulana Karenga, following the Watts Riots of 1965, to give people of African ancestry an occasion to celebrate themselves rather than only the history and culture of the people who had oppressed them.

Kwanzaa is similar to other African American holidays such as Pinkster, Juneteenth, and the Martin Luther King, Jr. birthday, where families and communities gather to perform community service; enjoy art, music, and communal feasts; honor ancestors; and study and meditate on African American and Pan-African history and culture. Anyone (regardless of race and ethnicity) who wishes to celebrate the good that people of African ancestry have brought into the world is welcome to participate in Kwanzaa observances.

Kwanzaa is different from the other holidays in that it lasts for seven days. On each day of the holiday, greetings that incorporate the *Nguzo Saba* (the Seven Principles) are exchanged; ceremonies are held that include the pouring of libation; and the *Nguzo Saba* principles are chanted, contemplated, and discussed. In addition, on the last day of the holiday, time is allowed for a period of self-assessment and meditation. The holiday concludes with gifts being exchanged, a communal feast, and a celebration.

The *Nguzo Saba* consists of the following seven principles of African culture. In Swahili (and English), the principles are:

- Day 1: *Umoja* [oo-MOH-jah] (unity)

- Day 2: *Kujichagulia* [KOO-jee-cha-goo-LEE-ah] (self-determination)

- Day 3: *Ujima* [oo-JEE-mah] (collective work and responsibility)

- Day 4: *Ujamaa* [oo-JAH-mah] (cooperative economics)

- Day 5: *Nia* [NEE-ya] (purpose)

- Day 6: *Kuumba* [koo-OOM-bah] (creativity)

- Day 7: *Imani* [ee-MAH-nee] (faith)

There are several ways the *Nguzo Saba* can be chanted. During the Kwanzaa holiday, the principle for each day can be chanted during the day as part of a greeting. The greeter says, *"Habari Gani"* [hah-BAR-ee GAH-nee] which means "What's happening?" The person being greeted responds with the principle for that day, for instance, *"Umoja!"* The greeter responds by exclaiming, *"Harambee"* [ha-RAHM-bay], which means "Let's come together!"

The principle for each day can also be chanted during gatherings: when libation is offered, as the kinara is lighted, and at the beginning of a group discussion on ways we can apply the day's principle in our everyday lives. In addition, *Harambee* and any *Nguzo Saba* principle can be chanted at any time during the year to help you free your mind, and to arouse in you and others a greater sense of our inherent goodness, genius and potential.

In addition to chanting, participating in the celebration and season of Kwanzaa each year is a wonderful way to support your efforts to free your mind. Greet family members and friends with the principle for each day. Then gather with them each evening in an intimate setting for the libation, as a candle on the kinara is lit, and as each person chants and shares what the principle for the day means to them and how they apply it in their life. Every participant will become more informed by the spontaneous insight and caring arising from the persons gathered, even if there are only two people present. Everyone will enjoy the celebration.

Please don't allow anyone to convince you that there is something wrong with celebrating your history and culture, your heroes and heroines, the people who contributed to the life you have today. Please don't allow anyone to convince you that since an educated black man who loves his people created Kwanzaa based on the authentic experience of black people, that somehow there must be something wrong with observing the holiday, that it shouldn't be taken seriously or that you need to be concerned about what other people might think if they found out that you cherish your heritage and black people. Remember that the source of all the wisdom in all the cultures of the world also resides in our people, and it resides in you as well as anyone else. If the wisdom of Kwanzaa helps you to free your mind, it really doesn't matter what anyone thinks about it.

To learn more about Kwanzaa, go to the Official Kwanzaa Web Site at: http://www.officialkwanzaawebsite.org/index.shtml.

Using Written Texts for Chanting

In addition to a word or phrase, written texts can be used for chanting. Find a poem, prayer, verse, or a short passage from a favorite writing that speaks to your heart. Read the words out loud once. Next, chant the text using one note or pitch for each syllable and with a steady and somewhat quick pace. Give yourself over to the flow of words and to any meaning or feelings that come up for you. When you reach the end of the text, chant the text again, if it is relatively short. Otherwise, you can chant another text or practice another technique.

Texts are ideal for use when chanting alone or with a group. If you lead a group in chanting a text, make sure everyone has the same text and that you chant loud enough so that everyone can hear and follow you. If you are following a chant leader, don't chant louder than the leader or get ahead.

Creating Your Own Chants

You can also create your own chants, ones that are suited to your needs. Here are some examples: Be *here* right *now*; Peace, be still; Let go; Yes, I can; and I'm Free, At Last. Whatever syllables, words, or phrases you use for chanting, use ones that are helpful to you. Use words that will reach you on a conscious and unconscious level. That is the way African American singer, dancer, actress and author Tina Turner describes her chanting practice: "[T]here are words you can say... as you say the words with rhythm the conscious tells the subconscious."[3]

In brief, use words that energize and elevate you. Chanting should lift you up, not bring you down!

Chanting During Sitting Meditation

If you want to chant at the beginning or conclusion of your regular sitting meditation session to help you to calm, focus, and uplift your mind, the following guidelines can be used:

1. Select a chant (for example, *Kujichagulia* [KOO-jee-cha-goo-LEE-ah] (self-determination)).

2. Sit up straight, but relaxed.

3. Allow your body to breathe deeply. As you breathe in, allow your belly to expand. As you breathe out, allow your belly to contract. Breathe from your belly rather than your chest.

4. Begin chanting your word, phrase, or text using one or two notes.

5. Let go of preoccupation with yourself. Give yourself fully to chanting, to the words, sounds, and rhythm as they reverberate through your body and space. If you feel inspired,

dwell in one note or quicken the tempo and pace or allow your body to naturally move or sway.

6. Stay present. When thoughts arise, bring your mind back to the chant, the sound and rhythm, the vibration and energy. Chant for several minutes. If you wish to increase your focus, increase the pace of your repetitions.

7. Stop chanting when you feel ready to do so. You can stop suddenly or gradually soften your voice until you are completely silent. You can then say the Yoruba word *Ashe* (See step 6 of the Affirmation Practice in chapter 22) or another personal concluding expression.

8. Conclude by sitting and breathe naturally. Although you may hear sounds or feel vibrations, just note them. Be aware of silence in space.

Make chanting a regular part of your sitting meditation session. Using the same chant or text will deepen your connection to the meaning it holds for you.

Chanting in Everyday Situations

In addition to chanting during your practice session, you can chant anywhere—at home, at work, on the bus or subway—as long as you are not disturbing others. This means that you may have to chant quietly, at the volume of a whisper. You can also chant during a ring walk, or while walking in the park, or to a specific destination.

If you want to chant while walking, it is best to use a single word or phrase that can be easily repeated and synchronized with your breathing or walking pace. For example, you can chant, either aloud or quietly, the phrase "Be here right now," with each syllable corresponding to a step: "Be" (left foot), "here" (right foot), "right" (left foot), "now" (right foot), "be" (left foot), etc.

Allow yourself to enjoy the movement of your breath through your body as you chant. After all, that's all the sound of your voice is—breath moving and vibrating through your body and filling space. That's what the sound is that you are creating, the rhythm and the words. Allow chanting to uplift your heart and mind whenever it is needed.

Using Beads

You may decide that as part of your chanting practice you are going to do a certain number of repetitions of a word or phrase. Say, for example, that you are going to chant "My people must go free" nineteen times. For this, you may want to know when you've completed nineteen repetitions. To help you keep track, you can count on your fingers or use pebbles or cowrie shells that are equal to the number of repetitions you want to do.

Or you can use strung beads. You can purchase strung beads such as a bracelet made with beads, string your own beads, or adapt prayer beads for this purpose. Try to find beads that are large enough for you to easily separate with your thumb while you are counting repetitions.

To use your strung beads, place a marker immediately before the bead you will use to start counting, and place a marker after the bead that will indicate you've completed the number of repetitions you intend to do. A marker can be a string, a clip, or a larger size bead. This may not be necessary if there are already markers on the strung beads you're using, as is often the case with prayer beads.

Now, hold the strung beads in either hand in front of your heart, draped over the middle joint of your index finger and with your thumb resting on top of the bead you will use to start counting. After each repetition of the chant, use your thumb to pull one bead over the finger, toward your body. Continue until you've reached the bead marker that indicates you have completed your intended number of repetitions.

You can also use strung beads as a reminder to stay awake. In this regard, simply use your strung beads as personal adornment. You can wear them around your neck or wrist. Occasionally, look at the beads, feel their texture, or count the beads while chanting silently.

Relating to your beads in this way can help you to remain alert and present. It can also help you to remain grounded in your heritage. After all, in Africa, particularly in West and Central Africa, beads have been used for centuries. They have been used for currency and also as personal adornment to convey age, wealth, and marital status and political, religious, and cultural affiliations. Beads have also been worn as charms for protection against illness and misfortune.

In fact, the use of beads as charms was transplanted and reinterpreted by African Americans during the colonial and antebellum periods. During these periods, blue beads—the predominant color of beads found at many sites inhabited by African Americans in the South—were worn to ward off the misfortunes of slavery and to attract blessings.

Today, whether you use blue beads or not, you can always use chanting to help you to uplift and protect your mind. Chanting can help you go beyond your thoughts and be completely present—right *here*, right *now*, as our ancestors have done for millennia. It can help you to unite your mind, breath, and body. Uniting your body, breath, and mind, will enable you to make the transformative and transcendent journey to freedom.

27. Singing

If we can laugh and sing a little
As we fight the good fight of freedom,
It makes it all go easier.

—Sojourner Truth, Former fugitive slave
quoted in *Sojourner Truth: Slave, Prophet, Legend* by
Carleton Mabee and Susan Mabee Newhouse

African American spirituals are among the most noble and dignified forms of music. They are songs created by slaves that concern what the Bible says about how to live a decent life. The songs also express faith and hope for deliverance from adversity. They can be likened to the bird's song in African American poet and novelist Paul Laurence Dunbar's "Why the Caged Bird Sings."

I know why the caged bird sings, ah me, when his wing is bruised and his bosom sore, when he beats his bars and he would be free; it is not a carol of joy or glee, but a prayer that he sends from his heart's deep core.[1]

The spirituals were not only a prayer and plea for deliverance. They were also a method used by slaves to secretly communicate with each other. According to folklore, songs such as "Steal Away" and "Swing Low, Sweet Chariot" contained hidden messages that signaled an opportunity to escape for anyone ready to flee. Similarly, the repeated singing of "O Canaan, sweet Canaan, I am bound for the land of Canaan" was not a message about reaching Heaven, but about reaching the North or Canada. Other songs, such as "Wade in the Water" and "Follow the Drinking Gourd," explained how to get to the North without being tracked by dogs and apprehended by slave catchers. For example, some of the lyrics from "Follow the Drinking Gourd" are below. The "Drinking Gourd" was another name for the North Star:

> When the sun comes back
> And the first quail calls
> Follow the Drinking Gourd.
> For the old man is waiting for to carry you to freedom,
> If you follow the Drinking Gourd.
> The river bank makes a mighty good road,
> The dead trees show you the way.
> Left foot, peg foot, traveling on
> Follow the Drinking Gourd.
> The river ends between two hills
> Follow the Drinking Gourd.[2]

Harriet Tubman used spirituals and other songs while escorting runaways to freedom. She'd hide her party whenever she needed to go ahead to scout or find food. Returning to them, often late at night, she would sing:

> Dark and thorny is the desert,
> Where the pilgrim makes his way,
> Yet beyond this vale of sorrow,
> Lies the fields of endless days.[3]

Tubman explained the secret meaning of this song:

> The first time I go by singing this hymn, they don't come out to me...until I listen to determine whether

the coast is clear; then when I go back and sing it again, they know it's safe to come out. But if I sing:

Moses go down in Egypt,
Tell oh Pharaoh let me go;
Hadn't been for Adam's fall,
Shouldn't have to die at all,

Then they know not to come out, for there's danger in the way.[4]

Undoubtedly, Tubman would have appreciated the attitude of African American gospel singer Mahalia Jackson, who, during the modern civil rights movement, said that, "Singing the old spirituals for blacks who are not ashamed of being black or from the South helps me to fight for my people."[5]

Basics of Singing Meditation

In your efforts to free your mind so you can uplift yourself and help your people, you may want to sing too—by joining singing with meditation.

In singing meditation, you use the sound, vibration, and energy of your voice as the object on which you rest your attention. As the song you are singing is about to end, gradually lower the volume of your voice until it dissolves in to silence. As your voice dissolves, rest your attention on your breath. Follow your exhalation out as it dissolves in to space. Then rest your attention on the silence. When thoughts or sounds arise, acknowledge them, view them as signals or cues for you to continue resting your attention on the silence. In silence, listen deeply and reverently. Glimpse the experience of oneness or communion. Be receptive to insight.

A Note About Silence

The silence you experience in singing meditation can be as powerful as the songs themselves. Like Spirituals, like the Suspension

Bridge, silence can lead you to the Promised Land, away from the strife and noisy distractions of your mind and the world, to a state of mind that is free of dwelling, fixating, and holding—calm and peaceful. This will help you to rest, discern, heal, and rejuvenate so that you can uplift yourself, your family, and your people. Just relax and continue resting your attention on the silence.

Many people enjoy this silence so much that they seek it in nature—away from sirens, car alarms, loud music, and so forth that bombard and overwhelm our minds. You may want to do this yourself—by visiting a park, garden, beach, forest, field, or your backyard. Of course, you may encounter the sound of thunder, rain, oceans, streams, birds, wind, insects, frogs or even mammals. But in between all those sounds is a rich silence in which you may also encounter greater calm and peace.

Finding a Song to Sing

To begin singing meditation, you'll need a song. Try to find one to which you know the lyrics and melody. Spirituals or any other kind of song that you have a heartfelt connection to will do—blues, gospel, hip-hop, jazz, pop, rap, reggae, or rhythm-and-blues. You may want to use "Lift Every Voice and Sing" by James Weldon Johnson. The lyrics below are the first stanza of the song. You can sing this stanza as many times as you wish. Of course, if you want the other stanzas or need the melody, you can find them on the Internet. (The second stanza can be found in chapter 8.)

Lift Every Voice and Sing

Lift every voice and sing, till earth and Heaven ring,
Ring with the harmonies of liberty;
Let our rejoicing rise, high as the listening skies,
Let it resound loud as the rolling sea.
Sing a song full of the faith that the dark past has taught us,

Sing a song full of the hope that the present has brought us,
Facing the rising sun of our new day begun,
Let us march on till victory is won.[6]

You can practice singing meditation because you were born with music in you. You simply need to let go and allow it to come out. Do not be concerned with the quality of your voice, whether your pitch is too high or low, or your singing style. Have you ever heard a child sing before he or she becomes self-conscious about it? Be like that child. Just express yourself freely.

Now, using the lyrics above or ones of your own choosing, let's practice singing meditation.

Singing Meditation

1. Take a seat in a space where your singing will not disturb others.

2. Take a few moments to slowly sweep your awareness through your body, from your head to your toes and toes to your head. Pay attention to your physical sensations, feelings, and state of mind, moment to moment, without judging.

3. When you are ready, begin singing your song in a mindful, heartfelt way. (You can sing the lyrics as many times as you wish.)

4. As you sing, rest your attention on the sounds of the words you are singing as they vibrate through your vocal cords, your head, neck, back, chest, shoulders, abdomen, and the space around you. Be aware of other sensations or emotions the song evokes.

5. As you feel inspired, bob your head, sway your body, tap your feet, wave your arms, or clap your hands to the song.

Be aware of your movements, too, even as you enjoy them. Be present.

6. As you conclude the song you are singing, taper off, gradually lowering the volume of your voice, and settle into a sitting meditation posture.

7. Looking straight forward with a soft gaze, rest your attention on your breath and follow your exhalations out. Allow your awareness to expand to include the silent space around you.

8. When thoughts, emotions, sensations or sounds arise, instead of viewing them as distractions or labeling them as "thoughts," just note them, and relate to them as signals or cues for you to continue resting your attention on the silence—and do that. Be right *here*, right *now*. Experience profound silence.

9. Continue practicing in this way. If this technique becomes too challenging after awhile, transition to the awakening or calming technique, and then resume this technique, beginning with step 7.

At the conclusion of the technique, before you move from your meditation posture, simply be aware of the space you are in for a few moments. Allow thoughts and perceptions to arise, abide, and fade. If you become distracted, return to an awareness of the space in the room or area. Simply be present with whatever arises. Just *be*, right *here*, right *now*.

Group Singing Meditation

In addition to singing alone, you can do singing meditation as a group practice. For this, you will need a song leader. To put participants at ease, the song leader should:

- select songs that are easy for participants to sing;

- be familiar with the lyrics and melodies;

- have copies of the songs as handouts; and

- explain to group members what singing meditation is about.

Call-and-response songs, reminiscent of the kind our ancestors sang, are ideal for use with group singing meditation. To get started with this technique, consider singing the following gospel song written by Harry Dixon Loes: "This Little Light of Mine." The lyrics have been slightly modified for our use.

The leader provides the instructions to the group for practicing singing meditation. After everyone has taken a seat and swept their body with their awareness, the leader sings his or her lines, and the group sings in response to the leader and uses the sound of the song, sung by the leader, themselves, and the group, as the object on which to rest their attention. If the leader sings loud, fast, soft, or slow, the group sings in the same way.

As singers feel inspired, they may harmonize their voices, bob their heads, sway their bodies, tap their feet, wave their arms, or clap their hands to the song. When the leader's voice softens, the group and the musical accompanist, if there is one, do the same: soften. As the leader establishes a sitting meditation posture and transitions to the remaining steps of the technique (steps 7 through 9, above) the group follows, and continues until the leader indicates that the practice of this technique has concluded.

Of course, you can think of "This Little Light" as your inherent dignity—your inherent goodness, your genius, and your potential.

Now, start singing, and enjoy!

This Little Light of Mine

Stanza #1

Leader: This little light of mine
Group: I'm gonna let it shine.
Leader: This little light of mine
Group: I'm gonna let it shine.
Leader: This little light of mine
Group: I'm gonna let it shine. Let it shine. Let it shine. Let it shine.

Stanza #2

Leader: Everywhere I go
Group: I'm gonna let it shine.
Leader: Everywhere I go
Group: I'm gonna let it shine.
Leader: Everywhere I go
Group: I'm gonna let it shine. Let it shine. Let it shine. Let it shine.

Stanza #3

Leader: All in my life (at this point, the leader might begin to sing more softly)
Group: I'm gonna let it shine.
Leader: All in my life (sung softer)
Group: I'm gonna let it shine.
Leader: All in my life (sung in a whisper)
Group: I'm gonna let it shine. Let it shine. Let it shine. Let it shine.[7]

The leader allows the song to conclude and leads the group in resting their minds in silence, being completely present, awake, and one with your environment.

Whether you do singing meditation alone or in a group, use the sound of your voice as a path and silence as a bridge to freedom. Then, allow your light to shine.

28. Dancing

We are almost a nation of dancers, musicians, and poets. Every great event, such as a triumphant return from battle, or other cause of public rejoicing, is celebrated in public dances, which are accompanied with songs and music suited to the occasion. The assembly is separated into four divisions, which dance either apart or in succession, and each with a character peculiar to itself. The first division contains the married men, who in their dances frequently exhibit feats of arms, and the representation of a battle. To these succeed the married women who dance into the second division. The young men occupy the third; and the maidens the fourth. Each represents some interesting scene of real life, such as a great achievement, domestic employment, a pathetic story, or some rural sport. And as the subject is generally found on some recent event, it is therefore ever new. This gives our dances a spirit and variety which I have scarcely seen elsewhere.

—Olaudah Equiano, *The Interesting Narrative of the Life of Olaudah Equiano*
Member of the Igbo tribe, former slave

When our ancestors heard rhythmic music, they quite naturally wanted to move their bodies; they wanted to get up and dance. Dancing was one of the ways they kept alive their African heritage and expressed their inherent dignity. As Lawrence W. Levine notes:

The basic characteristic of African dance, with its gliding, dragging, shuffling steps, its flexed, fluid bodily positions as opposed to the stiffly erect position of European dancers, its imitations of such animals as the buzzard and the eagle, its emphasis upon flexibility and improvisation, its concentration upon movement outward from the pelvic region which whites found lewd, its tendency to eschew bodily contact, and its propulsive, swinging rhythm, were perpetuated for centuries in the dances of American slaves.[1]

The slaveholders, however, didn't see anything dignified about our ancestors' dancing. They looked upon their dance with amusement, and considered it primitive, weird, comical, lustful, and wild. They viewed their dance as proof that black people were inferior. Yet, when the dances and the ritual ceremonies (of which many of the dances were a part) frightened or caused slaveholders to become fearful of insurrection, they banned slave gatherings, drumming, chanting, singing, and dancing.

Nevertheless, our ancestors continued to create music and dance in secret, especially on Saturdays and holidays. Inside cabins and in hollows and clearings in the woods, they could be found banjo playing, chanting, singing, moaning, clapping their hands, and stomping their feet. Former slave Isaac D. Williams observed that,

> Music was something we colored people had in our souls. It may not have been very fine, but the heart was there and it expressed all our best emotions, pervading our being and making the nerves tingle with pleasure while the very veins pulsated in sympathy. Thank the Lord for instilling in our souls this taste for the harmonious and for making us naturally light-hearted and cheerful under so many afflictions.... [2]

Of course, where there was music there was also dance, as Williams explains:

> Dance was the sunshine of slave life, and for a time we would drive dull care away and think not of its darker and gloomier shadows. I've seen some colored women grasp their dresses on each side, holding them so you could see their feet take every step known to the art, and do it as well as the most talented professional, all done easily and gracefully and with no apparent effort. There seemed to be a certain inborn grace and ease of movement possessed by many young colored girls... every motion was untrammeled and free.[3]

Through dance, our ancestors were able to let go of their preoccupation with what happened in the past and what might happen in the future. They rested their mind completely in the present moment. They took respite in *now*. *Now* provided them with relief from their trials and tribulations. As they danced, they worshipped, celebrated, socialized, and relaxed, and they expressed a range of emotions. Yes, they expressed sadness, but they also expressed gratitude, hope, inspiration, confidence, peace, love, and joy.

Positive Emotions

Expressing negative and positive emotions through dance enabled our ancestors to release bodily tension and stress. It enabled them to free their minds from attachment to thoughts that clouded their outlook. With a free mind, they were better able to see and reframe their situations in ways that helped them to carry on with their lives.

Like your ancestors, you can also use dance to free your mind so that you can carry on. To begin, find music that evokes in you one of these emotions:

- confidence—self-assuredness

- gratitude—appreciation or thankfulness

- hope—encouragement or optimism

- inspiration—upliftedness or elevation

- joy—happiness or gladness

- love—closeness or intimacy

- peace—calmness or contentment

- pride—a sense of excellence or achievement

As with singing meditation, you can select any style of music. But initially select music with which you are familiar, music that has roots deep inside you—African, spirituals, blues, gospel, jazz, soul, or reggae. Next, find a safe place where you can dance without injuring yourself, disturbing others, or being disturbed by others.

In dance meditation, we simply pay attention to our body as we dance to music, with moment to moment awareness of our posture, movements, sensations, and emotions, without judging ourselves or what we experience. In the process, we release bodily tension and stress and thoughts that cloud our outlook. With a free mind, we are then better able to understand, gain insight, and relate to situations in ways that help us to carry on with our lives.

In this technique, there isn't a right or wrong way to dance. There isn't any reason to be concerned about how you might be viewed. There's also no need to try to look sensuous, graceful, respectable, or cool. The only thing you need to do in dance meditation is to allow your body freedom of expression and to observe it continuously, moment to moment, without judgment.

Sometimes, as you dance, thoughts will arise, and you'll find yourself expressing some aspect of your own personal story or releasing a long held emotion. Remember to pay close attention to what you are experiencing as you dance. Just safely dance, express yourself, release tension, stress, and emotions. Heal your body, breath, and mind. Allow your heart to sing and dance in *now*.

Would you like to dance? Get your music ready, and let's join dance with meditation.

Dance Meditation

Until you are familiar with these instructions, you may want to record them and then play them back as needed or have a trusted friend read them to you so you can practice without interruption.

1. Stand with your feet shoulder-width apart, knees unlocked, and arms at your sides.

2. Let go of thoughts and rest your attention on your breath. Be aware of your in-breaths and out-breaths, the rising and falling of your chest and shoulders, and the expansion and contraction of your abdomen.

3. Become aware of your posture, sensations, and feelings in each part of your body. Begin with the heels, soles and toes of your feet; then slowly move your awareness upward to your ankles, and then slowly through your calves, knees, thighs, pelvis, abdomen, chest, shoulders, back, arms, hands, neck, head, and face. Then reverse this order, slowly moving your awareness through each part of your body from your scalp to the soles of your feet. Closely observe, without any judgment about it whatsoever, what you find or experience.

4. Slowly raise your right arm over your head and then slowly lower it; as you do this observe your posture, the movement, sensations, and pleasant or unpleasant feelings that accompany the lifting and lowering of your arm. Do the same with your left arm, right leg and then left leg as well, as you bend at the waist to the right and left and then return to a standing posture. Simply be aware of your posture, movement, sensations, and feelings.

5. Expand your awareness throughout your entire body, all at once. Be present in your body. Relax.

6. Start the music. Slowly move your body to the music, following your natural impulse to dance. As you dance, maintain an awareness of your postures, movements, sensations, and feelings. Simply be aware, moment to moment, of your dancing experience without judging.it.

7. Freely express yourself. If you feel like moving like a bird, do so. If you feel like shouting, groaning, or shrieking, go right ahead. If you feel like stamping, jumping, or clapping your hands, go ahead and do that too. If you feel like speaking out, tell about it. If you feel like crying, let your tears flow freely. If you feel like laughing, go ahead. If you feel like hollering, that's OK too. Express whatever arises in you without harming yourself or others. Even if you are feeling sad, angry, or discouraged, go ahead and express those emotions through dance; doing so can give rise to a more positive state of mind—provided you continue to observe your experience of dancing, your posture, movements, sensations, feelings, moment to moment, without judgment.

8. If you become dizzy or get out of breath, sit down. You can continue to dance, sway, tap your feet, or simply sit still and listen to the music, while maintaining awareness of your body.

9. If your attention wanders, bring it back to your breath, and regain your awareness of your body as it dances.

10. Dance more slowly as the music nears an end. Turn the music off when it ends, and then transition to walking to freedom or ring walk meditation (you may want to review

the instruction in chapter 8). Walk for a couple of minutes or more.

11. Return to the place you were standing when you began this meditation. Bring your attention to your breath and your awareness into your body by repeating steps 1, 2 and 3 of this technique.

12. Conclude this practice by transitioning to another meditation technique or resuming your activities. Drink water to avoid dehydration, and smile.

Dancing meditation can also be used to enact or reenact events, stories, or achievements, as was done by the Igbo tribe of which the former slave Olaudah Equiano was a member. You can do this, dancing alone or with a group, in a way that is either loosely scripted or not scripted; you might even want to dance while wearing an African mask that you've created, just to see how that feels. The main thing is to pay attention to your body—your posture, movement, sensations, and feelings—while you surrender to the dance. Allow emotions that are aroused to arise and surface. To paraphrase African American singer Lionel Richie: "Feel [the music] in your heart and feel it in your soul, let the music take control." This is what was done by our ancestors.

The Spirit of Dance

Carry the spirit of dance with you as you proceed through each day. Simply slow down, *smile,* and look for opportunities to be more fully present, and to arouse, embody, and express positive emotions such as confidence, gratitude, hope, inspiration, joy, love, peace, and pride:

- Arouse gratitude—upon waking up each morning and realizing that you and the people important to you are alive and well.

- Arouse hope—when you see youth on their way to school or someone on their way to a job interview.

- Arouse inspiration—when you hear that someone has excelled.

- Arouse compassion—when you hear or see someone who is injured, ill, or has experienced some other misfortune.

- Arouse joy—when you hear positive news.

- Arouse love—upon being greeted with a smile, touch, or embrace or while extending someone kindness.

- Arouse peace—when viewing art or any form of beauty, or when you have no problems to contend with at the moment.

- Arouse pride—when you pay a bill on time, do well on a test or a job interview, achieve any of your goals, or whenever you need it!

- Arouse confidence—whenever you are doubtful or uncertain.

Smile, let go, be present, and arouse positive emotions whenever something comes to mind that you appreciate!

Sometimes you might find it difficult to be present and arouse positive emotions. The sheer volume of negative information you receive from the news media, friends, family, and coworkers in the course of a day—tragedies, complaints, grievances, resentments, jealousies, hatreds, dislikes, and your own emotional disturbances—can weigh you down like heavy chains. It can cause you to lose sight of all the positive things in your life. When you feel weighed down, see if you can create some space for yourself. "Lighten up" by smiling, and move your body by walking, exercising or dancing. If necessary, dance away from the sources of negativity.

Of course, if *you* are a source of negativity, you can't dance away from yourself. But you can become more mindful of what you think, say, and do. Try to avoid polluting other people's minds with unwholesome thoughts and emotions, especially with outbursts of anger. By now you know that if you have a "problem" with anyone or anything, the first step to addressing it is to look at your own mind.

Meditate. Learn to *be* with whatever is happening in and around you, at all times, unconditionally. Move forward into an uninterrupted stream of moments of *now*. As you do, you'll realize that goodness is everywhere in every moment. Thus, around you at all times are opportunities to arouse and express positive emotions.

Mindfully dance. Be present. *Smile*. Live your life with gratitude, hope, inspiration, compassion, joy, love, peace, and confidence; doing this will positively help you to free your mind.[4]

TERMINUS: St. Catharines, Ontario, Canada

Harriet Tubman and her passengers were relieved and happy to finally arrive at the terminus—the end of the line—St Catharines. There, they found a picturesque town with shipyards, canals, dry docks, mills, factories, spas, orchards, gardens, outlying farms, and a mild climate. In 1850, the city had a population of about 7,000 residents, of whom about 1,000 were black and mostly fugitives.

Most of city's black population resided in a settlement on the outskirts of town. Whenever Tubman visited this area, she usually stayed with family members and friends. She also occasionally rented a room on North Street near the Bethel Chapel, African Methodist Episcopal Church, where she may have worshipped and had some influence on the settlement's development.

William Still, who visited St. Catharines, described the settlement this way:

> The colored settlement is a hamlet, situated on the outskirts of the village, and contains about 100 houses, 40 of which lie on North Street, the Broadway of the place. The houses are chiefly cottages, with from 3 to 6 rooms, and on lots of land nearly a quarter an acre each. Most of the dwellings are wood-colored, only a few of them having been

painted or white washed. Each family has a good garden, well-filled with vegetables, ducks, chickens, and a pig-pen, with at least one gat grunter [pig] getting ready for Christmas.[1]

Mary Ann Shadd Cary, who also visited, was pleased with what she saw:

> During my stay at St. Catharines, I had frequent opportunities of examining the general improvements of the place and was in no way more gratified than when viewing the snug homesteads of the colored people.[2]

Although homesteads were uplifted, incoming refugees needed help. They often were inadequately clothed, without money, in need of food, without trades or tools for work, unable to read and write, in need of housing and medical care for injuries and illness, and subject to racial discrimination by white Canadians. One of the people who helped them was Hiram Wilson, a white relief worker and brakeman in the Underground Railroad. He had a clear sense of his reason for being in the town: "I am to guard the Niagara Frontier and do all that can be done in this section of Canada for the welfare of the Refugees who are quite...rapidly increasing,"[3] Wilson was true to his word. Through his efforts many refugees arriving in Canada received the shelter, food, clothes, education, and employment they needed.

Tubman supported Wilson's efforts. But she also had to support herself. She worked as a cook, maid, and laundress and performed other temporary jobs. And when she had enough money to begin another rescue mission, she would quietly depart St.

Catharines. She would not be heard from for weeks and months, during which time she'd be reentering the South and conducting slaves out. Then, without notice, she'd reappear, be seen walking through the streets of the settlement with more passengers. In 1857, Wilson wrote to a friend about Tubman's arrival:

> In another instance 4 of the sable pilgrims of liberty came having a remarkable colored heroine for their conductress from the land of oppression to the "land of Promise," and to the bright noontide of British freedom.... We could not but admire the courage and fortitude of their benevolent guide nor refrain from cautioning her against too much adventure & peril, as this was but one of many instances of her deeds of daring.[4]

In 1858, the white radical abolitionist John Brown traveled to St. Catharines to meet with Tubman. He was vehemently opposed to slavery. He was active in efforts to ensure that Kansas territory was admitted to the Union as a free state. Upon his arrival in the black settlement, he had been involved in skirmishes in Kansas that had resulted in the deaths of proslavery men.

Brown talked to Tubman about his plan to raid the US armory at Harpers Ferry in Virginia. He planned to use the weapons and ammunition from the raid to create an armed force with slave recruits, and to send the force through the South to disrupt the institution of slavery. This is the same plan that Brown had discussed with his friend, Frederick Douglass. Douglass told him the plan was flawed and urged him not to undertake it. But Brown would not listen. He now asked Tubman to help him carry out the plan.

As they talked, Brown formed a highly favorable impression of Tubman. Later, he would describe her as "one of the best and bravest persons on the continent"[5] and, in a letter to his son, he referred to her as "General Tubman" and "the most of a man, naturally, that I ever met with."[6]

Tubman's willingness to meet with Brown and consider his plan was an indication of the strength of her convictions—"My people must go free." Clearly she was willing to consider any means by which that could happen.

However, she did not participate in the raid. Being always on the move, she couldn't be located when Brown's followers (five of whom were African Americans) launched their raid on the arsenal in the fall of 1859. The raid failed badly. Brown was captured, tried, and sentenced to death by hanging along with two African American accomplices, John Copeland and Shields Green (Green had been introduced to Brown by Douglass). In the meantime, when a letter to Brown signed by Douglass was found among Brown's belongings, Douglass instantly became the "most wanted" person in the country. He fled for his life to Canada and then England.

On December 2, 1859, when word of Brown's execution reached Tubman in Boston, she was distraught. She returned to St. Catharines and, after the frenzy surrounding Brown's raid and execution died down, resumed her activities. She established the Fugitive Aid Society of St. Catharines to benefit fugitives arriving in the town. She also traveled to antislavery conventions, fairs, and rallies to raise funds for her charity.

At the onset of the Civil War in 1861, Tubman was in Boston, probably to raise funds for her charity. While in the city, she accompanied wealthy friends to a private meeting with the governor of Massachusetts, John Andrew. He asked her to go south with soldiers from the state and help the Union army.

Traveling onboard the Union ship *Atlantic*, Tubman arrived in Beaufort, South Carolina, in the spring of 1862. According to Union General Rufus Saxton, her service to the Union army was exemplary:

> I can bear witness to the value of her services in South Carolina and Florida. She was employed in the hospitals and as a spy. She made many a raid inside the enemy's lines, displaying remarkable courage, zeal, and fidelity.[7]

While Tubman was down south with the Union army, abolitionists up north such as Frederick Douglass were lobbying President Abraham Lincoln to abolish slavery. Lincoln's ambivalence made Douglass uncomfortable. There were reports that the President's aim was to save the Union, and neither abolish nor maintain slavery, reports that he was actively recruiting free blacks to lead a black colonization movement to Central America, reports that he was going to free all the slaves in the South, and reports that he was going to allow Southerners to keep their slaves for forty years if they would lay down their arms and return to the Union.

Although Frederick Douglass knew that Lincoln "in his heart of hearts loathed and hated slavery," he also knew Lincoln "shared the prejudices of his white fellow countrymen against the Negro."[8] Douglass would later note:

> [President Lincoln] was preeminently the white man's President, entirely devoted to the welfare of the white man. He was ready and willing at any time during the first years of his administration to deny, postpone, and sacrifice the rights of humanity

in the colored people in order to promote the welfare of the white people in this country.... The race
to which we belong were not the special objects of
his consideration.[9]

As the year 1862 neared an end, no one knew what Lincoln
would do. However, he eventually came to the realization that
there was only one way to preserve the Union—abolish slavery.
Thus, on January 1, 1863, he took a first step in that direction
by allowing the Emancipation Proclamation to go into effect. It
freed slaves in all Southern states where Confederates were still
engaged in hostile action against the United States. The act also
authorized the induction of free blacks and emancipated slaves
into the US army.

Tubman's role as a spy in South Carolina during the summer of
1863 is noteworthy. Working in an army regiment with black soldiers, with several men under her supervision, she gathered intelligence that was used to plan a raid up the Combahee River. Then,
as a scout, she helped Colonel James Montgomery, the commander
of the Second Regiment South Carolina Volunteers, lead the unit in
the raid. The regiment was one of the first US military units consisting of black soldiers. The raid resulted in the liberation of over
seven hundred blacks who were being held by Confederates.

Tubman was very satisfied with what she saw during the raid:
slaveholders fleeing from approaching black Union soldiers and
slaves running jubilantly toward them. "I've never seen such a
sight," she commented.[10] She persuaded many of the men who
were liberated during the raid to enlist in the Union army.

In addition to the slaves freed during the Combahee River
Raid, there were hundreds of thousands of emancipated men,
women and children (often referred to as "contrabands") fleeing

their Confederate slaveholders throughout the South. Tubman dictated a letter to a friend up north that described the situation and explained what she was trying to do to help them:

> I have now been absent two years almost, and have just got letters from my friends in Auburn, urging me to come home. My father and mother are old and in feeble health, and need my care and attention. I hope the good people there will not allow them to suffer, and I do not believe they will. But I do not see how I am to leave at present the very important work to be done here. Among my other duties which I have, is the looking after the hospital here for contrabands. Most of those coming from the mainland are very destitute, almost naked. I am trying to find a place for those able to work, and provide for them as best I can, so as to lighten the burden on the Government as much as possible, while at the same time they learn to respect themselves by earning their own living.[11]

A month after the Combahee River Raid, Tubman's unit was near Charleston, South Carolina. She recalled serving a meal to Colonel Robert G. Shaw, the white commander of the all-black 54th Massachusetts Regiment—the first US military unit consisting of black soldiers to be raised in the North—before he led the regiment's ill-fated assault on Fort Wagner. She witnessed the battle:

> [W]e saw the lightening, and that was the guns; and then we heard the thunder, and that was the big guns; and then we heard the rain falling, and that

was the drops of blood falling; and when we came to get the crops, it was dead men that we reaped.[12]

After the assault on Fort Wagner, Tubman was assigned to a hospital where she nursed soldiers wounded during the battle. She described some of her work there:

> I'd go to the hospital, I would, early every morning. I'd get a big chunk of ice, I would, and put it in a basin, and fill it with water; then I'd take a sponge and begin. First man I'd come to, I'd thrash away the flies, and they'd rise, they would, like bees round a hive. Then I'd begin to bathe the wounds, and by the time I'd bathe off three or four, the fire and heat would have melted the ice and made the water warm, and it would be red as clear blood. Then I'd go and get more ice, I would, and by the time I got to the next ones, the flies would be round the first ones black and thick as ever.[13]

Tubman not only cared for wounded soldiers. She also cared for soldiers and contrabands that were sick. On one occasion, she was summoned from South Carolina to Florida to help doctors halt the spread of dysentery among black soldiers. According to Sarah H. Bradford, "Here she found thousands of sick soldiers and contrabands, and immediately gave up her time and attention to them."[14] Tubman recalled, "So I boiled up a great boiler of roots and herbs, and the General told a man to take two cans and go round and give it to all in the camp that needed it, and it cured them."[15]

Tubman also nursed men with small-pox and malignant fevers.

Regarding her work as a nurse, a surgeon wrote:

> I certify that I have been acquainted with Harriet Tubman for nearly two years; and my position as Medical Officer in charge of "contrabands" in this town and in [this] hospital, has given me frequent and ample opportunities to observe her general deportment; particularly her kindness and attention to the sick and suffering of her own race. I take much pleasure in testifying to the esteem in which she is generally held.[16]

Nancy and Josiah Henson
Source: Toronto Public Library

29. Serving

DEAR HARRIET: Most that I have done and suffered in the service of our cause has been in public, and I have received much encouragement at every step of the way. You, on the other hand, have labored in a private way. The midnight sky and the silent stars have been the witnesses of your devotion to freedom and of your heroism. Excepting John Brown—of sacred memory—I know of no one who has willingly encountered more perils and hardships to serve our enslaved people than you have.

—Frederick Douglass, Former fugitive slave
quoted in *Scenes in the Life of Harriet Tubman*
by Sarah H. Bradford

Harriet Tubman was not the only person who went into the South to conduct slaves to freedom. There were others. But because of the dangers involved, many of them were either arrested, imprisoned, or killed. Among the Underground Railroad conductors who fell in this category were white agents such as Delia Webster, Seth Concklin, and Calvin Fairbank, and African Americans such as Samuel D. Burris and Elijah Anderson.

John P. Parker was one of the conductors who succeeded without being caught. He was born enslaved, in Virginia. When he was eight years old, he was sold south and forced to walk all the way to Louisiana in a chain gang, barely able to keep up with the adults in the coffle. As he grew to manhood, he escaped from slavery several times, before finally gaining his freedom.

Parker eventually settled in Ripley, Ohio, with his wife, Miranda Boulden. He established a successful iron foundry business and started working with John Rankin and other railroad agents in the city. Over the years, Parker risked his life many times, rowing his boat across the Ohio River, making forays into Kentucky, and leading slaves across the river to Ripley, and to freedom.

Other efficient Underground Railroad networks existed, such ones overseen by Levi Coffin in Newport, Indiana, and later in Cincinnati. Many of the runaways reaching these networks after crossing the Ohio River were forwarded north to Canada.

After the passage of the Fugitive Slave Act of 1850, many conductors and other agents of the Underground Railroad curtailed their activities. They could be imprisoned, heavily fined, and have their property confiscated if they were caught. However, one hunted, disabled, poor, illiterate black woman, who deeply believed "My people must go free," continued.

Despite Tubman's unwavering efforts to rescue enslaved people, the institution of slavery was too big for her. In many cases it was too big even for the US government. Thus, as late as 1858—more than 50 years after the importation of slaves from Africa had been outlawed by the federal government—over 400 enslaved Africans from the Congo were found on board the *Wanderer* at Jekyll Island, Georgia. And, in the summer of 1859, over 100 enslaved Africans from the Gold Coast disembarked from the *Clotilde* at Mobile, Alabama.

Slavery was difficult to abolish. It was maintained by powerful political, economic, and social interests. Those interests succeeded in part because they kept a tight grip on the minds of people of African ancestry. Even Tubman is reported to have lamented, "I freed a thousand slaves, but I could have freed a thousand more if only they knew they were slaves."[1]

Tubman must have found it frustrating to encounter slaves who actually believed they were free. Yet, she never stopped trying to liberate them. She persevered because she understood what African American voting rights activist Fannie Lou Hamer would express one hundred years later: "Nobody's free until everybody's free."[2]

Like Tubman, you can also pave the way for others to become free. You can become a "Moses of your people." However, unlike Tubman, you do not have to quit your job, risk your life, or leave your family. You simply need to uplift your mind by letting go of thoughts that hold you down. Then uplift all areas of your life: spiritual, family, friendships, physical and mental health, finances, and career. By uplifting your mind and your personal existence, you will be uplifting your community. You will, by your example, show others the way to freedom.

30. Conducting

After I had tasted the blessings of freedom, my mind reverted to those whom I knew were groaning in captivity, and I at once proceeded to take measures to free as many as I could. I thought that, by using exertion, numbers might make their escape as I did, if they had some practical advice on how to proceed.

—Josiah Henson, *Truth Stranger Than Fiction*
Former fugitive slave

The Underground Railroad not only existed in the North, it also existed in the South—although in a different way.

In Florida, the Seminoles provided runaways from the Carolinas, Georgia, and Florida plantations with a refuge. Many of the runaways banded together to form maroon communities. Others assimilated into Seminole society, became Black Seminoles, and fought to defend the Seminole Nation from invasions by the US military.

When the US military succeeded in relocating the Seminoles to Indian Territory, and disarming them, Black Seminole John Horse led fellow Black Seminoles from the territory to Mexico to protect them from slave raiders. Many Maroons in Florida, unable to survive white attacks, fled to the Bahamas and Cuba.

The Seminoles were not alone in providing help to runaways. Quite a few whites helped as well. For example, Jonathan Walker risked imprisonment and death when he agreed to help seven enslaved men flee from Florida to the Bahamas. He used his boat to sail the men from Pensacola. But after sailing for two weeks, he and the men were captured and returned to Pensacola. Walker stood trial and was found guilty. For punishment, he was required to stand for public exhibition on the courthouse steps, have his hand branded with the letters "SS" to mark him as a slave stealer, and pay large fines and substantial court costs in order to obtain release from jail. After wealthy abolitionists helped obtain his release, Walker relocated to the North, where he was hailed as a hero.

Blacks in the South also aided runaways. The following account of Peter Smith's escape from slavery in Tennessee makes clear the role that blacks played.

> He travelled unmolested that day, and at night met with colored friends, who took him in and sheltered him until morning, when he resumed his journey being directed by his colored friends.... He pursued his journey for several days unmolested, and without eating, until he again met with some colored friends, who gave him some victuals [food], and advised him to push forward; and, after travelling several days unmolested, he was again urged by hunger to beg subsistence, but soon apprehending danger, and turned away, and travelled on until he again found a colored friend who gave him victuals.... He continued his journey again for several days.... till seeing a little colored girl, he hailed her, and requested her to tell an old colored man who was near there to come to him. Accordingly the old man came. He requested the old man to bring him victuals, but he persuaded him to come to the quarters with him, for they were all slaves there, and get dinner....[1]

Some of the "colored friends" that Smith encountered may have been free blacks. There were about 261,000 in the South in 1860. This was about 35,000 more than there were in the North.

These free blacks, about 40 percent of whom were mulattoes, lived under many of the same restrictive laws, codes, and practices that were used to regulate and control free blacks in the North: segregation and discrimination.[2]

Many free blacks in the South gravitated to cities where they could find work, such as in Baltimore, Alexandria, Richmond, Petersburg, Norfolk, Charleston, Savannah, and New Orleans. They became an indispensable segment of antebellum society, forming a subservient class that whites relied on for their high-quality, inexpensive labor. They worked as barbers, blacksmiths, bricklayers, butchers, carpenters, cooks, housekeepers, laundresses, millwrights, plasterers, shoemakers, tailors, waitresses, and so forth.

Most free blacks in the South, however, lived in rural areas. Although they were technically free, most of them lived in conditions similar to those experienced by slaves. They lived in shacks and cabins owned by slaveholders for whom they worked as sharecroppers and farmhands. The terms under which they worked essentially made them indentured servants or free slaves.

Whether residing in urban or rural areas, the moment-to-moment challenge of free blacks in the South was to avoid saying or doing anything that whites could interpret as a threat to their authority, dominance, security, or belief that they were superior. The punishment for doing so could be death.

Although free blacks made every effort to live in peace, whites simply were uncomfortable having African Americans around. Thus, in the 1850s, throughout the South, state legislatures debated what they should do with free blacks. Should they prohibit free blacks from entering the state? Should they expel all free blacks from the state? Should they deport all free blacks to Africa? Should they require all free blacks to "apprentice" with a white master for the duration of their lives? Or should they make all free blacks slaves?

Justifiably fearful that they could be enslaved because of a vote in one of these state legislatures, some free blacks fled from the Southern state they resided in. But fleeing was not easy. Several states prohibited free blacks from entering. Other states required black immigrants to post bonds. There was also the risk that if they attempted to relocate they could be mistaken for being runaways, snatched by slave catchers, sold to slave dealers, and sent back down south in chains.

Many free blacks decided to stay where they were. They were settled, did not see where conditions in the North were much better, and were opposed to breaking up their families and communities, and cutting ties to enslaved relatives on nearby plantations. Thus they stayed, and continued building strong families, churches, schools, businesses, and benevolent societies that served the needs of their people, and contributed to the white Southern society.

Many state lawmakers—although usually for selfish reasons—simply could not deny the inherent goodness, genius, and potential of black people. Seeing the indispensable economic and social benefits (to white society) of the presence of a free black population, they refused to back many of the most racist legislative schemes. Meanwhile, free blacks continued to live their lives with dignity, and help runaways like Peter Smith find their way north to freedom.

After making it across the Ohio River or the Mason-Dixon Line to a non-slaveholding state, many runaways succeeded in making it all the way to Canada, where they settled in the province of Ontario. Other runaways settled in the northern United States, many of them near Underground Railroad escape routes in the forested wilderness; in small towns such as Rocky Fork, New Philadelphia, and Miller Grove in Illinois; Lick Creek, Indiana; Poke Patch, Ohio;[3] or in thriving cities such as Philadelphia, New York City, and Boston.

After settling in the North, many fugitives joined free blacks and whites by serving as stationmasters. They allowed their homes, churches, stables and barns to be used as Underground Railroad stations. John P. Parker had this to say about the station-masters in Ripley, Ohio:

> He was watched by his neighbors, threatened by the authorities, and frequently betrayed by his friends. His work was all done under cover of the night. He had to use all manner of subterfuges to throw his watchers off his trail. In spite of law and man, these men in spite of hardships, and beset [with] difficul-ties, went on year after year in the work, which he believed was his burden [and] duty to perform. And he did perform it well.[4]

Indeed, the stationmasters did perform their work well. When runaways arrived at their stations, alone or accompanied by an Underground Railroad conductor or other agent, it was usually at night. Many of them wore tattered, coarse, and dirty clothing, and were shoeless. Some were unwashed and reeked of sweat; were missing some teeth; bore scars on their ankles, wrists, and neck from being shackled, and had marks on their faces and body from being flogged, or branded. They were hungry and exhausted.

The stationmasters welcomed them into dim, lamp-lighted spaces and gave them food and drink, water for bathing, clean clothes, and whatever was available to sleep on—a haystack, carpet, bedroll, or bed. In addition, if the station was the first one in the North the runaways had reached, the stationmasters helped them to select new names that would conceal their old identity and express their new identities as free men or women. Also, the stationmasters interviewed fugitives who were willing to talk, and recorded their information in a ledger: date of arrival, slave name, free name, physical description, an account of their life in slavery, an account of the escape and, later, the name of the station to which they were forwarded.

The ledger was used to help fugitives locate relatives or friends who might have gone through the station before them. However, after the Fugitive Slave Act of 1850 became law, most stationmasters destroyed their ledgers. They did this because if the ledger was found, the stationmaster could be convicted in court of aiding fugitives. He or she could then be fined, jailed, and forced to turn over all of his or her property to the court. Moreover, the freedom and lives of everyone identified in the ledger would be endangered.

One of the difficulties runaways had upon arriving at a station was overcoming their own feelings of distrust and fear. This was often the case if the stationmaster was white, as the following account from the runaway David Barrett makes clear:

> They invited me to sit down at the table with them. I refused, told them I could take a piece [of food] in my hand, but, no; nothing would satisfy them but to seat myself with them. The man told me he didn't set side tables for colored people. Said he, "If you are good enough to come into my house you are good enough to sit at my table and eat with me." I sat down at the table opposite him but was full of suspicion. I had never been accustomed to such treatment and knew

not what it meant. The good man, as he proved to be, closed his eyes to ask a blessing. Thought I, old man, you want me to shut my eyes and then you and your family will pounce upon me.

With my knife in one hand and my fork in the other, I sat facing him taking care to keep my eyes wide open, but in the enjoyment of a good wholesome breakfast and cheerful conversation, my fears soon left me.[5]

Depending on the circumstances, fugitives could remain at a station overnight or for days, weeks, months, or years until a way was found for them to safely continue their journey. But when it was time for them to leave, they were able to depart with a more positive outlook, having received clothing, food, directions or transportation to the next station, and genuine, heartfelt, unconditional kindness and caring.

When the fugitives reached their destination—the end of the line—an Underground Railroad brakeman/woman would help them to settle down. But making the transition to a life in freedom was not easy. In addition to finding a job, a place to live, food to eat, and clothing, many of the fugitives had to cope with symptoms of post-traumatic stress disorder—recurring recollections, depression, anxiety, flashbacks, agitation, and nightmares—the result of murders, sexual assaults, serious injuries, death threats, and other atrocities that they had experienced or witnessed during their years in slavery.

Reviving the Tradition of the Underground Railroad

After you have regularly practiced meditation for a while, you may want to follow the example of our ancestors by allowing your home to be used as a station—a place to which people can come and meditate to free their mind. You can do this, first, by gaining experience with the meditation principles and practices in this guidebook. Then you can invite family and friends to join you several times each year for meditation sessions.

For your group sessions, you can simply get everyone together and meditate informally. Or you can follow the form of the Underground Railroad. If you select this latter approach, the following Underground Railroad terms, adapted for your "station," can be used.

Underground Railroad Terms

- *Promised Land:* the uplifted mind, uplifted personal existence, and uplifted societal conditions that result from practicing meditation techniques.

- *Track:* the meditation principles and techniques used to reach the Promised Land.

- *Station:* the house or apartment where the group meditation session is held.

- *Ticket:* the invitation to participate in the meditation session.

- *Passenger:* the person who participates in the session.

- *Agent:* any meditator who helps to keep the station operating.

- *Conductor:* the person who leads the meditation practices during the session.

- *Stockholder:* the person who prepares a snack or light meal for passengers to enjoy after the practice session has concluded or provides other resources.

- *Stationmaster:* the person who allows his or her home to be used for group meditation.

- *Brakeman/Brakewoman:* an experienced meditator who helps new passengers arriving at the station to settle into a regular meditation practice when they request help.

- *Vigilance Committee:* agents who use principles and practices of meditation to ensure that all aspects of the station operate smoothly and to help passengers move toward freedom.

If you open a station, initially, you may have to assume all of the key roles: the conductor, stockholder, brakeman/woman, and stationmaster. But after you've held a few sessions, other participants who appreciate the importance of developing a free mind will be able to take over one or more of the roles.

Whatever role you take on, it is assumed that you are a person of initiative, integrity, and moral resolve. But remember one thing: you are not "the leader." Like Harriet Tubman, you are "the servant." In this capacity, your purpose is to elevate your family and friends. Your job is to help them bring forth their inherent goodness, genius, and potential. This means that you will need to listen to what they say their wants, needs, and values are and use persuasion to help them remove obstacles to the accomplishment of their goals. This also means that you will need to help them to find sources of strength within themselves that they can exert. Then you'll need to mobilize them and guide them as they go forward.

Operating the Station

After you have agents who are committed to supporting your station, you can use the schedule below to help you operate it smoothly. You will be able to find additional resources at www. freeyourmindguide.com.

Before the session

1. Stationmaster meets with agents, including the conductor, stockholder, and brakeman/woman, to plan the session. Topics for discussion include the practices that will be done by the group as well as the location, date, and time of the session, and who will be invited.[6]

2. Designated agents give out invitations.[7]

3. Stationmaster ensures that the practice environment is clean, uncluttered, and welcoming. A focal point should be created. This can be done very simply by placing a candle (not lit at first) on a table in front of the space where the passengers will practice.[8]

4. Stationmaster, conductor, stockholder, brakeman/woman and other agents arrive at the station to set up, an hour or so before the session begins.[9]

During the session

5. Stationmaster greets passengers at the door as they arrive.

6. Conductor invites participants to the practice area, makes introductory comments, pours libation, lights a candle, leads the group in practicing meditation techniques and, afterwards, leads a brief discussion on a topic related to meditation and freedom or invites participants to discuss a topic related to African American history and culture.[10]

7. Stockholder welcomes participants to enjoy a snack or meal.[11]

8. Passengers leave the station.[12]

After the session

9. Brakeman provides guidance to newcomers who request help in establishing a regular meditation practice.

10. Stationmaster meets with agent(s), conductor, stockholder, and the brakeman/woman after the session has concluded to discuss how the session went and to begin planning the next session.

Naming the Station

After your station has been operating for a while, you may want to invite your regular session participants to collaborate in selecting a name for the station. Ideally, the name will be one that inspires everyone to practice and deepen their connection to their heritage, such as *Richard Allen Station*, *Great Awakening Station*, *Harriet Tubman Station*, *54th Regiment Station*, or *Mountaintop Station*. Discussing the merits of possible station names can be an educational and fun thing to do.

Opening New Stations

If there are frequently more passengers than your home can accommodate, that could be a sign that it is time for one of the more experienced agents in your station to open a station of their own. Opening a new station will allow both stations to accommodate additional people. It will also help the Underground Railroad— the network of places to which people can come to meditate—to expand and become a way to freedom for others.

You may then choose to assist new stations that are opened by passengers who were introduced to meditation in your station. Or you may even choose to invite stationmasters of offshoot stations to assemble with their session participants for a larger meditation session. Although such a larger session would have to be carefully planned and implemented, creating a clean, peaceful, organized, kind, efficient, and uplifted environment where everyone can periodically meditate can be a great way to build a meditation community in your city or town.

Creating a Ledger

For your station, you may want to have a ledger available for first-time participants to print their names, if they desire to do so. As mentioned earlier, stationmasters of the Antebellum Period maintained a record of the men and women who entered their stations on the way to freedom. Inviting new arrivals to print their names in your ledger is simply a way for them to affirm their decision to meditate, and a way to revive an important tradition.

If you wish, you could begin your ledger with the names of some of the people who escaped from slavery. Then you could add your name and those of your fellow agents. You would then be inviting newcomers to join the long, inspiring lineage of people seeking freedom from all forms of slavery. This is also a way for them to support others who will enter the station later. As the number of names in the ledger increases, it can become a source of inspiration to all participants who see that they are part of a movement that is helping people to free their minds.

After everyone has left the station, place your ledger in a safe place. Fortunately, you do not have to bury it as William Still did, but it is a precious record nevertheless. Please don't undervalue your efforts to help your people. Your efforts to help your people are important, and the ledger—like the people whose names appear inside—is worthy of care and respect.

Being Vigilant

Although you and your fellow agents may be making great changes in your lives and want to share the benefits of meditation with others, it is worth remembering that the simple act of meditating can be very threatening to some people, especially if they have been misinformed about meditation or have a vested interest that they feel is threatened. If another person does not understand meditation or understands meditation but somehow sees what you are doing as a threat, he or she may try to persuade you to stop, obstruct your efforts, or act out in some other way. Since the agents in your station are Vigilance Committee members, they should always be mindful of the environment in which they are operating and relate to all situations with the aim of helping and not bringing harm of any kind to anyone.

Fostering Diversity

Although care should be taken when inviting people to your station, and it makes sense to invite like-minded people to meditate with you, be open to people you might otherwise dismiss because they aren't part of your usual crowd. Many enslaved people escaped to freedom with the help of people from different backgrounds. They were people of different races, with different occupations, nationalities, religious affiliations, ages, genders, income levels, sexual orientations, and so forth.

Intentionally engaging diversity by inviting people of diverse backgrounds to your session, exploring diversity issues with them, and encouraging them to engage with people from other backgrounds in their everyday lives can help everyone to let go of their biases.

Going beyond bias enables us to see that people of all backgrounds possess inherent goodness, genius, and potential. They can be kind and helpful, and can enrich our lives, and all of us can live free together as a beloved community.

31. Pilgrimaging

There was the long quarter, the quarter on the hill, the dwelling-house of my old master.... In connection with my old master's house was the kitchen where Aunt Katy presided, and where my head had received many a thump from her unfriendly hand. I looked into this kitchen with peculiar interest, and remember that it was there I last saw my mother.... The little closet in which I slept in a bag had been taken into the room; the dirt floor had disappeared under a plank. But upon the whole, the house is very much as it was in the olden time.

—Frederick Douglass,
Life and Times of Frederick Douglass
Former fugitive slave

In the 1860s, the United States was almost destroyed. Eleven Southern slaveholding states withdrew from the nation because Southerners were afraid that the newly elected US president, Abraham Lincoln, under the influence of Northern abolitionists, would abolish slavery. The Southern states created a separate nation called the Confederate States of America. The Confederate Constitution prohibited any law denying or impairing the right to own slaves.

During the civil war to reunite the United States, more than 650,000 Union and Confederate soldiers died. The war dead included more than 40,000 of the nearly 220,000 black Union soldiers and sailors. Notwithstanding the Union and Confederate dead, a far greater loss occurred among the migrating emancipated slaves. Hundreds of thousands of them died from yellow fever, smallpox, cholera, dysentery, malnutrition, and exposure because of an inadequate government response.[1]

During the war, black soldiers and sailors fought with exceptional valor, especially those who had been enslaved. Of note, two former slaves, Robert Blake and William Harvey Carney, were awarded the Congressional Medal of Honor.

After the US government approved a resolution to abolish slavery, defeated the Confederacy, readmitted the Southern states, and granted citizenship to all persons born or naturalized in the country, including former slaves, and extended the right to vote to black men—many former slaves returned to places where freedom had been longed for, fought for, and won. They returned in search of loved ones, to reminisce, and to pay respects to the men and women they had left behind.

Since many of these people are ancestors who continue to live on in your heart, you may want to pay your respects to them, too. You may want to stand in the same places they stood, walked, sat, worked, fought, wept, bled, and died, and gain insight into their lives. You may want to understand what they understood.

You may want to express your heartfelt gratitude for the sacrifices they made that have allowed you and your children to have the opportunities that exist today. You may want to let them know that you have not forgotten the crimes that made them weep. You may want to let them know that you have not forgotten the charge you received before your birth. Whatever you want to let them know, you can say it by going on a pilgrimage.

A pilgrimage is a journey to a historical site or exhibition that connects you to your history and culture. Mindfully preparing for the pilgrimage, traveling to the site, and visiting it can be a liberating thing to do. It can free your mind of its usual preoccupations and refresh and broaden your outlook. It can enlighten you as well as inspire you to carry on.

Planning and Going on the Pilgrimage

1. Find a site that is relevant to African American history or culture that you are interested in or which has heartfelt meaning for you. Here is a very small sampling of the possibilities: National Underground Railroad Freedom Center, Cincinnati, Ohio; Harriet Tubman Home and Harriet Tubman burial site in Auburn, New York; John P. Parker House in Ripley, Ohio; and the Smithsonian National Museum of African American History and Culture (opening on the National Mall in 2016) in Washington, DC. Of course, you can select sites related to any historical period. You might even find sites that have docents or guides who provide information about the people and events you will be traveling to commemorate.

   Whatever region you live in, with a little research, you will be able to find sites near you. The site can be a church, hospital, school, theater, home, monument, street corner, gallery, museum, cemetery, or field. You can get ideas from tourist bureaus, historical associations, museums, libraries, churches, family members, and friends. You will be surprised to discover the ways and places people of African ancestry have made their presence felt and contributed to your life.

2. Once you have decided where you want to go, make travel arrangements for your pilgrimage.

3. Study, contemplate, and meditate before departing:
   a. Do research on the pilgrimage site and the lives of the people associated with it.

b. Contemplate the relevance of the site to you as well as the events or people associated with it; develop a heartfelt connection to the challenges they faced and their triumphs.

c. Maintain a regular meditation practice.

4. Mindfully embark on your pilgrimage. If you travel with friends, you will certainly want to enjoy their company. However, it can be helpful to limit conversation around the site so that everyone may experience it with a mind that is fully present.

5. When you arrive at the pilgrimage site, pay attention to what's going on. Mindfully move through and around it. Appreciate its vivid qualities—the forms, smells, sounds, textures, feelings, and tastes. Imagine what the place may have been like for the people who inhabited it. Or, if your pilgrimage site is an exhibit, imagine what the items on display might have meant for the people who created, used, or were affected by them.

Relax. Be completely present in the place and with the items. Be at the same place, breathe the same air, walk on the same surfaces, feel and look at the same surfaces and objects, hear the same sounds, see the same sky or views that were experienced by your ancestors. Ask yourself: What is the relevance of this site and the people associated with it to me? What lessons can I learn? Is there something for which I need to express gratitude? What here is sacred? Allow yourself to experience whatever the site brings up in you. Sit quietly, meditate, pray, and mindfully and slowly walk through and around the site, feeling its living energy. Be completely present, open, and receptive. Tune in.

6. Before departing the site and returning home, show heart-felt gratitude by making an offering to the people who are the object of your pilgrimage. Leave something that symbolizes your intention to let go of anything to which you are bound. Your offering can be a note, a reverent bow, a cash donation, a spoken word or poem, an emotion, or a vow to use whatever insight you have gained from the pilgrimage.

7. Return home mindfully. When you get back, spend time in solitude, reflecting and meditating on your experience.

Sharing Your Pilgrimage Experience

Insights gained from your pilgrimage experience can be shared with members of your meditation group. Share what you saw, heard, tasted, felt, smelled, thought, and learned with friends and others who might appreciate hearing about it. That is what Malcolm X did when he went on his famous pilgrimage to Africa and the Middle East in 1964:

> You may be shocked by these words coming from me. But on this pilgrimage, what I have seen, and experienced, has forced me to *rearrange* much of my thought-patterns previously held, and to *toss aside* some of my previous conclusions. This was not too difficult for me. Despite my firm convictions, I have always been a man who tries to face facts, and to accept the reality of life as new experience and new knowledge unfolds it. I have always

kept an open mind, which is necessary to the flexibility that must go hand in hand with every form of intelligent search for truth.[2]

There is so much to be learned from a pilgrimage. What will you learn? How will you be affected? There is only one way to find out. Go, *now.*

GOING FORWARD

Look at your ankles and wrists, and feel your neck: There are no chains, shackles or ropes there. Run your hands over the flesh of your chest and your back; there are no welts there from branding or lacerations made by rawhide whips. Look out the window, right now, go ahead; there are no slave catchers with ropes waiting to apprehend you or yelping dogs waiting to devour you. There are no black people chained together trudging past your front door.

There is a very good likelihood that you grew up in the care of a loving mother, father, or guardian from whom you were never separated. You can go through the front door of most public places in this country and get the people there to respectfully satisfy your wants and needs. You can even board most modes of public transportation, sit down where you please, travel down most roads, and walk through most neighborhoods, without being stopped, questioned, searched, detained, or killed. No one is going to whip you if you are seen reading this book.

What about your children, nieces and nephews? They can go to school. They don't have to labor in the fields under a whip or dangerous conditions from sunrise to sunset. They are growing up in a society where there are opportunities for them to become whatever they want to be—US President, general, international diplomat, justice of the Supreme Court, chief executive officer of a big company, an astronaut, and so forth. There is nothing they can't do or become provided they have confidence in their inherent goodness, genius, and potential, and believe that their destiny is in their hands.

Our mothers, wives, sisters, and daughters—they can sleep safe and sound tonight in their beds without being sexually molested and raped by slaveholders and overseers. And black men don't have to stand by, powerless and humiliated, because they are unable to do anything to protect the members of their family.

Who were the primary actors in creating these conditions? Were they the abolitionists, the Underground Railroad agents, the Union soldiers, the politicians in the Congress, the state legislators, the US president?

The *primary* actors in our journey to freedom have always been people of African ancestry. This was true on the slave ships, on the plantations, on the slave escape routes, on the abolitionist speaker circuits, on the front lines of the Union Army, and in the halls of political power. Each of us must continue to be a primary actor today, especially in our efforts to free our minds. No one can fill this role for us.

Let's recall something *else* that Martin Luther King Jr., said: "As long as the mind is enslaved, the body can never be free."[1] Let's teach our children that.

Let us take the struggle for freedom to the next level. Let us learn to meditate. Let us go beyond a sense of limitation. Let us free our bodies *and* minds. When we do this, we will be able to overcome many of the challenges that we face.

Breath by breath, step by step, one by one, let us enter the Promised Land.

POSTSCRIPT

Harriet Tubman worked in military hospitals for a while after the war. The care that wounded black soldiers were receiving was so deplorable that she traveled to Washington, DC and complained about it to the Surgeon General of the United States Army, Joseph K. Barnes.

While in Washington, Tubman informed Secretary of State William Seward that she had not been compensated for her military service. This prompted him to ask Major General David Hunter to look into her claim. Her request for pay was denied.

Wanting to make a long overdue visit to her parents, Tubman headed to Auburn, traveling first near Philadelphia to visit the abolitionist and women's rights activist Lucretia Mott. Afterwards, she boarded a northbound train with a reduced-fare government pass.

"Come, hustle out of here! We don't carry niggers for half-fare,"[2] the conductor shouted to Tubman. When Tubman refused to rise from her seat, there was a scuffle. After choking her and twisting her arm, the conductor and three men succeeded in prying her out of the seat. "[Pitch] the nagur out!"[3] she heard as she was thrown on the floor of the adjoining baggage car.

The clash left Tubman disabled, with shoulder, arm, and hand injuries. As a result, when she arrived in Auburn, she was unable to provide for her parents and the destitute people in her home.

Frances Ellen Watkins Harper heard about the incident and mentioned it the next year at the Eleventh National Woman's Rights Convention. Harper wanted to remind attendees of the urgent need to press for equal rights for blacks and women:

> We have a woman in our country who has received the name of "Moses," not by lying about it, but by acting it out [applause].... That woman, whose courage and bravery won a recognition from our army and from every black man in the land, is excluded from every thoroughfare of travel.[4]

With the help of friends, Tubman and the members of her household were able to make it through the first winter after the war. Her own injury, however, did not keep her from organizing fairs to raise funds to help freedmen in the South. Her friends took note of her selflessness and wanted to do more to help her. They reasoned that if they published her biography, she could sell it, and that would help her make mortgage payments and pay other household expenses. Thus, a white writer, Sarah Hopkins Bradford, began interviewing Tubman and writing her biography. In 1869, *Scenes in the Life of Harriet Tubman* was published. Twelve hundred copies of the book were quickly sold.

Since by this time, Tubman's first husband, John, had died, she married Charles Nelson Davis. Davis was a former slave who had been a Union soldier during the Civil War. He farmed the couple's property, and worked in their orchard, and in his brickyard. But most of the time, since he was ill, Tubman was the household's primary source of income. She hired herself out as a maid and a cook, grew and sold fruit and vegetables, raised and sold chickens and pigs, and made and sold crafts such as baskets.

In the early 1870s Tubman experienced several setbacks. In 1871, her father, Benjamin Ross, died. The next year, her benefactor, former US Secretary of State William H. Seward, died. Then, in 1873, Tubman got caught up in a gold swindle. It ended with her being tied up and left in the woods. Rather than close her heart to helping others, she continued to help where she could. Thus, the following year, she and Davis adopted an orphaned infant, Gertie, whom they would raise to adulthood.

Around this time, Tubman became a regular attendee of the AME Zion Church, in Auburn. A visitor from South Carolina who attended one of the church services recalled:

> At the close of a thrilling selection she arose and commenced to speak in a hesitating voice....In a shrill voice, she commenced to give testimony to God's goodness and long suffering. Soon she was shouting, and so were others also. She possessed such endurance, vitality, and magnetism that I inquired and was informed it was Harriet Tubman—the "Underground Railroad Moses."[5]

Later, Tubman was beset with more troubles. In 1880, her mother, Harriet "Rit" Green, died. In the same year, forty pigs she had been raising to support her household died from poisoning. Then in, 1883, her wood frame house burned down. Although her husband helped to build a new brick home in 1884, afterward he became gravely ill with tuberculosis. Even Tubman became ill with respiratory problems, chronic headaches, and seizures.

Being in need of income to support her household and the indigents who regularly came to her front door for help, Tubman may have asked Sarah H. Bradford to reissue her biography. Bradford added material to the book and, in 1886, published *Harriet, the Moses of Her People*. Two years later, Davis died.

During her illness and misfortune, Tubman probably gave more thought to the well-being of others than she did to her own needs. After all, the political and economic gains made by African Americans following the civil war had been reversed.

US enforcement of blacks' civil rights had been halted in the South. White supremacists had regained control of Southern state and local governments. Jim Crow laws were being created to deprive blacks of the right to vote and force them into hard labor as sharecroppers and prisoners.

The constitutionality of racial segregation in public facilities had been upheld by state courts. And lynching had emerged as an American pastime as black men, women, and children were hung from trees, light posts and bridges, often at white community gatherings. Many others disappeared to hidden graves and the bottoms of rivers, never to be found, after being falsely accused of raping white women, failing to pay small debts, standing up for their rights, "sassing" white people, and "acting smart." This includes those who lost their lives because their white assailants were "afraid" or "uncomfortable."

Tubman had very good reasons to think about the well-being of others. Notions of white superiority/black inferiority were metastasizing like a cancer, spreading to government, law, business, religion, education, science, medicine, literature, art, music, and the hearts and minds of white people throughout the country. Whites in American society were continuing to "feast"—to borrow an expression used by Frederick Douglass—on the lives of African Americans, even though slavery had been abolished and they had been granted US citizenship and equal rights.

Postscript

In this environment, Tubman kept her house filled with the most vulnerable people in America—elderly, indigent, disabled, orphaned African Americans in need of shelter, a meal, medical care, and unconditional kindness.

In June 1896, one month after the US Supreme Court decided, in *Plessey vs. Ferguson*, that it was constitutional for states to require racial segregation in public facilities, Tubman bid on a twenty-five acre parcel of land adjacent to her property on which there was a brick building. She envisioned converting the building into "John Brown Hall," a dormitory and infirmary for impoverished sick, disabled, and elderly African Americans.

Tubman explained how the property was acquired:

> There was [all] white folks but me there...and there I was like a black berry in a pail of milk, but I was hid down in a corner, and no one knew who was bidding. The man began pretty low, and I kept going up by fifties; he got up to twelve hundred, thirteen hundred, fourteen hundred, and still that voice in the corner kept going up by fifties. At last, I got up to fourteen hundred and fifty, and then others stopped bidding, and the man said, "All done! Who is the buyer?" "Harriet Tubman," I shouted. "What! That old nigger?" they said. "Old woman, how [are] you going to pay for that lot of land?" "I'm going to tell the Lord Jesus all about it," I said.[6]

Tubman told everyone about the property because she needed them to contribute money for the mortgage and the renovation of the brick building for use as John Brown Hall.

She began to fundraise again. One outcome of the fundraising campaign is that it revived her national reputation. She began receiving invitations to attend women's rights gatherings in cities all across the North. Of course, she used these occasions to raise funds for John Brown Hall.

In July 1896, she attended a National League of Colored Women gathering in Washington as the featured speaker. She was introduced as "Mother Tubman." In connection with the event, the editors of the *Woman's Era*, an African American woman's newspaper, called her an "unsung 'Black Joan of Arc.'"

> Mrs. Tubman stood alone on the front of the rostrum, the audience, which not only filled every seat, but also much of the standing room in the aisles, rose as one person and greeted her with the waving of handkerchiefs and the clapping of hands. This was kept up for at least a minute, and Mrs. Tubman was much affected by the hearty reception given her. When the applause had somewhat subsided, Mrs. Tubman acknowledged the compliment paid her in appropriate words, and at the request of some leading officers of the Convention related a little of her war experience. Despite the weight of advancing years, Mrs. Tubman is the possessor of a strong and musical voice, which last evening penetrated every portion of the large auditorium in which the Convention was held....[7]

A few months later, Susan B. Anthony, the white women's rights and suffrage activist, led Tubman to the podium of the predominantly white New York State Women's Suffrage Association

Meeting in Rochester and introduced her as the "great Black Liberator." "Yes, ladies," Tubman said to those gathered, many of whom were of the view that black women needed to be pushed out of the suffrage movement in order for women's suffrage to prevail. "I was the conductor of the Underground Railroad for eight years, and I can say what most conductors can't say—I never run my train off the track," and she added, "and I never lost a passenger."[8] When asked whether she believed women should vote, her response was, "I suffered enough to believe it."[9]

Undoubtedly, Tubman was invited to these gatherings because she was an inspirational figure. She was living proof that disadvantaged and oppressed people—men and women—regardless of their circumstances, can triumph over adversity and oppression. She understood the reasons for the invitations, so she allowed herself to be used. She knew that we often need others to inspire and help us.

Bradford wrote, "Harriet's charity for all the human race is unbounded."[10] Indeed it was. But she had a special interest in the welfare of African Americans. Thus, in 1897, when the Queen of England invited Tubman to attend her Golden Jubilee Celebration, she declined the invitation. She kept her attention focused on helping African Americans in Auburn.

Although Tubman wanted to bring her vision for John Brown Hall into reality, she realized that she could not do it alone. She needed help. Therefore, she offered to donate the land and John Brown Hall to AME Zion Church on the condition that it use the property to help Auburn's impoverished, homeless, sick, disabled, and elderly African American residents.

While the church was considering her proposal, Tubman continued fundraising at suffrage and temperance gatherings all across the North, from Chicago to New York City and Washington to Boston. Almost imperceptibly, friends who were helping her raise funds ceased referring to the project as John Brown Hall. They began calling it simply "Harriet Tubman Home."

Although Tubman was traveling and fundraising, she did not possess any personal wealth. The only thing she had to her name was the mortgaged land that she was trying to bequeath to Auburn's black community, a mortgaged house, and a tiny widower's pension from the military. What little she had she gave away to people who needed it. Thus, when Bradford visited her home in 1900 and found her living in poverty, she was appalled. To generate income for Tubman's personal support, Bradford added more material to *Harriet, the Moses of Her People*, and, in 1901, reissued the book.

Two years later, Tubman turned over the deed to her property to the AME Zion Church. The church took over fundraising for the mortgage and property taxes, but the church officers abandoned Tubman's plan to renovate the brick building and, instead, they drew up plans for the construction of a more suitable wood frame facility, and began overseeing its construction.

Tubman continued to receive invitations to help various social and charitable causes. In 1905, she arrived in Boston to attend a fundraising reception in her honor that had been organized by the Women's Christian Temperance Union. A reporter wrote,

> During the evening this rare old woman told extremely interesting reminiscences of the exciting events in which she participated. For a woman of so great age she is remarkably erect, her voice is clear, her manner bright, and her wit keen....She arrived in town yesterday morning from Auburn, N.Y., and told her friends she guessed it would be the last time she would be up this way.[11]

At the time, Tubman was one of the few noteworthy anti-slavery activists still alive. Susan B. Anthony, Henry Bibb, Henry "Box" Brown, William Wells Brown, Mary Ann Shadd Cary, Frederick Douglass, Mary and Emily Edmonson, Henry Highland Garnet, Thomas Garrett, William Lloyd Garrison, Sarah and Angelina Grimké, Josiah Henson, Harriet Jacobs, Lucretia Coffin Mott, John P. Parker, Robert Purvis, Sarah Parker Remond, Wendell Phillips, William H. Seward, Gerrit Smith, Elizabeth Cady Stanton, Harriet Beecher Stowe, Sojourner Truth, and Jonathan Walker were among the notable abolitionists resting in their graves. But, in 1907, when a newspaperman from the *New York Herald* arrived in Auburn to interview Tubman, he was surprised to find that "after 80 years of service to her people and to the cause of justice, she is closing her life in poverty."[12]

In 1908, the Harriet Tubman Home for Aged and Infirm Negroes was officially dedicated. The dedication ceremony was attended by several hundred members of Auburn's black community. Many of those assembled had been beneficiaries of her many years of social work and charity. Tubman told the gathering:

> I did not take up this work for my own benefit, but for those of my race who need help. The work is now well started and I know God will raise up others to take care of the future. All I ask is united effort, for "united we stand, divided we fall."[13]

Tubman was nearly ninety. She withdrew from involvement in the management of the home. But she soon had a falling out with the church over the Home's admission policies:

[W]hen I give the home over to Zion Church what you suppose they done? Why, they make a rule that nobody should come in without they have a hundred dollars. Now I wanted to make a rule that nobody should come in unless they didn't have no money at all.[14]

Tubman's health was declining, and she didn't have any money at all. In 1911, the great heroine of the age was admitted to Harriet Tubman Home. Her vigor continued to fade. As death drew near, she summoned her caregivers to her bedside. They sang songs, and she bestowed on them her blessings. Then, on March 10, 1913, around 8:30 p.m., like a conductor slipping away into the night, she passed away.

Several hundred members of Auburn's black community gathered at Harriet Tubman Home on March 13th, where Tubman's body lay in state. Later her casket was removed to the Thompson Memorial AME Zion Church, where it lay open, draped with the American flag, surrounded by floral arrangements. Many of the more than 1,000 people who attended the church service followed Tubman's flag-draped casket to Fort Hill Cemetery, where her body was interred.

Immediately after the funeral, the City of Auburn did something that had never been done in the United States; it commissioned a memorial plaque for a woman who had been enslaved, Tubman. The plaque was ready for installation at the city's courthouse the following June. On that occasion, US flags were flown from municipal buildings and homes throughout the city, as the great African American educator Booker T. Washington arrived and addressed an overflow crowd as the event's principal speaker. In his remarks, he noted:

In the ten millions of black people scattered throughout this country, there are many great souls, heroic souls, that the white race does not know about. Harriet Tubman brought these two races nearer together and made it possible for the white race to know the black race and to place a different estimate upon it.[15]

After Washington's comments, the Harriet Tubman Memorial Plaque was unveiled, and the Mayor of Auburn, Charles W. Brister, proudly stepped forward to accept it on behalf of a grateful city:

In accepting this tablet we reaffirm in a public way our belief that in the fullness of time character shall be measured by its true standards irrespective of its origins or its surroundings....Measured by such a standard, the woman whose memory is today honored and perpetuated must be ranked with the great characters of history....Not because the subject of this memorial was a woman, nor because she was black, is this tribute tendered, but rather to commemorate the inherent greatness of her character.[16]

Although Harriet Tubman has entered the pantheon of our heroes and heroines of the past, she returns to us through inspirational stories about her life in books, film, theater, music, and art. She does just what she did as a conductor: She returns again and again to inspire those who are shackled and bound—even by thoughts—to let go, steal away, leave what enslaves you behind, and come away to freedom.

Harriet Tubman
*Source: Collection of the Smithsonian National Museum
of African American History and Culture,
Gift of Charles L. Blockson*

FURTHER READINGS
FOR EXPLORATION AND
INSPIRATION

Adiele, Faith. *Meeting Faith: The Forest Journals of a Black Buddhist Nun*. New York: W. W. Norton & Company, 2004.

Akbar, Na'im. *Community of Self*. Tallahassee, FL: Mind Productions, 1991.

Alston, Robbin. *The Art of Feeling Good: The Power of Ase Yoga*. Bloomingdale, IN: iUniverse, 2012.

Arewa, Caroline Shola. *Opening to the Spirit: Contacting the Healing Power of the Chakras & Honoring African Spirituality*. London: Thorsons, 1998.

Ashby, Muata and Karen "Dja" Ashby. *Egyptian Yoga: Postures of the Gods and Goddesses*. Miami, FL: Cruzian Mystic Books, 2005.

Baldoquin, Hilda Gutierrez, ed. *Dharma, Color, and Culture: New Voices in Western Buddhism*. Berkeley, CA: Parallax Press, 2004.

Bynum, Edward. *The African Unconscious*. New York: Teachers College Press, 1999.

Chodron, Pema, and Alice Walker. *Pema Chodron and Alice Walker in Conversation: On the Meaning of Suffering and the Mystery of Joy*. Louisville, CO: Sounds True, Inc., 2005.

DeGruy, Joy. *Post Traumatic Slave Syndrome: America's Legacy of Enduring Injury and Healing.* Portland, OR: Joy DeGruy Publications, 2005.

Devi-Doolin, Daya. *Yoga Meditation and Spiritual Growth for the African American Community: If You Can Breathe You Can Do Yoga and Find Inner and Outer Peace.* Padaran Publications, Phoenix, AZ: Amber Communications Group, Inc., 2014.

Doumbia, Adama and Naomi Doumbia. *The Way of the Elders: West African Spirituality & Tradition.* Saint Paul, MI: Llewellyn Publications, 2004.

Frederick Douglass Family Initiatives (FDFI). Accessed October 28, 2014. http://www.fdfi.org/aboutus.html

Ferguson, Gaylon. *Natural Wakefulness: Discovering the Wisdom We Were Born With.* Boston: Shambhala, 2009.

Grant, Robert. *The Way of the Wound: A Spirituality of Trauma and Transformation.* Oakland, CA: Robert Grant, 1996.

Hanh, Thich Nhat. *Together We Are One: Honoring Our Diversity, Celebrating Our Connection.* Parallax Press, 2010.

Holmes, Barbara A. *Joy Unspeakable: Contemplative Practices of the Black Church.* Minneapolis, MN: Fortress Press, 2004.

Horne, David L. "SRDC Practicing MA'AT in Organizing the African Diaspora." *Sixth Region Diaspora Caucus.* Accessed June 18, 2015. http://srdcinternational.org/?p=2372.

Jacq, Christian. *The Wisdom of Ptah-Hotep: Spiritual Treasures From the Age of the Pyramids.* London: Constable & Robinson Ltd., 2006.

Johnson, Charles. *Taming the Ox: Buddhist Stories and Reflections on Politics, Race, Culture, and Spiritual Practice.* Boston: Shambhala Publications, 2014.

Kabat-Zinn, Jon. *Full Catastrophe Living: Using the Wisdom of Your Body and Mind to Face Stress, Pain, and Illness.* New York: Dell Publishing, 1990.

Khandro Rinpoche. *This Precious Life: Tibetan Buddhist Teachings on the Path to Enlightenment.* Boston, MA: Shambhala, 2005.

Kiau, Kimbwandelende Kia Bunseki. *Self-Healing Power and Therapy: Old Teachings From Africa.* New York: Vantage Press, 1991.

Lozoff, Bo. *We're All Doing Time: A Guide to Getting Free.* Durham, NC: Human Kindness Foundation, 2001.

Masters, Jarvis. *Finding Freedom: Writings from Death Row.* Junction City, CA: Padma Publishing, 1997.

Mipham, Sakyong. *Turning the Mind into an Ally.* New York: Riverhead Books, 2003.

Mumford, George. *The Mindful Athlete: Secrets to Pure Performance.* Berkeley, CA: Parallax Press, 2015.

Rangdrol, Lama Choyin. *Traitors, Converts, and Heathens.* Oakland: RainbowDharma, 2007.

Reininger, Gustave, ed. *The Diversity of Centering Prayer.* New York: Continuum Publishing Company, 1999.

Simmons, Russell, and Chris Morrow. *Success Through Stillness: Meditation Made Simple.* New York: Gotham Books, 2014.

Tolle, Eckhart. *The Power of Now: A Guide to Spiritual Enlightenment.* Novato, CA: New World Library, 1999.

Williams, Angel Kyodo. *Being Black: Zen and the Art of Living with Fearlessness and Grace.* New York: Viking Press, 2000.

Willis, Jan. *Dreaming Me: An African American Woman's Spiritual Journey.* New York: Riverhead Books, 2001.

ACKNOWLEDGMENTS

I want to express heartfelt gratitude to my parents, and to the many teachers and guides I have met throughout my life. This includes the teachers and students in the Mindrolling Lotus Garden and Shambhala communities. I especially wish to thank those individuals who offered suggestions during the early phase of writing. This guidebook would not have been possible without their kindness.

I also want to thank my brothers, sister, children and their families as well as other relatives and friends for providing encouragement, serving as models, and contributing financially to this project. In particular, I thank my daughters—Andrea for early advice that has influenced the overall development of this guidebook, Krishnia for repeatedly asking me about the status of the book, which helped me to complete it, and Tamara for splendid model photography. I am deeply grateful to all of them for their generosity.

I wish to thank Zaire Oglesby and Donte Watts for reading the manuscript at different stages in the writing process and offering feedback. I also wish to thank G. Francis Johnson for reading, offering feedback, and suggesting the book title. Special thanks to Carolyn G. Francis for proofreading the final manuscript. I am deeply grateful to all of these wonderful people for their help and advice.

Finally I wish to thank Linda Gail Francis for her invaluable contributions. In no small way, it is because of her patience, kindness, encouragement, and editing of the manuscript that *Free Your Mind* is now available.

NOTES

Note: Throughout *Free Your Mind,* I have normalized the dialect used by previous authors when quoting Harriet Tubman and other former slaves. –C.R.

Preface
1   William Wells Brown, *Clotel: Or, The President's Daughter,* Chapter XIX.
2   James M. Washington, ed., *A Testament of Hope: The Essential Writings and Speeches of Martin Luther King, Jr.* (New York: HarperSanFrancisco, 1991), 246.

Introduction
1   Rakesh Kochhar and Richard Fry, "Wealth inequality has widened along racial, ethnic lines since end of Great Recession," *Pew Research Center* (2014).
2   Tami Luhby, "5 disturbing stats on black-white inequality," *The Real Economy* (August 21, 2014).
3   Todd Minton and Daniela Golinelli, "Jail Inmates at Midyear 2013—Statistical Tables (Revised)," *Bureau of Justice Statistics* (May 2014), 7.
4   Michael Lipka, "Many US congregations are still racially segregated, but things are changing," *Pew Research Center* (December 8, 2014).

5   Lynn Sweet, "Obama's NAACP Speech Transcript," *Chicago Sun-Times* (New York, July 17, 2009).

6   Angela Davis Quotes," Goodreads.com.

7   James M. Washington, ed., *A Testament of Hope*, 246.

8   "Marcus Garvey Quotes," Afieldnegro.com.

9   Matt Rossano, "Did Meditating Make Us Human?", 47–58.

TERMINAL: Dorchester County, Maryland

1   Earl Conrad, *Harriet Tubman* (Washington, DC: Associated Publishers, 1943), 3.

2   Sarah H. Bradford, *Scenes in the Life of Harriet Tubman* (1869) (Auburn, NY: General Books, 2009), 7.

1. Being

1   Joslyn Pine, *Book of African-American Quotations* (Mineola, NY: Dover Publications, Inc., 2011), 169.

2. Calming

1   In meditation, there are different sitting postures that you can use, none of which is "better" or "worse" than the others: sitting in a chair, kneeling with the help of a bench, or sitting cross-legged on cushions or the floor. The cross-legged posture known as the lotus posture shown on the cover of this guidebook can be challenging to assume and maintain. I do not recommend it for meditation beginners. However, you can find a wealth of information about this posture and others, as well as meditation benches and cushions, online.

2   Philip Galanes, "For Arianna Huffington and Kobe Bryant: First Success. Then Sleep," *New York Times*, September 26, 2014. http://www.nytimes.com/2014/09/28/fashion/arianna-huffington-kobe-bryant-meditate.html?_r=0.

3. Developing

1 Pine, *Book of African-American Quotations*, 44.

2 Pine, *Book of African-American Quotations*, 103.

3 Nelson Mandela, *Conversations with Myself* (New York: Farrar, Straus, and Giroux, 2010), viii.

TERMINAL: Wilmington, Delaware

1 Bradford, *Scenes in the Life of Harriet Tubman*, 9.

2 Fergus M. Bordewich, *Bound for Canaan* (New York: Harper Collins), 347.

3 James A. McGowan, *Station Master on the Underground Railroad: The Life and Letters of Thomas Garrett* (Moylan, PA: The Whimsie Press, 1977), 65.

4 Bradford, *Scenes in the Life of Harriet Tubman*, 21.

4. Breathing

1 "Frederick Douglass' *North Star*," *Western Literary Messenger*, (March 28, 1848).

2 Center for MultiCultural Health, "African Americans and Tobacco," 3.

5. Thinking

1 "Charles Barkley Quotes," Goodreads.com.

TERMINAL: Philadelphia, Pennsylvania

1 Bradford, *Scenes in the Life of Harriet Tubman*, 9.

2 Bradford, *Scenes in the Life of Harriet Tubman*, 9.

3 Milton C. Sernett, *Harriet Tubman: Myth, Memory, and History* (Durham, NC: Duke University Press), 42.

4 William Still, *Underground Railroad* (Oxford: Benediction Classics, 2008), 295.

5   McGowan, *Station Master on the Underground Railroad*, 95.

6   Bradford, *Scenes in the Life of Harriet Tubman*, 11.

7   Still, *Underground Railroad*, 295.

8   Still, *Underground Railroad*, 79-80.

9   "William Still Dead," *New York Times* (July 15, 1902).

6. Reading

1   Frederick Douglass, *My Bondage and My Freedom* (1855) (New York: Penguin Group, 2003), 201.

2   Pine, *Book of African-American Quotations*, 44.

3   Pine, *Book of African-American Quotations*, 131.

4   Sweet, "Obama's NAACP Speech Transcript," July 17, 2009.

5   Bob Blaisdell, *Selected Writings and Speeches of Marcus Garvey* (Mineola, NY: Dover Publications, 2004). iv.

7. Awakening

1   US Census Bureau, *Population of the United States in 1860* (Washington, DC: Government Printing Office, 1864), xii.

2   David Walker, *Walker's Appeal* (Atlanta, GA: Two Horizons Press, 2012), 57.

3   Bradford, *Scenes in the Life of Harriet Tubman*, 10.

TERMINAL: New York, New York

1   Bradford, *Scenes in the Life of Harriet Tubman*, 12.

2   Sarah H. Bradford, *Harriet: The Moses of Her People* (1886) (Bedford: Applewood Books, 1993), 8.

3   Bradford, *Scenes in the Life of Harriet Tubman*, 23.

4   Jean M. Humez, *Harriet Tubman: The Life and the Life Stories*, (Madison, WI: University of Wisconsin Press, 2003), 24.

5   Frances Smith Foster, ed., *A Brighter Coming Day: A Frances Ellen Watkins Harper Reader* (New York, NY: The Feminist Press at the City University of New York, 1990), 101.

8. Walking

1   Larry Gara, *The Liberty Line: The Legend of the Underground Railroad* (Lexington, KY: University of Kentucky Press, 1996), 47-48.

2   William W. Brown, *Narrative of William W. Brown, a Fugitive Slave* (1848), Reprinted in Barnes and Noble Classics. *The Great Escapes: Four Narratives* (New York: Barnes and Noble, 2007), 55-56.

3   James Weldon Johnson, *"Lift Every Voice and Sing"* (Wikipedia, 2014).

9. Exercising

1   Bradford, *Harriet: The Moses of Her People*, 73-74.

2   Solomon Northup, *Twelve Years a Slave*, edited by Henry Louis Gates, Jr. (New York: Penguin, 2012), 92.

3   Bibb, *Narrative of the Life and Adventures of Henry Bibb, An American Slave*, 42-43.

4   "Recollections of Slavery by a Runaway Slave," *The Emancipator,* August 23, 1838. From the Advocate of Freedom, http://docsouth.unc.edu/neh/runaway/runaway.html.

5   "Babacar Khane" (Wikipedia, 2013).

6   Ashby, Muata and Karen "Dja" Ashby. *Egyptian Yoga: Postures of the Gods and Goddesses*. Miami, FL: Cruzian Mystic Books, 2005, 20.

TERMINAL: Albany, New York

1   Bradford, *Scenes in the Life of Harriet Tubman*, 22.
2   Bradford, *Scenes in the Life of Harriet Tubman*, 12.
3   Bradford, *Scenes in the Life of Harriet Tubman*, 13.

10. Paying Attention

1   Samuel H. Williamson and Lewis P. Cain, "Measuring Slavery in 2011," *Measuring Worth* (2013).
2   James Daley, *Great Speeches by African Americans: Frederick Douglass, Sojourner Truth, Dr. Martin Luther King, Jr., Barack Obama, and Others* (Mineola, NY: Dover Publications, 2006), 10.
3   Michael Wayne, "The Black Population of Canada West on the Eve of the American Civil War: A Reassessment Based on the Manuscript Census of 1861," *Histoire sociale / Social History*, 465–488.
4   Wayne, "The Black Population of Canada West," 465–488.
5   Frederick Douglass, *Life and Times of Frederick Douglass* (1892) (Mineola, NY: Dover Publications, Inc., 2003), 201.
6   Pine, *Book of African-American Quotations*, 28.
7   "Oprah Winfrey Quotes," Goodreads.com.

11. Contemplating

1   John Marks, "Abdication and Acceptance: Slave-Trading in Antebellum Lynchburg" (2007), 5.
2   Williams, *Sunshine and Shadow of Slave Life: Reminiscences as told by Isaac D. Williams to "Tege,"* 59.
3   John P. Parker, *His Promised Land: The Autobiography of John P. Parker, Former Slave and Conductor of the Underground Railroad* (New York: W. W. Norton & Company, 1996), 39–40.
4   Iyanla Vanzant, *Acts of Faith: Daily Meditations for People of Color* (New York: Simon & Schuster, 1993), 1.

TERMINAL: Syracuse, New York

1   Sernett, *North Star Country*, 178.
2   Daley, *Great Speeches by African Americans*, 10.
3   Bradford, *Scenes in the Life of Harriet Tubman*, 40-41.
4   Bradford, *Scenes in the Life of Harriet Tubman*, 21.

12. Overcoming

1   Bradford, *Scenes in the Life of Harriet Tubman*, 11.

13. Practicing

1   If you decide to create a meditation shrine, you can even use photos of inspirational people you regard as worthy of honor, such as your parents, elders, or even ancestors, like Harriet Tubman and Frederick Douglass. The point is not to worship these people, but to draw inspiration from them, who they were, and what they were able to do with their lives.

   In this regard, it's often helpful to place a reminder of your parents on your shrine. Regardless of whether they were "perfect" or not (they usually are not), regardless of whether they overcame the legacy of slavery or succumbed to it (we all have succumbed at one time or another), *they* are how you got here. They are your link to your past and the key to your future.

   When you honor your parents, you are not just honoring them; you are also honoring all ten thousand generations of your family. These are people who used their mind to survive. Many of them used it to survive slavery, Jim Crow, contemporary racism, and as a result you are here reading this guidebook. You are their beneficiary. When you honor your parents, you are also honoring yourself. After all, you *are* them. And they *are* you. You may not always like it, but you and they *are* inseparable.

Since we are inseparable from our ancestors, they are always present in us. Like us, they possess inherent dignity. They possess unlimited inherent goodness, genius and potential, whether their lives have shown that or not. Moreover, they can help us to become even stronger and wiser than they were (or are). That's one of the effects that Barack Obama, Sr. had on his son. When he grew up, Barack Obama, Jr. resolved to become a better husband, parent, and public servant than his father ever was.

2   Malcolm X, *Autobiography of Malcolm X*, 450.

TERMINAL: Auburn, New York

1   Humez, *Harriet Tubman: The Life and Life Stories*, 134.
2   Benjamin Quarles, *Black Abolitionists* (New York: Da Capo Press, 1969), 63.
3   For more on the Pearl Incident, see Mary Kay Ricks, *Escape on the Pearl: The Historic Bid for Freedom on the Underground Railroad* (New York: Harper, Perennial, 2007).
4   Shirley Yee, *Black Woman Abolitionists: A Study in Activism, 1828-1860* (Knoxville, TN: The University of Tennessee Press, 1992), 21.
5   Sernett, *Harriet Tubman, Myth, Memory, and History*, 50.
6   Humez, *Harriet Tubman, The Life and Life Stories*, 38.

14. Bravery

1   Frederick Douglass, *Narrative of the Life of Frederick Douglass, an American Slave* (1845) (New York: Barnes & Noble, 2003), 77-78.
2   Frederick Douglass, *Life and Times of Frederick Douglass: His Early Life as a Slave, His Escape from Bondage, and His Complete History* (1892) (New York: Gramercy Books, 1992), 106.

15. Creating

1   Recollections of Slavery by a Runaway Slave," *The Emancipator*, October 11, 1838.
2   Northup, *Twelve Years a Slave*, p. 72-73.
3   Lawrence W. Levine, *Black Culture and Black Consciousness* (Oxford, NY: Oxford University Press, 2007), 14.
4   Pine, *Book of African-American Quotations*, 21.
5   Pine, *Book of African-American Quotations*, 106.

16. Developing Helpful Mindsets and Habits

1   Pine, *Book of African-American Quotations*, 5.
2   For more on the role played by the black community during the abolitionist movement, read Benjamin Quarles, *Black Abolitionists* (New York: Da Capo Press, 1969).
3   Howard Thurman, "The Sound of the Genuine," Baccalaureate Address, Spelman College, Atlanta, May 4, 1980.

17. Affecting Life

1   The Compromise of 1787, among other things, guaranteed the right to own slaves, and gave the states the right to count a slave as three-fifths of a person in determining political representation in the House of Representatives.
2   The Compromise of 1793 protected slaveholding rights and authorized slave owners and slave hunters to go across state lines to apprehend and return to bondage any black person suspected of being a slave.
3   The Compromise of 1820 permitted slavery to expand into the North, with the admission of Missouri to the Union as a slave state, and into the West, with the extension of the Mason-Dixon Line at 36°30′ north latitude, which essentially divided the country into free and slave states.

4 The Compromise of 1850 ended the domestic slave trade in Washington, DC (not the institution of slavery), established special judicial commissions to hear cases regarding fugitive slaves, required law enforcement officials and citizens to assist in the recapture and return of alleged slaves, prohibited persons accused of being slaves from giving testimony or evidence at judicial hearings on their status, and imposed severe fines and prison terms on anyone found aiding runaway slaves.

5 The Compromise of 1854 allowed further expansion of slavery in the North, above the Mason-Dixon Line, by allowing the residents of the newly organized Kansas and Nebraska Territories to decide by "popular sovereignty" whether slavery would be permitted.

6 The Dred Scott Decision of 1857 affirmed that people of African ancestry were beings of "an inferior order" and had "no rights which the white man was bound to respect."

7 Washington, ed., *A Testament of Hope*, 254.

8 Pine, *Book of African-American Quotations*, 40.

9 Washington, *A Testament of Hope*, 246.

10 "Tupac Shakur Quotes," Goodreads.com.

TERMINAL: Rochester, New York

1 Bradford, *Scenes in the Life of Harriet Tubman*, 10.

2 Bradford, *Harriet: The Moses of Her People*, 11.

3 Bradford, *Harriet: The Moses of Her People*, 76.

4 Bradford, *Harriet: The Moses of Her People*, 5.

5 Bradford, *Scenes in the Life of Harriet Tubman*, 41.

6 Bradford, *Scenes in the Life of Harriet Tubman*, 10.

7 Beverly Lowry, *Harriet Tubman: Imagining a Life* (New York: Anchor Books, 2007), 193.

8   Douglass, *The Life and Times of Frederick Douglass*, 190.
9   Forner, *Life and Writings of Frederick Douglass*, 280.

18. Forgiving

1   Josiah Henson, *Truth Stranger Than Fiction: Father Henson's Story of His Own Life* (New York: Barnes & Noble, 2008), 43.
2   Bradford, *Scenes in the Life of Harriet Tubman*, 7.
3   Conrad, *Harriet Tubman*, 10.
4   Douglass, *Life and Times of Frederick Douglass*, 321-322.
5   Desmond Mpilo Tutu, *No Future Without Forgiveness* (New York: Doubleday, 1999), 282.

20. Helping

1   Henson, *Truth Stranger Than Fiction*, 59.
2   Brown, *Narrative of William W. Brown*, 57.
3   Douglass, *Narrative of the Life of Frederick Douglass*, 93.
4   Bradford, *Scenes in the Life of Harriet Tubman*, 9.
5   Booker T. Washington, *Up From Slavery, An Autobiography* (New York: Barnes and Noble, 2003), 146.
6   Bradford, *Harriet: The Moses of Her People*, 89-90.

TERMINAL: Buffalo, New York

1   Brown, *Narrative of William Wells Brown*, Chapter XII.
2   Frederick Douglass, "West India Emancipation Speech" (New York, August 3, 1857).
3   Bradford, *Scenes in the Life of Harriet Tubman*, 38-39.
4   Kate Clifford Larson, *Bound for the Promised Land: Harriet Tubman, Portrait of an American Hero* (New York: One World, 2004), 54.

21. Dressing

1   Pine, *Book of African-American Quotations*, 43.

22. Affirming

1   Bradford, *Harriet: The Moses of Her People*, 92.

2   Bradford, *Harriet: The Moses of Her People*, 92.

3   Bradford, *Harriet: The Moses of Her People*, 93.

4   Ben Carson, Twitter post, May 17, 2011.

5   Shawn Weston, "Thoughts from an Art Director: The Muhammad Ali Guide to Being #1" (June 29, 2013).

6   Weston, "Thoughts from an Art Director," June 29, 2013.

7   Weston, "Thoughts from an Art Director," June 29, 2013.

8   "Barack Obama's New Hampshire Primary Speech," *New York Times* (June 28, 2013).

9   Malcolm X, *The Autobiography of Malcolm X*, 450.

23. Imagining

1   Bradford, *Scenes in the Life of Harriet Tubman*, 7–8.

2   Carter Woodson, *The Mis-Education of the Negro* (Chicago: African American Images, 2000), 84-85.

3   Na'im Akbar, *Chains and Images of Psychological Slavery* (Tallahassee, FL: New Mind Productions, 1984), 39–40.

4   Ivory A. Toldson, "What Black High School Grads Need to Hear," *The Root* (May 21, 2013).

5   Here are 100 notable people of African ancestry: Dorothy Height, Asa Philip Randolph, Patricia Bath, Lorraine Hansberry, Arthur Mitchell, Sophia Packard, Wangari Muta Maathai, Harriet Giles, Benjamin Banneker, Rosa Parks, Richard Allen, Marian Anderson, B. B. King, Ella Baker, Jill E. Brown-Hiltz, Maria Stewart, David Walker, William Grant Still, Althea Gibson, Nat King Cole, Frances Ellen Watkins Harper, Mary

Ann Shadd Cary, Nat Turner, Ella Fitzgerald, Martin R. Delaney, Mahalia Jackson, Alice Coachman, James Cleveland, Sarah E. Goode, Booker T. Washington, W.E.B. Dubois, Marcus Garvey, Guion Bluford, Ann Nixon Cooper, Alain L. Locke, Carter G. Woodson, Tupac Shakur, Medgar Evers, Sadie Tanner Mossell, Malcolm X, Hattie McDaniel, Maya Angelou, George Washington Carver, Charles R. Drew, Phillis Wheatley, Gordon Parks, Zora Neale Hurston, Martin Luther King, Jr., Rebecca Lee Crumpler, Ralph J. Bunche, Jessie Redmon Fauset, Bayard Rustin, Gwendolyn Brooks, James Baldwin, Robert Hayden, Fannie Lou Hamer, William H. Carney, Benjamin O. Davis, Sr., Langston Hughes, Sadie Tanner Mossell Alexander, Ralph Ellison, Alex Haley, Matthew A. Henson, Shirley Chisholm, Mamie Till-Bradley, Joseph H. Rainey, Barbara Jordan, Adam Clayton Powell, George W. Gibbs, Jr., Nannie Helen Burroughs, Charles Hamilton Houston, Sojourner Truth, Thurgood Marshall, Jesse Owens, Patricia Harris, P.B.S. Pinchback, Willie T. Barrow, Jackie Robinson, Arthur Ashe, Ida B. Wells-Barnett, Jack Johnson, Wilt Chamberlain, Bessie Coleman, Paul Laurence Dunbar, Ruth Simmons, Madame C. J. Walker, Count Basie, Duke Ellington, Wilma Rudolph, Mary McLeod Bethune, John H. Johnson, Reginald F. Lewis, Pearl Bailey, Alvin Ailey, Josephine Baker, Sammy Davis, Jr., Mary Church Terrell, Daisy Bates, your mother, and your father. However, you may want to do your own research and select notable people of African ancestry who inspire you. Read their biographies and about their struggles and triumphs. Remember, if they can bring forth their inherent goodness, genius and potential, so can you. You possess the same inherent goodness, genius, and potential they did.

6   Washington, ed., *A Testimony of Hope*, 254.

24. Drawing Near

1   Levine, *Black Culture and Black Consciousness*, 58.

2   Bradford, *Harriet: The Moses of Her People*, 23.

3   Larson, *Bound for the Promised Land*, 234.

25. Praying

1   Dred Scott v. Sandford, 60 United States (1857), 393.

2   Henry Brown, *Narrative of the Life of Henry Box Brown* (1851) (New York: Barnes and Noble, 2007), 207–208.

3   John W. Blassingame, ed., *Slave Testimony: Two Centuries of Letters, Speeches, Interviews and Autobiographies* (Baton Rouge, LA: Louisiana State University Press, 1977), 462.

4   Bradford, *Harriet, the Moses of Her People*, 105-106.

5   Bradford, *Scenes in the Life of Harriet Tubman*, 7.

6   Marcus Garvey Quotes" Afieldnegro.com.

7   Russell Simmons, "Why I Meditate," *Huffington Post*, April 26, 2010.

TERMINAL Niagara Falls, New York

1   Bradford, *Harriet, the Moses of Her People*, 50-51.

2   Still, *Underground Railroad*, 754.

3   Rosemary Sadlier. *Harriet Tubman: Freedom Seeker, Freedom Leader* (Toronto: Dudurn), 76.

4   McGowan, *Station Master of the Underground Railroad*, 107-108.

26. Chanting

1   Spiritual Workshop, "Tunes and Beats Before 1865," June 29, 2013.

2   Isaac D. Williams, *Sunshine and Shadow of Slave Life: Reminiscences*, 16.

27. Singing

1 Tina Turner Quotes, BrainyQuote.com
2 Pine, *Book of African-American Quotations*, 53.
3 Maryland Public Television. "Follow the Drinking Gourd."
4 Bradford, *Scenes in the Life of Harriet Tubman*, 12.
5 Bradford, *Scenes in the Life of Harriet Tubman*, 12.
6 Pine, *Book of African-American Quotations*, 99.
7 James Weldon Johnson, "Lift Every Voice and Sing" (Wikipedia, 2014)
8 Spiritual Workshop, "This Little Light of Mine," April 27, 2014.

28. Dancing

1 Levine, *Black Culture and Black Consciousness*, 16.
2 Isaac D. Williams, *Sunshine and Shadow of Slave Life: Reminiscences of a Runaway Slave as told by Isaac D. Williams to "Tege,"* 62.
3 Williams, *Sunshine and Shadow of Slave Life*, 61-62.
4 For more on positivity, see Barbara L. Fredrickson, *Positivity: Top-Notch Research Reveals the 3-to-1 Ratio That Will Change Your Life* (New York: Three Rivers Press, 2009).

TERMINUS: St. Catharines, Ontario, Canada

1 Sadlier, *Harriet Tubman*, 87.
2 Sadlier, *Harriet Tubman*, 86.
3 Sadlier, *Harriet Tubman*, 94.
4 Humez, *Harriet Tubman, The Life and Life Stories*, 25.
5 Bradford, *Scenes in the Life of Harriet Tubman*, 3.
6 Larson, *Bound for the Promised Land*, 157–158.
7 Bradford, *Scenes in the Life of Harriet Tubman*, 25.
8 Douglass, *Life and Times of Frederick Douglass*, 357.
9 Douglass, *Life and Times of Frederick Douglass*, 354.

10 Bradford, *Harriet: The Moses of Her People*, 100.

11 Bradford, *Scenes in the Life of Harriet Tubman*, 33-34.

12 Sernett, *Harriet Tubman, Myth, Memory, and History*, 93.

13 Humez, *Harriet Tubman, The Life and Life Stories*, 62.

14 Bradford, *Harriet: The Moses of Her People*, 98.

15 Larson, *Bound for the Promised Land*, 224-225.

16 Bradford, *Harriet: The Moses of Her People*, 139-140.

29. Serving

1 Henry Louis Gates, Jr. and Kwame Anthony Appiah, *Africana: The Encyclopedia of the African and African American Experience* (Philadelphia: Running Press, 2003), 299.

2 Pine, *Book of African-American Quotations*, 81.

30. Conducting

1 Blassingame, *Slave Testimony*, 246–247.

2 An excellent source on free blacks in the South: Ira Berlin, *Slaves Without Masters: The Free Negro in the Antebellum South* (New York: The New Press, 2007), 343–390.

3 Cheryl Janifer LaRoche, "On the Edge of Freedom: Free Black Communities, Archaeology, and the Underground Railroad" (doctoral dissertation, University of Maryland Baltimore County, 2004), 1–351.

4 Parker, *His Promised Land*, 74.

5 Blassingame, *Slave Testimony*, 192-193.

6 The group might want to practice together daily, weekly, or only on holidays or special days in honor of notable people or important events in African American history and culture. Depending on when a session is held, it can last anywhere from sixty minutes any day or four to eight hours on weekends and holidays. Even a full weekend retreat can be scheduled with various meditation

techniques interspersed with yoga, storytelling, mask drawing, contemplation, talks, reading, walking outdoors, group discussion, snacks and socializing, rest periods, and periods for quietly doing chores or eating meals without talking. Whatever the frequency or times selected for your sessions, the information should be put on a calendar, and distributed so that everyone knows when and where the group will gather to practice.

7 Remember that "inviting" should not be confused with marketing or recruiting. No one should ever be asked to pay a fee or make a donation to join a session, and there certainly is no reason to proselytize. After all, meditation is not a religion. It is not a belief. It is a technique. Therefore, there is nothing to convert anyone to. The merits of the technique can be easily determined through regular meditation practice.

8 Prepare the space for someone on a long and difficult journey who just needs a clean, beautiful space in which to rest, or for someone who is on the way to becoming a "Moses" of our people.

9 All agents should be kind, uplifted, and joyful, and work with the station master to ensure that no one is ever subject to any kind of abuse.

10 The libation ceremony is an offering to departed people of African ancestry and living elders. This involves picking up a chalice (a cup) filled with water, inviting each passenger to call out the name of a revered ancestor, and pouring a little water into a potted plant for each ancestor mentioned, until the chalice is empty. Keep the session free of doctrine. As much as possible, speak from your own experience. That is the only thing any of us can truly be an authority on.

11 Serving a sampling of ethnic food and having African and African American music, art, and dance can enhance the post-session environment and create a healing communal experience.

12 Your passengers should feel supported when they leave your station. If they don't feel this way, you should meet with the other agents in your station to determine why that is so and what can be done about it.

31. Pilgrimaging

1 For more on the hundreds of thousands of emancipated slaves who died during the epidemic in the years following the start of the Civil War, read Jim Downs, *Sick From Freedom: African-American Illness and Suffering during the Civil War and Reconstruction* (New York: Oxford University Press, 2012).

2 Malcolm X, *Autobiography of Malcolm X*, 391.

Going Forward

1 Washington, *A Testament of Hope*, 246.

Postscript

1 Bradford, *Scenes in the Life of Harriet Tubman*, 19.

2 Bradford, *Scenes in the Life of Harriet Tubman*, 19.

3 Larson, *Bound for the Promised Land*, 235.

4 Humez, *Harriet Tubman, The Life and Life Stories*, 92.

5 Humez, *Harriet Tubman, The Life and Life Stories*, 94.

6 Humez, *Harriet Tubman, The Life and Life Stories*, 99-100.

7 Humez, *Harriet Tubman, The Life and Life Stories*, 101.

8 Conrad, *Harriet Tubman*, 217.

9 Bradford, *Scenes in the Life of Harriet Tubman*, 41.

10 Humez, *Harriet Tubman, The Life and Life Stories*, 113.

11 Conrad, *Harriet Tubman*, 191.

12 Humez, *Harriet Tubman, The Life and Life Stories*, 106.

13 Larson, *Bound for the Promised Land*, 285.

14 Sernett, *Harriet Tubman, Myth, Memory, and History*, 192.

15 Sernett, *Harriet Tubman, Myth, Memory, and History*, 190.

BIBLIOGRAPHY

Akbar, Na'im. *Chains and Images of Psychological Slavery.* Tallahassee, FL: New Mind Productions, 1984.

Akbar, Na'im. *Community of Self.* Tallahassee, FL: Mind Productions, 1991.

Ashby, Muata, and Karen "Dja" Ashby. *Egyptian Yoga: Postures of the Gods and Goddesses.* Miami, FL: Cruzian Mystic Books, 2005.

"Babacar Khane." *Wikipedia.* July 21, 2012 (7:45 a.m.) Accessed December 21, 2014. http://en.wikipedia.org/wiki/Babacar_Khane.

"Barack Obama's New Hampshire Primary Speech." *New York Times.* Accessed December 2, 2014. http://www.nytimes.com/2008/01/08/us/politics/08text-obama.html?pagewanted=all&_r=0.

Berlin, Ira. *Slaves without Masters: The Free Negro in the Antebellum South.* New York: New Press, 2007.

"Black Settlement in Ontario." *Ontario Heritage Trust.* Accessed December 22, 2014. http://www.heritagetrust.on.ca/Slavery-to-Freedom/History/Black-settlement-in-Ontario.aspx.

Bibb, Henry. *Narrative of the Life and Adventures of Henry Bibb, An American Slave,* Bennington, NH: Flying Chipmunk Publishing, 1849.

Blaisdell, Bob. *Selected Writings and Speeches of Marcus Garvey.* Mineola, NY: Dover Publications, 2004.

Blassingame, John W., ed. *Slave Testimony: Two Centuries of Letters, Speeches, Interviews and Autobiographies.* Baton Rouge, LA: Louisiana State University Press, 1977.

Blight, David W. *Passages to Freedom: The Underground Railroad in History and Memory.* New York: Smithsonian Books, 2004.

Bradford, Sarah H. *Harriet: The Moses of Her People* (1886). Bedford, MA: Applewood Books, 1993.

——. *Scenes in the Life of Harriet Tubman* (1869). Auburn, NY: General Books, 2009.

Brown, Henry Box. *Narrative of the Life of Henry Box Brown* (1851). Reprinted in Barnes and Noble Classics. *The Great Escapes: Four Narratives.* New York: Barnes and Noble, 2007.

Brown, William Wells. *Clotel: Or, The President's Daughter. Project Gutenberg.* Accessed December 22, 2014. http://www.gutenberg.org/cache/epub/2046/pg2046.html.

——. *Narrative of William W. Brown, a Fugitive Slave* (1848). Reprinted in Barnes and Noble Classics. *The Great Escapes: Four Narratives.* New York: Barnes and Noble, 2007.

——. *Narrative of William Wells Brown,* Chapter XII. *University of Missouri-St. Louis.* Accessed December 22, 2014. http://www.umsl.edu/virtualstl/phase2/1850/events/perspectives/documents/wwbrown/wwbrown12.html.

——. "The American Slave Trade" (1848). Reprinted in Barnes and Noble Classics. *The Great Escapes: Four Narratives.* New York: Barnes and Noble, 2007.

Carson, Ben. Twitter post. May 17, 2011. 5:05 p.m. Accessed December 22, 2014. https://twitter.com/bencarson3.

Center for MultiCultural Health. "African Americans and Tobacco: The Historical Journey." *Searching for Answers: Health without Harm in the Black Community* 1, no. 1 (Fall

2006), 1-4. Accessed December 22, 2014. http://www.cschc. org/newsletter/documents/Tobacconewsletter.pdf.

Clinton, Catherine. *Harriet Tubman: The Road to Freedom*. New York: Back Bay Books, 2005.

Co, Master Stephen. *Power Breathing: Prana Practices for Health and Vitality*. Boulder, CO: Sounds True, 2011.

Conrad, Earl. *Harriet Tubman*. Washington, DC: Associated Publishers, 1943.

Copage, Eric V. *Black Pearls: Daily Meditations, Affirmations, and Inspirations for African-Americans*. New York: Quill, William Murrow, 1993.

Craft, William. *Running a Thousand Miles for Freedom; Or, The Escape of William and Ellen Craft from Slavery* (1860). Reprinted in Barnes and Noble Classics. *The Great Escapes: Four Narratives*. New York: Barnes and Noble, 2007.

Daley, James, ed. *Great Speeches by African Americans: Frederick Douglass, Sojourner Truth, Dr. Martin Luther King Jr., Barack Obama, and Others*. Mineola, NY: Dover Publications, 2006.

Davis, Sue. "General Harriet Tubman." *Ann Arbor Sun*. (Ann Arbor, MI) October 1970. Accessed June 29, 2013. http://old-news.aadl.org/node/193017.

DeGraft-Hanson, Kwesi. "Unearthing the Weeping Time: Savannah's Ten Broeck Race Course and 1859 Slave Sale." *Southern Spaces,* February 18, 2010. Accessed December 22, 2014. http://www.southernspaces.org/2010/unearth-ing-weeping-time-savannahs-ten-broeck-race-course-and-1859-slave-sale#sthash.1V12YawN.dpuf.

Doran, Michael F. "Negro Slaves of the Five Civilized Tribes." *Latin American Studies*. Accessed December 22, 2014. http://www.latinamericanstudies.org/slavery/Slaves-Five-Civilized-Tribes.pdf.

Downs, Jim. *Sick From Freedom: African-American Illness and Suffering during the Civil War and Reconstruction*. New York: Oxford University Press, 2012.

Douglass, Frederick. *Life and Times of Frederick Douglass: His Early Life as a Slave, His Escape from Bondage, and His Complete History* (1892). New York: Gramercy Books, 1993.

——. *Narrative of the Life of Frederick Douglass, an American Slave* (1845). New York: Barnes & Noble, 2003.

——. *My Bondage and My Freedom* (1855). New York: Penguin Group, 2003.

——. "West India Emancipation Speech," delivered at Canandaigua, New York, August 3, 1857. University of Rochester, Frederick Douglass Project, Writings. Accessed December 22, 2014. http://www.lib.rochester.edu/index.cfm?PAGE=4398.

Equiano, Olaudah. *The Interesting Life of Olaudah Equiano or Gustavus Vassa, the African* (1814). Reprinted in Henry Louis Gates, Jr., ed. *Classic Slave Narratives*. New York: Signet Classics, 2002.

"Follow the Drinking Gourd." *Pathway to Freedom: Maryland and the Underground Railroad*. Accessed September 9, 2013. http://pathways.thinkport.org/secrets/gourd2.cfm.

Foster, Frances Smith, ed. *A Brighter Coming Day: A Frances Ellen Watkins Harper Reader*. New York, NY: The Feminist Press at the City University of New York, 1990.

Fredrickson, Barbara L., PhD. *Positivity: Top-Notch Research Reveals the 3-to-1 Ratio That Will Change Your Life*. New York: Three Rivers Press, 2009.

Galanes, Philip, "For Arianna Huffington and Kobe Bryant: First Success. Then Sleep." *New York Times*. September 26, 2014. http://www.nytimes.com/2014/09/28/fashion/arianna-huff-ington-kobe-bryant-meditate.html?_r=0.

Gara, Larry. *The Liberty Line: The Legend of the Underground Railroad.* Lexington, KY: University Press of Kentucky, 1996.

Garvey, Marcus. *Selected Writings and Speeches of Marcus Garvey,* edited by Bob Blaisdell. Mineola: Dover Publications, 2004.

Gates, Henry Louis, Jr., and Kwame Anthony Appiah. *Africana: The Encyclopedia of the African and African American Experience.* Philadelphia: Running Press, 2003.

Henson, Josiah. *Truth Stranger Than Fiction: Father Henson's Story of His Own Life.* New York: Barnes & Noble, 2008.

Humez, Jean M. *Harriet Tubman: The Life and the Life Stories.* Madison: University of Wisconsin Press, 2003.

Isiguzo, Andrew Ifeanyi. "African Culture and Symbolism: A Rediscovery of the Seam of a Fragmented Identity." *Council for Research in Values and Philosophy.* Accessed December 22, 2014. http://www.crvp.org/seminar/05-seminar/Andrew%20 Ifeanyi%20Isiguzo.htm.

Johnson, James Weldon. "Lift Every Voice and Sing." *Wikipedia.* May 12, 2014, 9:54 p.m. Accessed December 22, 2014. http:// en.m.wikipedia.org/wiki/Lift_Every_Voice_and_Sing.

Kochhar, Rakesh and Richard Fry. "Wealth inequality has widened along racial, ethnic lines since end of Great Recession." *Pew Research Center.* December 12, 2014. Accessed December 14, 2014. http://www.pewresearch.org/fact-tank/2014/12/12/ racial-wealth-gaps-great-recession/.

Lacy, J. Tolberette, *Vanguard for Vistas: Freshmen Orientation Activities.* Augusta, GA: Paine College, 1972.

LaRoche, Cheryl Janifer. "On the Edge of Freedom: Free Black Communities, Archaeology, and the Underground Railroad." Doctoral dissertation, University of Maryland Baltimore County, 2004. Accessed December 22, 2014. http://drum.lib. umd.edu/handle/1903/1676.

Larson, Kate Clifford. *Bound for the Promised Land: Harriet Tubman, Portrait of an American Hero*. New York: One World, 2004.

Levin, Lawrence W. *Black Culture and Black Consciousness*. Oxford, NY: Oxford University Press, 2007.

Lipka, Michael. "Many U.S. congregations are still racially segregated, but things are changing." *Pew Research Center*. December 8, 2014. Accessed December 31, 2014. http://www.pewresearch. org/fact-tank/2014/12/08/many-u-s-congregations-are-still-racially-segregated-but-things-are-changing-2/.

Lowry, Beverly. *Harriet Tubman: Imagining a Life*. New York: Anchor Books, 2007.

Luhby, Tami. "5 disturbing stats on black-white inequality." *The Real Economy*. August 21, 2014. Accessed December 14, 2014. http://money.cnn.com/2014/08/21/news/economy/black-white-inequality/?iid=EL.

Mabee, Carleton, and Susan Mabee Newhouse. *Sojourner Truth: Slave, Prophet, Legend*. New York: New York University Press, 1993.

Malcolm X. *The Autobiography of Malcolm X*. New York: Random House, 1965.

Mandela, Nelson. *Conversations with Myself*. New York: Farrar, Straus, and Giroux, 2010.

Marks, John. "Abdication and Acceptance: Slave-Trading in Antebellum Lynchburg." *Agora*, 16 (Spring 2007). Accessed December 22, 2014. http://www.agorajournal.org/2007/marksslavery.pdf.

Mayfield, Curtis. "Check Out Your Mind." Accessed December |22, 2014. http://www.songlyrics.com/curtis-mayfield/check-out-your-mind-lyrics/.

McGowan, James A. *Station Master on the Underground Railroad: The Life and Letters of Thomas Garrett*. Moylan, PA: Whimsie Press, 1977.

Minton, Todd and Daniela Golinelli. "Jail Inmates at Midyear 2013—Statistical Tables (Revised)." May 2014. *Bureau of Justice Statistics*. Office of Justice Programs. US Department of Justice. Accessed December 14, 2014. http://www.bjs.gov/content/pub/pdf/jim13st.pdf.

New York Times, "William Still Dead." *New York Times*, July 15, 1902. Accessed December 22, 2014. http://query.nytimes.com/gst/abstract.html?res=F00810F6385412738DDDAC0994DF405B828CF1D3 and http://hd.housedivided.dickinson.edu/node/15393.

Northup, Solomon. *Twelve Years a Slave*. Edited by Henry Louis Gates, Jr. New York: Penguin, 2012.

Parker, John P. *His Promised Land: The Autobiography of John P. Parker, Former Slave and Conductor of the Underground Railroad*. Edited by Stuart Seely Sprague. New York: W. W. Norton & Company, 1996.

Pease, William H. and Jane H. Pease. *Black Utopia: Negro Communal Experiments in America*. Madison, WI: State Historical Society of Wisconsin, 1963.

Pine, Joslyn, ed., *Book of African-American Quotations*. Mineola, NY: Dover Publications, Inc., 2011.

Public Broadcasting Service. "The Weeping Time." Accessed December 22, 2014. http://www.pbs.org/wgbh/aia/part4/4p2918.html.

Quarles, Benjamin. *Black Abolitionists*. New York: Da Capo Press, 1969.

"Recollections of Slavery by a Runaway Slave." *The Emancipator,* October 11, 1838. Accessed April 27, 2014. http://docsouth.unc. edu/neh/runaway/runaway.html.

Ricks, Mary Kay. *Escape on the Pearl: The Historic Bid for Freedom on the Underground Railroad.* New York: Harper, Perennial, 2007.

Rossano, Matt J. "Did Meditating Make Us Human?" *Southeastern Lousiana University.* Accessed September 7, 2013. http:// www2.southeastern.edu/Academics/Faculty/mrossano/ recentpubs/meditating.pdf.

Sadlier, Rosemary. *Harriet Tubman: Freedom Seeker, Freedom Leader.* Toronto: Dudurn, 2012.

Schmidt, Lorna. "Tobacco Use Among African Americans." *Campaign for Tobacco-Free Kids.* December 2, 2014. http:// www.tobaccofreekids.org/research/factsheets/pdf/0006.pdf.

Sernett, Milton C. *Harriet Tubman: Myth, Memory, and History.* Durham: Duke University Press, 2007.

——. *North Star Country: Upstate New York and the Crusade for African American Freedom.* Syracuse, NY: Syracuse University Press, 2002.

Shapiro, Thomas, Tatjana Meschede, and Sam Osoro. "The Roots of the Widening Racial Wealth Gap: Explaining the Black-White Economic Divide." *Institute on Assets and Social Policy.* February 2013. Accessed December 2, 2014. http://iasp. brandeis.edu/pdfs/Author/shapiro-thomas-m/racialwealth-gapbrief.pdf.

Sheilds, John, ed. *The Collected Works of Phillis Wheatley.* New York: Oxford University Press, 1988.

Simmons, Russell. "Why I Meditate." *Huffington Post.* April 26, 2010. http://www.huffingtonpost.com/russell-simmons/why-i-meditate_b_474689.html

Spiritual Workshop. "Tunes and Beats Before 1865." *Negro Spirituals.* Accessed December 22, 2014. http://www.negro-spirituals.com/song.html.

———. "This Little Light of Mine," *Negro Spirituals.* Accessed December 22, 2014. http://www.negrospirituals.com/news-song/this_little_light_of_mine.html.

Still, William. *The Underground Railroad:* Oxford: Benediction Classics, 2008.

Stine, Linda France, Melanie A. Cabake, and Mark D. Groover. "Blue Beads as African-American Cultural Symbols." *University of Florida.* Accessed December 22, 2014. http://www.clas.ufl.edu/users/davidson/arch%20of%20aa%20life%20and%20culture/Week%2007-08/Stine%20et%20al.%201996.pdf.

Sweet, Lynn. "Obama's NAACP speech, New York, July 16, 2009. Transcript." *Chicago Sun-Times.* July 17, 2009. Accessed December 22, 2014. http://blogs.suntimes.com/sweet/2009/07/obamas_naacp_speech.html.

Thurman, Howard. *Meditations of the Heart.* Boston: Beacon Press, 1981.

———. "The Sound of the Genuine," *Crossings Reflection #4.* The Crossings Project. University of Indianapolis. Accessed December 29, 2014. http://eip.uindy.edu/crossings/publications/reflection4.pdf. Based on excerpts from Howard Thurman's Baccalaureate Address, Spelman College, May 4, 1980, edited by Jo Moore Stewart, *The Spelman Messenger,* Vol. 96 No. 4 (Summer 1980), 14-15.

Toldson, Ivory A., "What Black High School Grads Need to Hear." *The Root.* May 21, 2013. Accessed December 22, 2014. http://www.theroot.com/articles/culture/2013/05/high_

school_graduation_speeches_what_blacks_teens_need_to_hear.html.

"Tupac Shakur Quotes." Goodreads.com. Accessed December 22, 2014. http://www.goodreads.com/quotes/.

Tutu, Desmond Mpilo. *No Future Without Forgiveness*. New York: Doubleday, 1999.

US Census Bureau. "Population of the United States in 1860." Washington, DC: Government Printing Office, 1864. Accessed December 2, 2014. http://www2.census.gov/prod2/decennial/documents/1860a-01.pdf.

Vanzant, Iyanla. *Acts of Faith: Daily Meditations of People of Color.* New York: Simon & Schuster, 1993.

Wachob, Jason. "Kareem Abdul-Jabbar: Yoga as Preventative Medicine." *MindBodyGreen*. Accessed June 29, 2013. http://www.mindbodygreen.com/0-1907/Kareem-AbdulJabbar-Yoga-as-Preventative-Medicine.html.

Walker, David. *Walker's Appeal, in Four Articles, Together with a Preamble, To The Citizens of the World, But In Particular, and Very Expressly To Those Of The United States of America,* 2nd edition. 1830. Atlanta: Two Horizons Press, 2012.

Washington, Booker T. *The Story of My Life and Work*. New York: Barnes and Noble, 2008.

Washington, Booker T. *Up From Slavery: An Autobiography*. New York: Barnes and Noble, 2003.

Washington, James M., ed. *A Testament of Hope: The Essential Writings and Speeches of Martin Luther King Jr.* New York: HarperSanFrancisco, 1991.

Wayne, Michael. "The Black Population of Canada West on the Eve of the American Civil War: A Reassessment Based on the Manuscript Census of 1861." *Histoire sociale / Social History*.

Accessed January 26, 2014. http://pi.library.yorku.ca/ojs/ index.php/hssh/article/viewFile/16644/15502.

Western Literary Messenger. "Frederick Douglass' North Star." *Western Literary Messenger.* Volume 10. March 18, 1848. Accessed December 3, 2014. http://books.google.com/ books?id=IpMAAAAMAAJ&pg=RA1-PA99&dq=Wester+liter ary+messenger,+north+star&hl= en&sa=X&ei=QTF- VOvvJ4uYNrClgbAF&ved=0CB8Q6AEwA A#v =onepage&q=Wester%20literary%20messenger%2C%20 north%20star&f=false.

Weston, Shawn. "Thoughts from an Art Director: The Muhammad Ali Guide to Being #1." *ShawnWeston.* Accessed on June 29, 2013. http://shawnweston.com/best/.

Williams, Isaac D. *Sunshine and Shadow of Slave Life. Reminiscences as told by Isaac D. Williams to "Tege."* Accessed December 22, 2014. http://docsouth.unc.edu/neh/iwilliams/iwilliams.html.

Williamson, Samuel H., and Lewis P. Cain. "Measuring Slavery in 2011." *Measuring Worth.* Accessed December 22, 2014. http:// www.measuringworth.com/slavery.php.

Woodson, Carter G. *The Mis-Education of the Negro.* Chicago: African American Images, 2000.

Yee, Shirley J. *Black Women Abolitionists: A Study in Activism, 1828–1860.* Knoxville: University of Tennessee Press, 1992.

INDEX

Note: Page numbers followed by p indicate photographs; those followed by i indicate illustrations.

of, 220-222, 379-381;
community development,
222-224, 381
Free Colored School, 142
Freedom's Journal, 224
Free Your Mind (guidebook),
message of, 2; using, 10
Fugitive Aid Society of St.
Catharines, 368
Fugitive Slave Act of 1793, 97
Fugitive Slave Act of 1850:
provisions of, 147-148;
enforcement of, 169; risks
posed by, 375, 376, 383;
resistance to, 149-150,
170-171, 196-197; migration
caused by, 97, 148-149, 271,
328
"Fugitive Slave's Apostrophe
to the North Star"
(Pierpont), 191-192

G

Gara, Larry, 104
Garner, Margaret and Robert,
245-246
Garnet, Henry Highland, 283,
409
Garrett, Thomas, 55-56, 57p,
76-77, 172, 331

Garrison Literary and
Benevolent Society of New
York, 224
Garrison, William Lloyd, 92,
170, 203, 241, 409
Garvey, Marcus, 18, 87, 320
Gaye, Marvin, 151
George, Letitia, 77
Gertie (Tubman's adopted
daughter), 403
Gibbs, Jacob R., 100
Giles, Charlette, 112
Green, Shields, 368
Green, Harriet "Rit"
(Tubman's mother), 25,
403
Grimké, Sarah and Angelina,
194-195, 409

H

habits: developing helpful
ones, 226-230, taking
positive actions, 232-234
Haiti, 30
Hamer, Fannie Lou, 377
harm, repairing, 234-236
Harper, Frances Ellen
Watkins, 100-102, 103p,
328, 402
Harpers Ferry Armory, raid
on, 141, 367-368

18800261R00265

Made in the USA
Middletown, DE
01 December 2018